PHYSICAL EDUCATION

Don Webster
Lecturer in Sports Studies,
South Tyneside College

Letts
EDUCATIONAL

Letts Educational
Aldine Place
London W12 8AW
Tel: 020 8740 2266
Fax: 020 8743 8451
e-mail: mail@lettsed.co.uk

First published 1997
Reprinted 1999 (twice)

Text © Don Webster 1997
Design and illustrations © BPP (Letts Educational) Ltd 1997

Typesetting, illustrations and layout by Ian Foulis and Associates, Saltash, Cornwall.

All our Rights Reserved. No part of this publication may be reproduced, stored in a retrieval system, or transmitted, in any form or by any means, electronic, mechanical, photocopying, recording or otherwise, without the prior permission of Letts Educational.

British Library Cataloguing in Publication Data
A CIP record for this book is available from the British Library.

ISBN 1 85805 437 0

Printed in Great Britain by Bath Press Colourbooks, Glasgow

Acknowledgements

In the preparation of this book I have been greatly assisted by Anne Webster, Douglas J M Adams, The Boldon Ladies Football team, Guildford Spectrum Leisure Centre, Guildford Flames Ice Hockey team, and Carly Quinn, Cheryl Kennedy, Emma Leggett, Jane Hawkins and Mark Nicholson and colleagues from South Tyneside College. To Richard Carr, Wayne Davies and Vicky Parker my thanks for their editorial assistance and Carol Thibaut for her helpful criticism.

The author and Letts Educational are grateful to the following Examination Boards for their permission to reproduce questions from their examination papers: Northern Ireland Council for the Curriculum Examinations and Assessment, Southern Examining Group, Midland Examining Group, and Northern Examinations and Assessment Board. Please note that the Examination Boards accept no responsibility for the accuracy or method of working in the answers given to sample questions.

Every effort has been made to trace copyright holders and to obtain their permission for the use of copyright material. The authors and publishers will gladly receive information enabling them to rectify any error or omission in subsequent editions.

Contents

Starting points

Introduction   1
How to use this book   1
GCSE Physical Education   1
Analysis of courses available   2
Using the material   16
Learning and remembering   16
Revision programmes   16
Preparing for examinations   17

The human body's make-up relating to movement

1   The human body   18
1.1   The skeletal system   18
1.2   The muscular system   19
1.3   The nervous system   19
1.4   The circulatory system   20
1.5   The respiratory system   21
1.6   The digestive system   21

2   The skeleton   22
2.1   Functions of the skeleton   22
2.2   Skeletal system   22
2.3   Bones   24
2.4   Major types of joint   25
2.5   Synovial joints   27
2.6   Bone development   28
2.7   Ligaments   28
2.8   Cartilage   29
Principal topics covered   29
Questions on this chapter   30

3   Muscles of the body   31
3.1   Muscle types   31
3.2   Skeletal muscles at work   32
3.3   Skeletal muscles and movement   32
3.4   Muscles and energy   33
3.5   Effects of exercise on muscles   35
Principal topics covered   35
Questions on this chapter   36

4   The control of movement   37
4.1   The central nervous system (CNS)   37
4.2   The nerves   37
4.3   Nervous co-ordination   39
4.4   Reflex actions   39

Principal topics covered   40
Questions on this chapter   40

5   The circulatory system   41
5.1   The heart   41
5.2   The pulse   42
5.3   The blood vessels   43
5.4   Watch pocket valves   44
5.5   Blood structure   45
5.6   Functions of the blood   45
5.7   Blood pressure   46
5.8   Effects of exercise   47
Principal topics covered   47
Questions on this chapter   47

6   The respiratory system   48
6.1   The respiratory tract   49
6.2   Gaseous exchange   50
6.3   Mechanism of breathing   50
6.4   Lung capacity   51
6.5   Effects of exercise   52
Principal topics covered   53
Questions on this chapter   53

7   Digestion and diet   54
7.1   The alimentary canal   55
7.2   Peristalsis   55
7.3   Diet   56
7.4   Balanced diet   57
7.5   Diet and exercise   57
Principal topics covered   59
Questions on this chapter   59

Capabilities and limitations of the human body

8   Fitness   60
8.1   What is fitness?   60
8.2   Physical fitness   60
8.3   Components of physical fitness   61
8.4   Strength   61
8.5   Speed   62
8.6   Stamina   62
8.7   Suppleness   62
8.8   Motor fitness   63
8.9   Influences on fitness   64
Principal topics covered   64
Questions on this chapter   64

9	Improving fitness	65
9.1	Overload	65
9.2	Progression	66
9.3.	Specificity	66
9.4	Reversibility	66
9.5	Training threshold	67
9.6	Training methods	67
9.7	Training sessions	72
9.8	Rest periods	73
Principal topics covered		73
Questions on this chapter		73

10	Acquisition of skill	74
10.1	Skill defined	74
10.2	Open and closed skills	74
10.3	Processing information	75
10.4	Overloading the processing mode	76
10.5	Factors affecting performance	77
Principal topics covered		78
Questions on this chapter		78

11	Effects on fitness	79
11.1	Food and diet	79
11.2	Lifestyle	79
11.3	Illness and injury	79
11.4	Physical make-up	81
11.5	Personal history	83
11.6	Environmental conditions	83
11.7	Drug use and abuse	84
Principal topics covered		85
Questions on this chapter		85

12	Measurement in sport	86
12.1	Tests for suppleness	86
12.2	Tests of strength	89
12.3	Tests of endurance	93
Principal topics covered		95
Questions on this chapter		95

13	Sports related injuries	96
13.1	Safe practice	96
13.2	What to do in the event of an injury	96
13.3	Soft tissue injuries	99
13.4	Hard tissue injuries	100
13.5	Miscellaneous injuries	101
13.6	Injuries associated with specific sports	102
Principal topics covered		104
Questions on this chapter		104

Development and organisation of sport

14	Administration of sport	105
14.1	Structure of sport	105
14.2	Governing bodies of sport	106
14.3	Central Council for Physical Recreation (CCPR)	107
14.4	Sports Council	107
14.5	British Olympic Association (BOA)	109
14.6	International Olympic Committee (IOC)	109
14.7	International Sports Federations (ISF)	109
14.8	Development of international competitions	110
14.9	Recreational quangos	110
Principal topics covered		111
Questions on this chapter		111

15	Providers of sports facilities	112
15.1	National providers	113
15.2	Local providers	113
15.3	Voluntary providers	116
15.4	Commercial providers	116
15.5	Finance of sport	116
15.6	Obtaining money in sport	117
15.7	Spending in sport	117
Principal topics covered		118
Questions on this chapter		118

16	Participation in sport	119
16.1	Leisure, recreation, sport	119
16.2	Leisure time	120
16.3	Reasons for sports participation	120
16.4	Growth in sports participation	121
16.5	User groups in sport	121
16.6	Factors affecting sports participation	122
16.7	Promotional campaigns	124
Principal topics covered		125
Questions on this chapter		125

17	Development of international competition	126
17.1	Codification of rules	126
17.2	International competitions	127
17.3	Modern Olympic Games	127
Principal topics covered		128
Questions on this chapter		128

18	Major influences on sport	129
18.1	Finance of sport	129
18.2	Amateur v professional	131
18.3	The professional amateur	132
18.4	Sponsorship in sport	132
18.5	The media in sport	134
18.6	Politics and sport	135
	Principal topics covered	137
	Questions on this chapter	137

19	Changing attitudes in sport	138
19.1	Attitude towards winning	138
19.2	Abuse of drugs	139
19.3	Spectatorism	139
19.4	Crowd violence	140
	Principal topics covered	141
	Questions on this chapter	141

20	Social concepts in sport	142
20.1	Discrimination in sport	142
20.2	Women in sport	144
20.3	The disabled and sport	147
	Principal topics covered	148
	Questions on this chapter	148

Coursework (for NEAB candidates only)

21	Analytical investigation	149
21.1	Sample analytical investigations	150
21.2	Presentation	152
21.3	Suitable topics for investigation	152

22	Performance improvement programme	154
22.1	Sample performance improvement programmes	154
22.2	General advice	159

Test yourself

23	Test yourself: questions	160
	Questions Type A	161
	Questions Type B	162
	Questions Type C	165

24	Test yourself: answers	167
	Answers Type A	167
	Answers Type B	169
	Answers Type C	176

25	Answers to chapter questions	179
Index		190

Starting points

Introduction

How to use this book

This revision guide has been prepared for those who need help in reaching a standard of work appropriate to that needed for a high level pass in the GCSE examination for Physical Education. It provides:

- advice on what your syllabus requires
- advice on how to learn
- what to learn, in an easy-to-follow form
- advice on how to answer questions from the examination
- practice in answering examination questions.

First, you should find out which syllabus your school or college is following. Your teacher will be the best person to ask. As there are several GCSE Physical Education courses, each with a similar title, it is essential that you obtain this information correctly. Each course is described in outline in the section called GCSE Physical Education.

Secondly, look carefully at the section called Analysis of Courses Available. From this you will be able to find out the following information about your particular course.

- the address of the Examination Board
- what you need to know for the syllabus, topic by topic
- the number and lengths of the papers to be sat
- the amount of the course that is assessed by the teacher
- the amount, if any, of the coursework to be submitted for assessment.

The Analysis of Courses Available should be regarded only as a helpful guide as boards may make minor alterations to their syllabuses each year. You should therefore obtain an up-to-date copy of the syllabus for your course from the examination board that is offering it. (Examination boards charge for these but it will be a good investment.) It is also wise to ask them to send you copies of past papers. From these you will be able to judge more easily what the special features of your syllabus are. Your teacher should be prepared to give you advice on all the units that need to be studied.

If you are a private candidate not attending a school or college you will have to find a centre that offers the course that you wish to be examined in. You should first decide which syllabus you want to follow, then contact the relevant board, advise them of your intentions and they will tell you which centres in your area offer the syllabus you are interested in. Then you should contact one of these centres and get them to agree to internally mark your coursework and enter you for the examination. A charge will be made for entering the examination.

GCSE Physical Education

The aims of this type of course are to enable candidates to improve:
1. their ability to plan, perform and evaluate physical activities
2. their knowlege, skills and understanding of a range of physical activities.

The attainment of these aims is through a combination of a written examination, practical coursework and sometimes written coursework, both of which are internally assessed and externally moderated.

Starting points

Assessment objectives indicate the skills and abilities which are to be assessed. They are listed at the beginning of each syllabus and reflect the aims of the course. They also relate to the general and common requirements of the National Curriculum and extend the Key Stage 4 programme of study as appropriate.

A Scheme of Assessment table provided in each syllabus will indicate the relationship between the assessment components and assessment objectives. Weightings are given to each assessment objective.

There are *four* types of course available that fall under the 'umbrella' title of **Physical Education**.

1. *All* the boards listed below offer a GCSE course entitled **Physical Education**. This is a full GCSE course with a pass standard comparable with any GCSE pass in any other full course.
2. *Three* of the boards listed below also offer a GCSE course entitled **Physical Education - Games**. This is a full GCSE course with a pass standard comparable with any GCSE pass in any other full course.
3. *Three* of the boards listed below also offer a GCSE course entitled **Physical Education - Short Course**. In each case this is an abridged version of the full course on offer and the standard of pass is equivalent to approximately half of a full GCSE Physical Education pass.
4. *Three* of the boards listed below offer a course entitled **Physical Education-Games (short course)**. The standard of this course is similar to that of the other short courses on offer.

As the titles of these courses are very similar and could lead to confusion, it is essential that you establish which course you are following (see Table A).

Table A: Physical Education courses available and their syllabus numbers

	Physical Education (full course)	Physical Education - Games (full course)	Physical Education (short course)	Physical Education - Games (short course)
ULEAC (EDEXEL)	1825	1826	3825	3826
SEG	2680	2685		1485
MEG	1680	1681		3680
NEAB	1271		2271	
NICCEA	no number			
WJEC	no number		no number	

Analysis of courses available

University of London Examinations and Assessment Council (ULEAC or EDEXEL)

Address: Stewart House, 32 Russell Square, London WC1B 5DN
Tel no: 0171 331 4000

Syllabus topic		Covered in Unit no	✔
1	**Human body**		
	Skeletal system	1.1	
	Muscular system	1.2	
	Nervous system	1.3	
	Circulatory system	1.4	
	Respiratory system	1.5	
	Digestive system	1.6	
2	**The skeleton**		
	Functions of the skeleton	2.1	
	Skeletal system	2.2	
	Bones	2.3	
	Major types of joints	2.4	

	Synovial joints	2.5	
	Bone development	2.6	
	Ligaments	2.7	
	Cartilage	2.8	
3	**Muscles of the body**		
	Muscle types	3.1	
	Skeletal muscle fibres at work	3.2	
	Skeletal muscle fibres and movement	3.3	
	Muscles and energy	3.4	
	Effects of exercise on muscles	3.5	
4	**Control of movement**		
	Central nervous system	4.1	R
	Nerves	4.2	R
	Nervous co-ordination	4.3	R
	Reflex actions	4.4	R
5	**Circulatory system**		
	Blood circulation	5	
	Heart	5.1	
	Pulse	5.2	
	Blood vessels	5.3	
	Watch pocket valves	5.4	
	Blood structure	5.5	
	Functions of blood	5.6	
	Blood pressure	5.7	
	Effects of exercise on the system	5.8	
6	**Respiratory system**		
	Respiratory tract	6.1	
	Gaseous exchange	6.2	
	Mechanism of breathing	6.3	
	Lung capacity	6.4	
	Effects of exercise	6.5	
7	**Digestion and diet**		
	Alimentary canal	7.1	R
	Peristalsis	7.2	R
	Diet	7.3	
	Balanced diet	7.4	
	Diet and exercise	7.5	
8	**Fitness**		
	What is fitness?	8.1	
	Physical fitness	8.2	
	Components of fitness	8.3	
	Strength	8.4	
	Speed	8.5	
	Stamina	8.6	
	Suppleness	8.7	
	Motor fitness	8.8	
	Influence on fitness	8.9	
9	**Improving fitness**		
	Overload	9.1	
	Progression	9.2	
	Specificity	9.3	
	Reversibility	9.4	
	Training threshold	9.5	
	Training methods	9.6	
	Training sessions	9.7	
	Rest periods	9.8	
11	**Effects on fitness**		
	Food and diet	11.1	
	Lifestyle	11.2	
	Illness and injury	11.3	
	Physical make-up	11.4	
	Personal history	11.5	
	Environmental conditions	11.6	
	Drug use and abuse	11.7	
12	**Measurement in sport**		
	Tests of suppleness	12.1	
	Tests of strength	12.2	
	Tests of endurance	12.3	
13	**Sports related injuries**		
	Safe practice	13.1	
	What to do	13.2	
	Soft tissue injuries	13.3	
	Hard tissue injuries	13.4	

Starting points

	Miscellaneous injuries	13.5	
	Injuries associated with specific sports	13.6	
16	**Participation in sport**		
	Leisure, recreation and sport	16.1	
	Leisure time	16.2	
	Reasons for sports participation	16.3	
	Growth of sports participation	16.4	
	User groups in sport	16.5	
	Factors affecting sports participation	16.6	
	Promotional campaigns	16.7	

R = Recommended; all other topics listed are essential.

ULEAC Exam breakdown

Physical Education (1825)

1 written paper	1¾ hrs	40% of total marks
practical:	5 activities from 3+ groups	25% of total marks
course assessment:	analysis of performance	10% of total marks
	final assessment	25% of total marks

Physical Education – Games (1826)

1 written paper	1¾ hrs	40% of total marks
practical:	5 activities from 3 groups (at least one from each group)	60% of total marks

Physical Education (short course) (3825)

1 written paper	1 hr	40% of total marks
practical:	2 activities from 2 groups	25% of total marks
course assessment:	analysis of performance	10% of total marks
	final assessment	25% of total marks

Physical Education-Games (short course) (3826)

1 written paper	1 hr	40% of total marks
practical:	2 activities from 3 groups (not from same group)	60% of total marks

Southern Examining Group (SEG)

Address: Stag Hill House, Guildford, Surrey, GU2 5XJ

Syllabus topic		Covered in Unit no	✔
1	**Human body**		
	Skeletal system	1.1	
	Muscular system	1.2	
	Nervous system	1.3	
	Circulatory system	1.4	
	Respiratory system	1.5	
	Digestive system	1.6	
2	**The skeleton**		
	Functions of the skeleton	2.1	
	Skeletal system	2.2	
	Bones	2.3	
	Major types of joints	2.4	
	Synovial joints	2.5	
	Bone development	2.6	
	Ligaments	2.7	
	Cartilage	2.8	
3	**Muscles of the body**		
	Muscle types	3.1	
	Skeletal muscle fibres at work	3.2	
	Skeletal muscle fibres and movement	3.3	
	Muscles and energy	3.4	
	Effects of exercise on muscles	3.5	
4	**Control of movement**		
	Central nervous system	4.1	R
	Nerves	4.2	R

		Nervous co-ordination	4.3		R
		Reflex actions	4.4		R
5		**Circulatory system**			
		Blood circulation	5		
		Heart	5.1		
		Pulse	5.2		
		Blood vessels	5.3		
		Watch pocket valves	5.4		
		Blood structure	5.5		
		Functions of blood	5.6		
		Blood pressure	5.7		
		Effects of exercise on the system	5.8		
6		**Respiratory system**			
		Respiratory tract	6.1		
		Gaseous exchange	6.2		
		Mechanism of breathing	6.3		
		Lung capacity	6.4		
		Effects of exercise	6.5		
7		**Digestion and diet**			
		Alimentary canal	7.1		R
		Peristalsis	7.2		R
		Diet	7.3		
		Balanced diet	7.4		
		Diet and exercise	7.5		
8		**Fitness**			
		What is fitness?	8.1		
		Physical fitness	8.2		
		Components of fitness	8.3		
		Strength	8.4		
		Speed	8.5		
		Stamina	8.6		
		Suppleness	8.7		
		Motor fitness	8.8		
		Influence on fitness	8.9		
9		**Improving fitness**			
		Overload	9.1		
		Progression	9.2		
		Specificity	9.3		
		Reversibility	9.4		
		Training threshold	9.5		
		Training methods	9.6		
		Training sessions	9.7		
		Rest periods	9.8		
10		**Acquisition of skill**			
		Skill defined	10.1		
		Open and closed skills	10.2		
		Processing information	10.3		
		Overloading the processing model	10.4		
		Factors affecting performance	10.5		
11		**Effects on fitness**			
		Food and diet	11.1		
		Lifestyle	11.2		
		Illness and injury	11.3		
		Physical make-up	11.4		
		Personal history	11.5		
		Environmental conditions	11.6		
		Drug use and abuse	11.7		
12		**Measurement in sport**			
		Tests of suppleness	12.1		
		Tests of strength	12.2		
		Tests of endurance	12.3		
13		**Sports related injuries**			
		Safe practice	13.1		
		What to do	13.2		
		Soft tissue injuries	13.3		
		Hard tissue injuries	13.4		
		Miscellaneous injuries	13.5		
		Injuries associated with specific sports	13.6		
14		**Administration of sport**			
		Structure of sport	14.1		
		Governing bodies of sport	14.2		
		Central Council for Physical Recreation	14.3		
		Sports Council	14.4		

Starting points

	British Olympic Association	14.5	
	International Olympic Committee	14.6	
	International Sports Federation	14.7	
	Development of international competitions	14.8	
	Recreational quangos	14.9	
15	**Providers of sports facilities**		
	National providers	15.1	
	Local providers	15.2	
	Voluntary providers	15.3	
	Commerical providers	15.4	
	Finance of sport	15.5	
	Obtaining money in sport	15.6	
	Spending in sport	15.7	
16	**Participation in sport**		
	Leisure, recreation and sport	16.1	
	Leisure time	16.2	
	Reasons for sports participation	16.3	
	Growth of sports participation	16.4	
	User groups in sport	16.5	
	Factors affecting sports participation	16.6	
	Promotional campaigns	16.7	
17	**Development of international competition**		
	Codification of rules	17.1	R
	International competitions	17.2	
	Modern Olympic Games	17.3	
18	**Major influences on sport**		
	Finance of sport	18.1	
	Amateur v professional	18.2	
	The professional amateur	18.3	
	Sponsorship in sport	18.4	
	The media in sport	18.5	
	Politics and sport	18.6	
19	**Changing attitudes in sport**		
	Attitude towards winning	19.1	
	Abuse of drugs	19.2	
	Spectatorism	19.3	
	Crowd violence	19.4	
20	**Social concepts in sport**		
	Discrimination in sport	20.1	
	Women in sport	20.2	
	The disabled and sport	20.3	

R = Recommended; all other topics listed are essential.

SEG Exam breakdown

Physical Education (2680)
1 written paper   2 hrs   40% of total marks
practical: 4 activities from 3+ groups   60% of total marks

Physical Education-Games (2685)
1 written paper   2 hrs   40% of total marks
practical: 4 activities   60% of total marks
                   (at least 1 from each of 3 groups)

Physical Education-Games (short course) (1485)
1 written paper   1 hr   40% of total marks
practical: 2 activities from 2 groups   60% of total marks

Midland Examining Group (MEG)

Syllabus topic		Covered in Unit no	✔
1	**Human body**		
	Skeletal system	1.1	
	Muscular system	1.2	
	Nervous system	1.3	
	Circulatory system	1.4	
	Respiratory system	1.5	
	Digestive system	1.6	

2	**The skeleton**		
	Functions of the skeleton	2.1	
	Skeletal system	2.2	
	Bones	2.3	
	Major types of joints	2.4	
	Synovial joints	2.5	
	Bone development	2.6	
	Ligaments	2.7	
	Cartilage	2.8	
3	**Muscles of the body**		
	Muscle types	3.1	
	Skeletal muscle fibres at work	3.2	
	Skeletal muscle fibres and movement	3.3	
	Muscles and energy	3.4	
	Effects of exercise on muscles	3.5	
4	**Control of movement**		
	Central nervous system	4.1	R
	Nerves	4.2	R
	Nervous co-ordination	4.3	R
	Reflex actions	4.4	R
5	**Circulatory system**		
	Blood circulation	5	
	Heart	5.1	
	Pulse	5.2	
	Blood vessels	5.3	
	Watch pocket valves	5.4	
	Blood structure	5.5	
	Functions of blood	5.6	
	Blood pressure	5.7	
	Effects of exercise on the system	5.8	
6	**Respiratory system**		
	Respiratory tract	6.1	
	Gaseous exchange	6.2	
	Mechanism of breathing	6.3	
	Lung capacity	6.4	
	Effects of exercise	6.5	
7	**Digestion and diet**		
	Alimentary canal	7.1	R
	Peristalsis	7.2	R
	Diet	7.3	
	Balanced diet	7.4	
	Diet and exercise	7.5	
8	**Fitness**		
	What is fitness?	8.1	
	Physical fitness	8.2	
	Components of fitness	8.3	
	Strength	8.4	
	Speed	8.5	
	Stamina	8.6	
	Suppleness	8.7	
	Motor fitness	8.8	
	Influence on fitness	8.9	
9	**Improving fitness**		
	Overload	9.1	
	Progression	9.2	
	Specificity	9.3	
	Reversibility	9.4	
	Training threshold	9.5	
	Training methods	9.6	
	Training sessions	9.7	
	Rest periods	9.8	
10	**Acquisition of skill**		
	Skill defined	10.1	
	Open and closed skills	10.2	
	Processing information	10.3	
	Overloading the processing model	10.4	
	Factors affecting performance	10.5	
11	**Effects on fitness**		
	Food and diet	11.1	
	Lifestyle	11.2	
	Illness and injury	11.3	
	Physical make-up	11.4	
	Personal history	11.5	
	Environmental conditions	11.6	

Starting points

	Drug use and abuse	11.7	
12	**Measurement in sport**		
	Tests of suppleness	12.1	
	Tests of strength	12.2	
	Tests of endurance	12.3	
13	**Sports related injuries**		
	Safe practice	13.1	
	What to do	13.2	
	Soft tissue injuries	13.3	
	Hard tissue injuries	13.4	
	Miscellaneous injuries	13.5	
	Injuries associated with specific sports	13.6	
14	**Administration of sport**		
	Structure of sport	14.1	
	Governing bodies of sport	14.2	
	Central Council for Physical Recreation	14.3	
	Sports Council	14.4	
	British Olympic Association	14.5	
	International Olympic Committee	14.6	
	International Sports Federation	14.7	
	Development of international competitions	14.8	R
	Recreational quangos	14.9	R
15	**Providers of sports facilities**		
	National providers	15.1	
	Local providers	15.2	
	Voluntary providers	15.3	
	Commerical providers	15.4	
	Finance of sport	15.5	
	Obtaining money in sport	15.6	
	Spending in sport	15.7	
16	**Participation in sport**		
	Leisure, recreation and sport	16.1	
	Leisure time	16.2	
	Reasons for sports participation	16.3	
	Growth of sports participation	16.4	
	User groups in sport	16.5	
	Factors affecting sports participation	16.6	
	Promotional campaigns	16.7	
17	**Development of international competition**		
	Codification of rules	17.1	
	International competitions	17.2	
	Modern Olympic Games	17.3	
18	**Major influences on sport**		
	Finance of sport	18.1	
	Amateur v professional	18.2	
	The professional amateur	18.3	
	Sponsorship in sport	18.4	
	The media in sport	18.5	
	Politics and sport	18.6	R
19	**Changing attitudes in sport**		
	Attitude towards winning	19.1	R
	Abuse of drugs	19.2	
	Spectatorism	19.3	R
	Crowd violence	19.4	R
20	**Social concepts in sport**		
	Discrimination in sport	20.1	
	Women in sport	20.2	
	The disabled and sport	20.3	

R = Recommended; all other topics listed are essential.

MEG Exam breakdown

Physical Education (1680)
1 written paper   2 hrs   40% of total mark
practical: 4 activities from 3+ groups   50% of total marks
planning, performing, evaluating, analysing and improving   10% of total marks

Physical Education-Games (1681)
1 written paper	2 hrs	40% of total marks
practical:	4 activities from 3 groups	50% of total marks
planning, performing, evaluating, analysing and improving		10% of total marks

Physical Education-Games (short course) (3680)
1 written paper	1½ hrs	40% of total marks
practical:	2 activities from 2 groups	50% of total marks
planning, performing, evaluating, analysing and improving		10% of total marks

Northern Examinations and Assessment Board (NEAB)

Address: 31/33 Springfield Avenue, Harrogate, North Yorkshire, HG1 2HW
Tel no: 01423 840015

Syllabus topic		Covered in Unit no	✔
1	**Human body**		
	Skeletal system	1.1	
	Muscular system	1.2	
	Nervous system	1.3	
	Circulatory system	1.4	
	Respiratory system	1.5	
	Digestive system	1.6	
2	**The skeleton**		
	Functions of the skeleton	2.1	
	Skeletal system	2.2	
	Bones	2.3	
	Major types of joints	2.4	
	Synovial joints	2.5	
	Bone development	2.6	
	Ligaments	2.7	
	Cartilage	2.8	
3	**Muscles of the body**		
	Muscle types	3.1	
	Skeletal muscle fibres at work	3.2	
	Skeletal muscle fibres and movement	3.3	
	Muscles and energy	3.4	
	Effects of exercise on muscles	3.5	
4	**Control of movement**		
	Central nervous system	4.1	
	Nerves	4.2	
	Nervous co-ordination	4.3	
	Reflex actions	4.4	
5	**Circulatory system**		
	Blood circulation	5	
	Heart	5.1	
	Pulse	5.2	
	Blood vessels	5.3	
	Watch pocket valves	5.4	
	Blood structure	5.5	
	Functions of blood	5.6	
	Blood pressure	5.7	
	Effects of exercise on the system	5.8	
6	**Respiratory system**		
	Respiratory tract	6.1	
	Gaseous exchange	6.2	
	Mechanism of breathing	6.3	
	Lung capacity	6.4	
	Effects of exercise	6.5	
7	**Digestion and diet**		
	Alimentary canal	7.1	
	Peristalsis	7.2	
	Diet	7.3	
	Balanced diet	7.4	
	Diet and exercise	7.5	

Starting points

8	**Fitness**		
	What is fitness?	8.1	
	Physical fitness	8.2	
	Components of fitness	8.3	
	Strength	8.4	
	Speed	8.5	
	Stamina	8.6	
	Suppleness	8.7	
	Motor fitness	8.8	
	Influence on fitness	8.9	
9	**Improving fitness**		
	Overload	9.1	
	Progression	9.2	
	Specificity	9.3	
	Reversibility	9.4	
	Training threshold	9.5	
	Training methods	9.6	
	Training sessions	9.7	
	Rest periods	9.8	
10	**Acquisition of skill**		
	Skill defined	10.1	R
	Open and closed skills	10.2	R
	Processing information	10.3	R
	Overloading the processing model	10.4	R
	Factors affecting performance	10.5	R
11	**Effects on fitness**		
	Food and diet	11.1	
	Lifestyle	11.2	
	Illness and injury	11.3	
	Physical make-up	11.4	
	Personal history	11.5	
	Environmental conditions	11.6	
	Drug use and abuse	11.7	
12	**Measurement in sport**		
	Tests of suppleness	12.1	
	Tests of strength	12.2	
	Tests of endurance	12.3	
13	**Sports related injuries**		
	Safe practice	13.1	
	What to do	13.2	
	Soft tissue injuries	13.3	
	Hard tissue injuries	13.4	
	Miscellaneous injuries	13.5	
	Injuries associated with specific sports	13.6	
14	**Administration of sport**		
	Structure of sport	14.1	
	Governing bodies of sport	14.2	
	Central Council for Physical Recreation	14.3	
	Sports Council	14.4	
	British Olympic Association	14.5	
	International Olympic Committee	14.6	
	International Sports Federation	14.7	
	Development of international competitions	14.8	
	Recreational quangos	14.9	
15	**Providers of sports facilities**		
	National providers	15.1	
	Local providers	15.2	
	Voluntary providers	15.3	
	Commercial providers	15.4	
	Finance of sport	15.5	
	Obtaining money in sport	15.6	
	Spending in sport	15.7	
16	**Participation in sport**		
	Leisure, recreation and sport	16.1	
	Leisure time	16.2	
	Reasons for sports participation	16.3	
	Growth of sports participation	16.4	
	User groups in sport	16.5	
	Factors affecting sports participation	16.6	
	Promotional campaigns	16.7	
17	**Development of international competition**		
	Codification of rules	17.1	R
	International competitions	17.2	R
	Modern Olympic Games	17.3	

18	Major influences on sport		
	Finance of sport	18.1	
	Amateur vs professional	18.2	
	The professional amateur	18.3	
	Sponsorship in sport	18.4	
	The media in sport	18.5	
	Politics and sport	18.6	
19	Changing attitudes in sport		
	Attitude towards winning	19.1	
	Abuse of drugs	19.2	
	Spectatorism	19.3	
	Crowd violence	19.4	
20	Social concepts in sport		
	Discrimination in sport	20.1	
	Women in sport	20.2	
	The disabled and sport	20.3	

R = Recommended; all other topics listed are essential.

NEAB Exam breakdown

Physical Education (1271)

1 written paper	2 hrs	30% of total marks
practical:	4 activities from 3+ groups	50% of total marks
analytical investigation		20% of total marks

Physical Education (short course) (2271)

1 written paper	1½ hrs	40% of total marks
practical:	2 activities from 2 groups	50% of total marks
personal improvement programme		10% of total marks

* *Also see coursework requirements in Chapter 21 and 22*

Northern Ireland Council for the Curriculum Examinations and Assessment (NICCEA)

Address: Clarendon Dock, 29 Clarendon Road, Belfast BT1 3BG
Tel no: 01232 26 1200

Syllabus topic		Covered in Unit no	✔
1	Human body		
	Skeletal system	1.1	
	Muscular system	1.2	
	Nervous system	1.3	
	Circulatory system	1.4	
	Respiratory system	1.5	
	Digestive system	1.6	
2	The skeleton		
	Functions of the skeleton	2.1	
	Skeletal system	2.2	
	Bones	2.3	
	Major types of joints	2.4	
	Synovial joints	2.5	
	Bone development	2.6	
	Ligaments	2.7	
	Cartilage	2.8	
3	Muscles of the body		
	Muscle types	3.1	
	Skeletal muscle fibres at work	3.2	
	Skeletal muscle fibres and movement	3.3	
	Muscles and energy	3.4	
	Effects of exercise on muscles	3.5	
4	Control of movement		
	Central nervous system	4.1	
	Nerves	4.2	
	Nervous co-ordination	4.3	
	Reflex actions	4.4	
5	Circulatory system		
	Blood circulation	5	
	Heart	5.1	
	Pulse	5.2	

Starting points

	Blood vessels	5.3	
	Watch pocket valves	5.4	
	Blood structure	5.5	
	Functions of blood	5.6	
	Blood pressure	5.7	
	Effects of exercise on the system	5.8	
6	**Respiratory system**		
	Respiratory tract	6.1	
	Gaseous exchange	6.2	
	Mechanism of breathing	6.3	
	Lung capacity	6.4	
	Effects of exercise	6.5	
7	**Digestion and diet**		
	Alimentary canal	7.1	
	Peristalsis	7.2	
	Diet	7.3	
	Balanced diet	7.4	
	Diet and exercise	7.5	
8	**Fitness**		
	What is fitness?	8.1	
	Physical fitness	8.2	
	Components of fitness	8.3	
	Strength	8.4	
	Speed	8.5	
	Stamina	8.6	
	Suppleness	8.7	
	Motor fitness	8.8	
	Influence on fitness	8.9	
9	**Improving fitness**		
	Overload	9.1	
	Progression	9.2	
	Specificity	9.3	
	Reversibility	9.4	
	Training threshold	9.5	
	Training methods	9.6	
	Training sessions	9.7	
	Rest periods	9.8	
10	**Acquisition of skill**		
	Skill defined	10.1	
	Open and closed skills	10.2	
	Processing information	10.3	
	Overloading the processing model	10.4	
	Factors affecting performance	10.5	
11	**Effects on fitness**		
	Food and diet	11.1	
	Lifestyle	11.2	
	Illness and injury	11.3	
	Physical make-up	11.4	
	Personal history	11.5	
	Environmental conditions	11.6	
	Drug use and abuse	11.7	
12	**Measurement in sport**		
	Tests of suppleness	12.1	
	Tests of strength	12.2	
	Tests of endurance	12.3	
13	**Sports related injuries**		
	Safe practice	13.1	
	What to do	13.2	R
	Soft tissue injuries	13.3	R
	Hard tissue injuries	13.4	R
	Miscellaneous injuries	13.5	R
	Injuries associated with specific sports	13.6	R
14	**Administration of sport**		
	Structure of sport	14.1	
	Governing bodies of sport	14.2	
	Central Council for Physical Recreation	14.3	
	Sports Council	14.4	
	British Olympic Association	14.5	
	International Olympic Committee	14.6	
	International Sports Federation	14.7	
	Development of international competitions	14.8	
	Recreational quangos	14.9	

15	**Providers of sports facilities**		
	National providers	15.1	
	Local providers	15.2	
	Voluntary providers	15.3	
	Commercial providers	15.4	
	Finance of sport	15.5	
	Obtaining money in sport	15.6	
	Spending in sport	15.7	
16	**Participation in sport**		
	Leisure, recreation and sport	16.1	
	Leisure time	16.2	
	Reasons for sports participation	16.3	
	Growth of sports participation	16.4	
	User groups in sport	16.5	
	Factors affecting sports participation	16.6	
	Promotional campaigns	16.7	
17	**Development of international competition**		
	Codification of rules	17.1	R
	International competitions	17.2	R
	Modern Olympic Games	17.3	
18	**Major influences on sport**		
	Finance of sport	18.1	
	Amateur v professional	18.2	
	The professional amateur	18.3	
	Sponsorship in sport	18.4	
	The media in sport	18.5	
	Politics and sport	18.6	
19	**Changing attitudes in sport**		
	Attitude towards winning	19.1	
	Abuse of drugs	19.2	
	Spectatorism	19.3	
	Crowd violence	19.4	
20	**Social concepts in sport**		
	Discrimination in sport	20.1	
	Women in sport	20.2	
	The disabled and sport	20.3	

R = Recommended; all other topics listed are essential.

NICCEA Exam breakdown

Physical Education (no number)

2 written papers	1½ hrs each	20% each of total marks
practical:	4 activities from 8 groups	50% of total marks
performance, evaluation and improvement		10% of total marks

Welsh Joint Education Committee (WJEC)

Address: 245 Western Avenue, Cardiff CF5 2YX
Tel no: 01222 562 231

Syllabus topic		Covered in Unit no	✔
1	**Human body**		
	Skeletal system	1.1	
	Muscular system	1.2	
	Nervous system	1.3	
	Circulatory system	1.4	
	Respiratory system	1.5	
	Digestive system	1.6	
2	**The skeleton**		
	Functions of the skeleton	2.1	R
	Skeletal system	2.2	R
	Bones	2.3	R
	Major types of joints	2.4	R
	Synovial joints	2.5	R
	Bone development	2.6	R
	Ligaments	2.7	R
	Cartilage	2.8	R
3	**Muscles of the body**		
	Muscle types	3.1	R

Starting points

		Skeletal muscle fibres at work	3.2	R
		Skeletal muscle fibres and movement	3.3	R
		Muscles and energy	3.4	R
		Effects of exercise on muscles	3.5	R
4	**Control of movement**			
		Central nervous system	4.1	R
		Nerves	4.2	R
		Nervous co-ordination	4.3	R
		Reflex actions	4.4	R
5	**Circulatory system**			
		Blood circulation	5	
		Heart	5.1	
		Pulse	5.2	
		Blood vessels	5.3	
		Watch pocket valves	5.4	
		Blood structure	5.5	
		Functions of blood	5.6	
		Blood pressure	5.7	
		Effects of exercise on the system	5.8	
6	**Respiratory system**			
		Respiratory tract	6.1	
		Gaseous exchange	6.2	
		Mechanism of breathing	6.3	
		Lung capacity	6.4	
		Effects of exercise	6.5	
7	**Digestion and diet**			
		Alimentary canal	7.1	R
		Peristalsis	7.2	R
		Diet	7.3	
		Balanced diet	7.4	
		Diet and exercise	7.5	
8	**Fitness**			
		What is fitness?	8.1	
		Physical fitness	8.2	
		Components of fitness	8.3	
		Strength	8.4	
		Speed	8.5	
		Stamina	8.6	
		Suppleness	8.7	
		Motor fitness	8.8	
		Influence on fitness	8.9	
9	**Improving fitness**			
		Overload	9.1	
		Progression	9.2	
		Specificity	9.3	
		Reversibility	9.4	
		Training threshold	9.5	
		Training methods	9.6	
		Training sessions	9.7	
		Rest periods	9.8	
10	**Acquisition of skill**			
		Skill defined	10.1	
		Open and closed skills	10.2	
		Processing information	10.3	
		Overloading the processing model	10.4	
		Factors affecting performance	10.5	
11	**Effects on fitness**			
		Food and diet	11.1	
		Lifestyle	11.2	
		Illness and injury	11.3	
		Physical make-up	11.4	
		Personal history	11.5	
		Environmental conditions	11.6	
		Drug use and abuse	11.7	
12	**Measurement in sport**			
		Tests of suppleness	12.1	
		Tests of strength	12.2	
		Tests of endurance	12.3	
13	**Sports related injuries**			
		Safe practice	13.1	
		What to do	13.2	
		Soft tissue injuries	13.3	
		Hard tissue injuries	13.4	

	Miscellaneous injuries	13.5	
	Injuries associated with specific sports	13.6	
14	**Administration of sport**		
	Structure of sport	14.1	
	Governing bodies of sport	14.2	
	Central Council for Physical Recreation	14.3	
	Sports Council	14.4	
	British Olympic Association	14.5	
	International Olympic Committee	14.6	
	International Sports Federation	14.7	
	Development of international competitions	14.8	
	Recreational quangos	14.9	
15	**Providers of sports facilities**		
	National providers	15.1	
	Local providers	15.2	
	Voluntary providers	15.3	
	Commercial providers	15.4	
	Finance of sport	15.5	
	Obtaining money in sport	15.6	
	Spending in sport	15.7	
16	**Participation in sport**		
	Leisure, recreation and sport	16.1	
	Leisure time	16.2	
	Reasons for sports participation	16.3	
	Growth of sports participation	16.4	
	User groups in sport	16.5	
	Factors affecting sports participation	16.6	
	Promotional campaigns	16.7	
17	**Development of international competition**		
	Codification of rules	17.1	R
	International competitions	17.2	R
	Modern Olympic Games	17.3	R
18	**Major influences on sport**		
	Finance of sport	18.1	
	Amateur v professional	18.2	
	The professional amateur	18.3	
	Sponsorship in sport	18.4	
	The media in sport	18.5	
	Politics and sport	18.6	
19	**Changing attitudes in sport**		
	Attitude towards winning	19.1	
	Abuse of drugs	19.2	
	Spectatorism	19.3	
	Crowd violence	19.4	
20	**Social concepts in sport**		
	Discrimination in sport	20.1	
	Women in sport	20.2	
	The disabled and sport	20.3	

R = Recommended; all other topics listed are essential.

WJEC Exam breakdown

Physical Education (no number)
Paper 1 video-based questions		10% of total marks
Paper 2 written	2 hrs	30% of total marks
practical:	4 activities from 3 of the National Curriculum areas	

Physical Education (short course) (no number)
1 written paper	1 ½ hrs	40% of total marks
practical:	2 activities from 2 of the National Curriculum areas	

Scottish Qualifications Authority (formerly SEB)

Address: Ironmills Road, Dalkeith, Midlothian EH22 1LE
Tel no: 0131 663 6601

The Scottish Qualifications Authority offer Physical Education for assessment at three levels, Foundation, General and Credit, and papers include questions relating to differing activities as shown on a video. Some questions are based on an analysis of the activity seen and these are followed by questions of a broader nature. These latter questions require a wider knowledge of the subject area. They often ask for information relating to training, training methods, aspects of fitness and the basic anatomy of physical performance.

In preparing for this examination you should concentrate on the section of this study guide relating to the Capabilities of the Human Body, ch 8 to 11. The section dealing with the Body's Make Up Relating to Movement, ch 1-6, provides a good underpinning knowledge of the subject.

Starting points

Using the material

Work through only those units that you need for your syllabus and do not try to cover too many topics at one sitting. Remember that the marks available in the examination account for 40% of the total available marks for the final grade award (30% in the case of the NEAB syllabus). The remainder of your marks are awarded for practical coursework that is assessed in your school or college. The examination is an important part of the total assessment and can alter radically any grade predicted on the basis of your coursework.

Learning and remembering

The best way to learn about most aspects of physical education is through practical experience. However it is not always possible to acquire all the knowledge necessary for this subject by practical means. It is therefore necessary to learn facts by reading texts such as this and be able to recall them for examination purposes.

The important points dealt with in this book are summarised at the end of each chapter under the heading *Principal topics covered*. Read the relevant unit first, making sure that you understand it, then use the summary points as topic points for your own notes or as memory prompts for revision. Summary points should help you to recall the detail of the unit. Reading through them and making notes from memory on the topics concerned will also help you to see which units need to be studied again. *The learning of summary points should not be seen as a substitute for learning the contents of the unit.*

Memory aids:

1 Repetition
By writing or saying something aloud over and over again, you can often learn a fact 'parrot fashion'. This method has its drawbacks, as you might not understand what you can remember.

2 Mnemonics
These are devices to aid memory, such as the use of a word whose letters remind you of important items of information. There are examples of mnemonics in this text: the RICE formula (standing for: rest, ice, compression, elevation) in Unit 14 is one. If you make up your own mnemonic, use a word which is distinctive and easy to remember.

3 Flow diagrams
These are made by starting with a key word and linking others to it by lines. The lines may radiate outwards like a diagram of the sun, up and down like a ladder, or link words in a circle. This flow diagram to show the main components of fitness is an example.

```
STRENGTH ─────────╲         ╱───────── STAMINA
                   ►FITNESS◄
SUPPLENESS ───────╱         ╲───────── SPEED
```

Revision programmes

At the end of your course, but before your final examination, you will need to revise thoroughly. You should have already covered the course units to be studied. All that is now needed is that you 'refresh' your memory and add to it. You should devise a realistic revision programme that will be effective. Your programme should:

- allow you to show yourself what you already know about a topic
- show what you need to concentrate on for a given topic
- be timetabled in such as way that you work for several time slots over a number of days.

Take some practical measures to help ensure that your revision strategy is effective. Choose a workplace which does not offer too many distractions, so that you can concentrate fully on the task you have set yourself in the time slot you have allowed. Make sure that you get some fresh air and exercise regularly during your revision period: a short walk is ideal. It is important not to get stale as this makes concentration more difficult. Try to ensure that you get enough sleep, too.

Most people who read a new piece of text will, on average, be able to recall only 15% to 20% of it a week later. However, you should not be put off by this. When you re-read the same piece of text, your recall increases by a similar amount. Thus repeated revision of the text will dramatically increase your memory of the facts. During revision periods it is advisable to start off by writing down all that you can remember about a given topic. Then aim to build on this knowledge.

Remember:

- All of us have different 'concentration times': you can find out how long yours is by trying the following test. Concentrate hard while reading a text which is new to you. When you find that your mind begins to wander, you are reaching the end of your concentration time. This will probably be between 20 and 40 minutes.
- Each person will learn and be able to recall facts at a different rate.
- Make a realistic estimate of how much you feel you can revise each week over a long period and set yourself targets.
- Divide your time into study periods of approximately 30 minutes with short breaks between them.
- Test yourself to see if you are reaching your own targets. If not, perhaps you are trying to do too much: you may need to re-define your targets.
- The use of revision notes, flow charts and simple tables will aid memory.
- If you find that you do not understand a topic, do not be afraid to ask your teacher. He or she should be happy to help.
- Do not leave your revision too late: use half-term holidays and any other breaks that you get.

To help you keep track of your revision programme, you might like to construct a topic card like this:

SYLLABUS	MEG Physical Education (full course)		
Topic	Unit covered	Revised	Self-tested
Circulatory system	5	✓	✓
Heart	5.1	✓	✓
Pulse	5.2	✓	

Use a different card for each separate topic. Each card then represents a stage in your revision programme.

Place a tick in each of the final columns as you complete each section of your topic. As each is completed you can see the progress you are making with your revision. It gives enormous satisfaction to see the list of ticks grow, and it reminds you of your progress.

These cards can also serve as quick revision reminders just before you sit your examination. A quick glance through them should jog your memory.

Preparing for examinations

It is very important that, having worked hard throughout the year and having revised thoroughly, you do yourself justice in the written examination. Here are some tips to help you.

1. Give yourself plenty of practice in reading examination papers so that you are familiar with the style of language employed and know the kind of response you are expected to give when terms such as 'explain', 'describe' or 'discuss' are used.

2. Take advantage of all opportunities to answer examination questions. This is not only a good way of getting used to working to time, but also helps to focus revision.

3. Accustom yourself to using the marks available for each question as an indication of how detailed your answer should be.

4. Above all, go into the examination with a positive attitude.

The human body's make-up relating to movement

Chapter 1
The human body

The scientific aspects of physical education focus on the human body. The human body is a very complex machine which is made up of many parts. Although each part has its own individual job to do, no part can work in isolation from the other parts.

When parts of the body work closely together in a specific process, they and their activity are known as a **system** within the body.

From the range of body systems which can be identified, the following six are of importance to this study and will be looked at in greater depth in succeeding chapters. They are:

1.1 The skeletal system

This includes all the bones of the body, their attachments, the joints and their range of movement. (See Fig. 1.1, which shows the main parts of the human skeleton.)

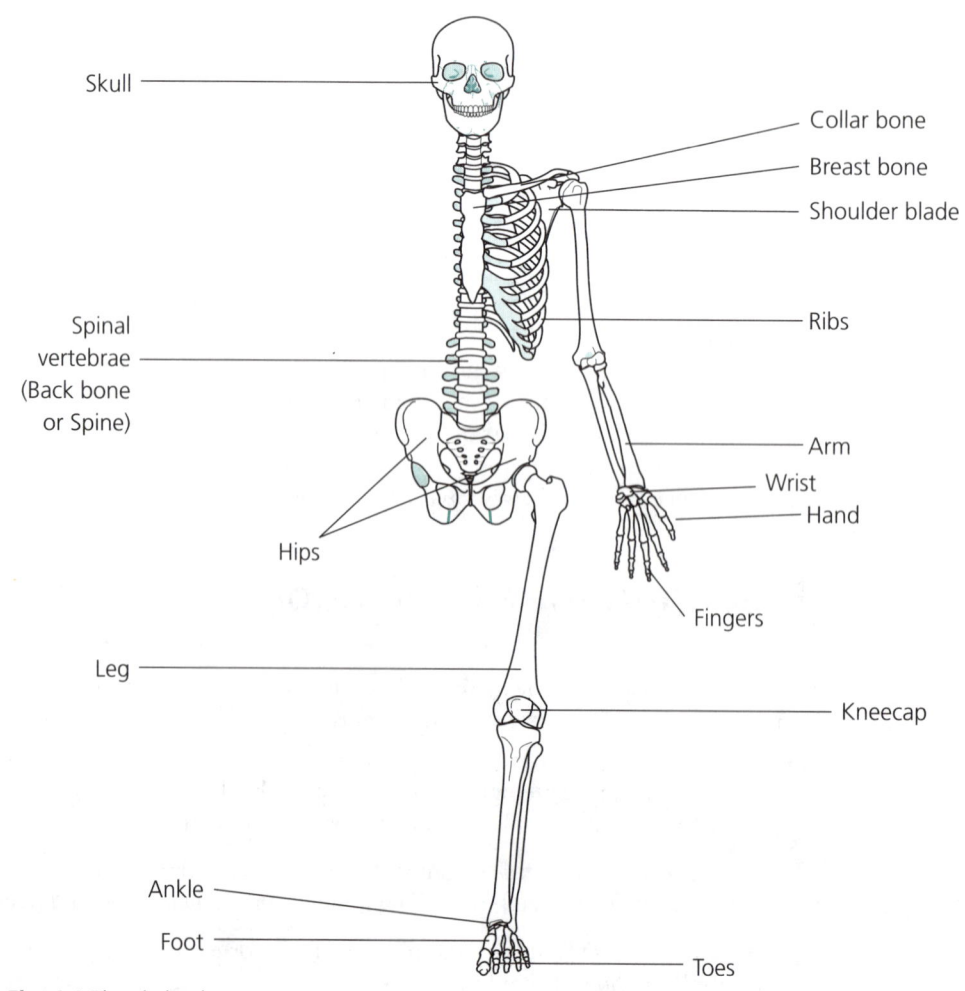

Fig. 1.1 The skeletal system

1.2 The muscular system

This includes the three main types of muscles and their attachment to bones (where appropriate). It also involves the production of energy. (See Fig. 1.2.)

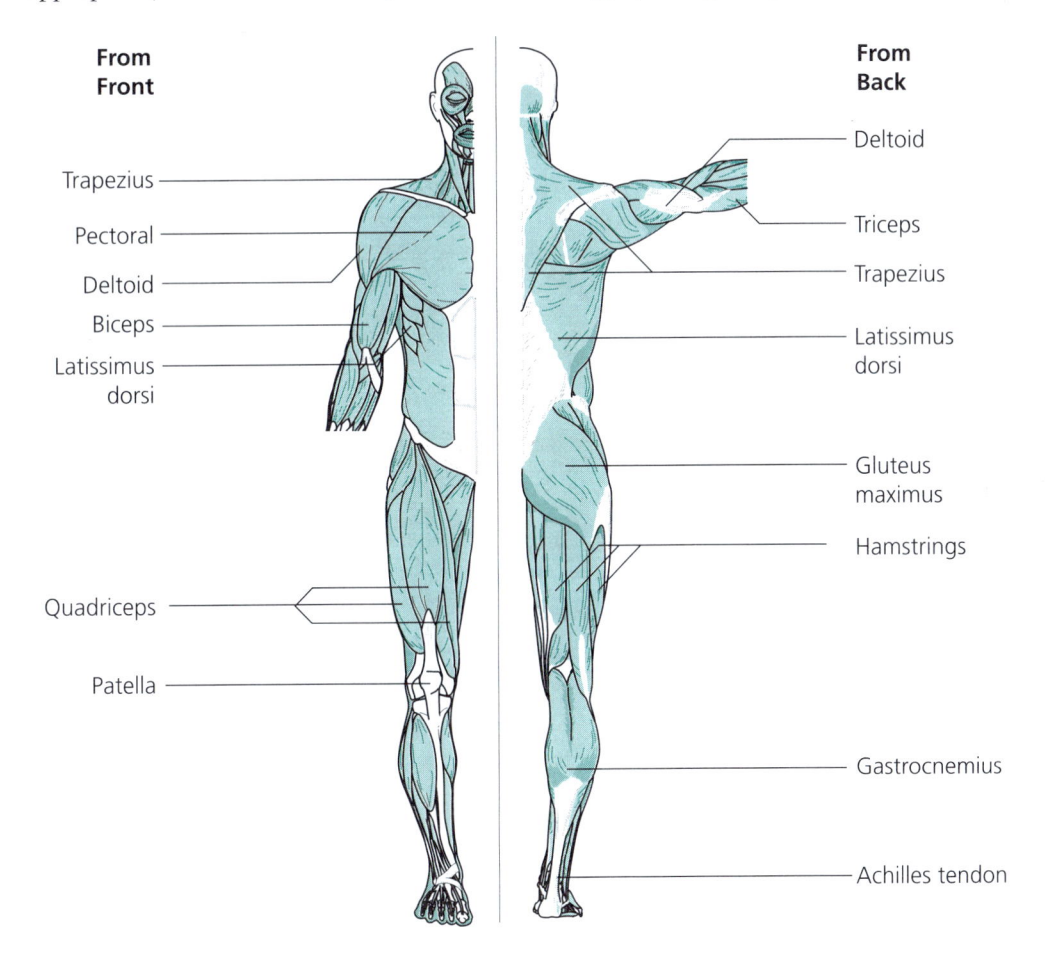

From Front
- Trapezius
- Pectoral
- Deltoid
- Biceps
- Latissimus dorsi
- Quadriceps
- Patella

From Back
- Deltoid
- Triceps
- Trapezius
- Latissimus dorsi
- Gluteus maximus
- Hamstrings
- Gastrocnemius
- Achilles tendon

Fig. 1.2 The muscular system

1.3 The nervous system

This includes the brain, brain stem and spinal cord (the Central Nervous System), where all decisions are made; and the nerves of the body, which carry information and instructions from the CNS to all parts of the body and vice versa. (See Fig. 1.3.)

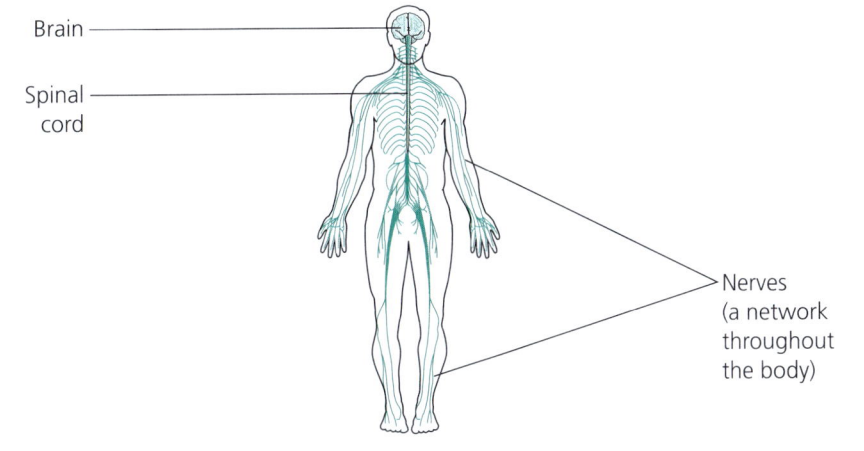

- Brain
- Spinal cord
- Nerves (a network throughout the body)

Fig. 1.3 The nervous system

The human body's make-up relating to movement

1.4 The circulatory system

This includes the heart, the blood and blood vessels, and the transport of gases to and from the various parts of the body. (See Fig. 1.4 which shows the main organs through which blood circulates in the human body.)

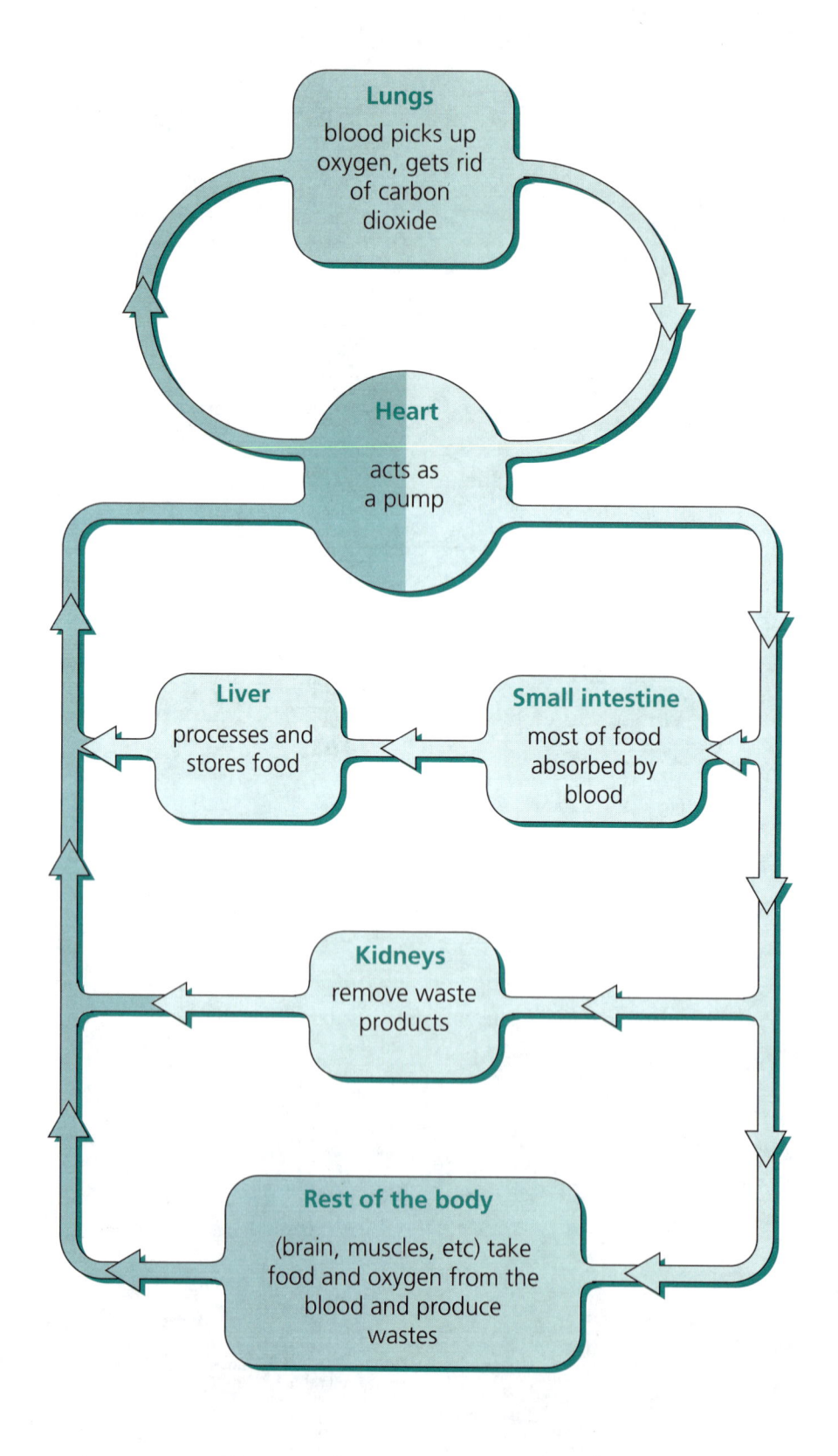

```
           Lungs
      blood picks up
      oxygen, gets rid
         of carbon
          dioxide

           Heart
          acts as
          a pump

    Liver              Small intestine
processes and           most of food
 stores food            absorbed by
                           blood

          Kidneys
        remove waste
          products

       Rest of the body
     (brain, muscles, etc) take
     food and oxygen from the
       blood and produce
             wastes
```

Fig. 1.4 The circulatory system

1.5 The respiratory system

This includes the nasal passages, the windpipe and lungs, all aspects of the breathing process and the transfer of gases to and from the blood. (See Fig. 1.5.)

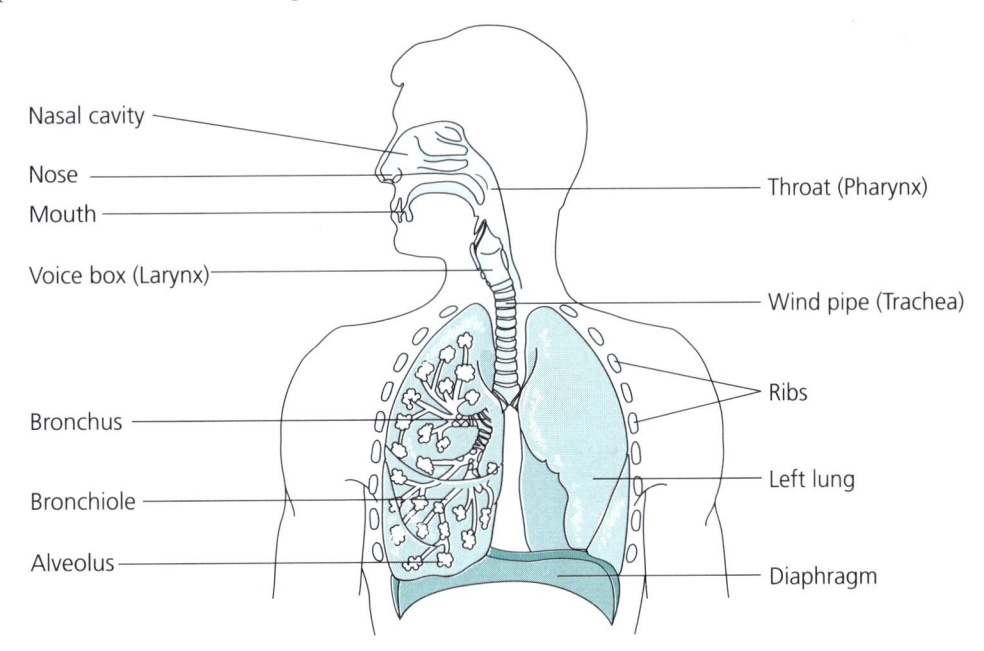

Labels: Nasal cavity, Nose, Mouth, Voice box (Larynx), Bronchus, Bronchiole, Alveolus, Throat (Pharynx), Wind pipe (Trachea), Ribs, Left lung, Diaphragm

Fig. 1.5 The respiratory system

Examiner's tip
You should be able to list the main parts of the nervous, circulatory, respiratory and digestive systems and place them with accuracy on an outline of the body.

1.6 The digestive system

This includes food intake through the mouth via the gullet to the stomach, its passage through the intestines and its disposal as waste matter through the anus. (See Fig. 1.6.)

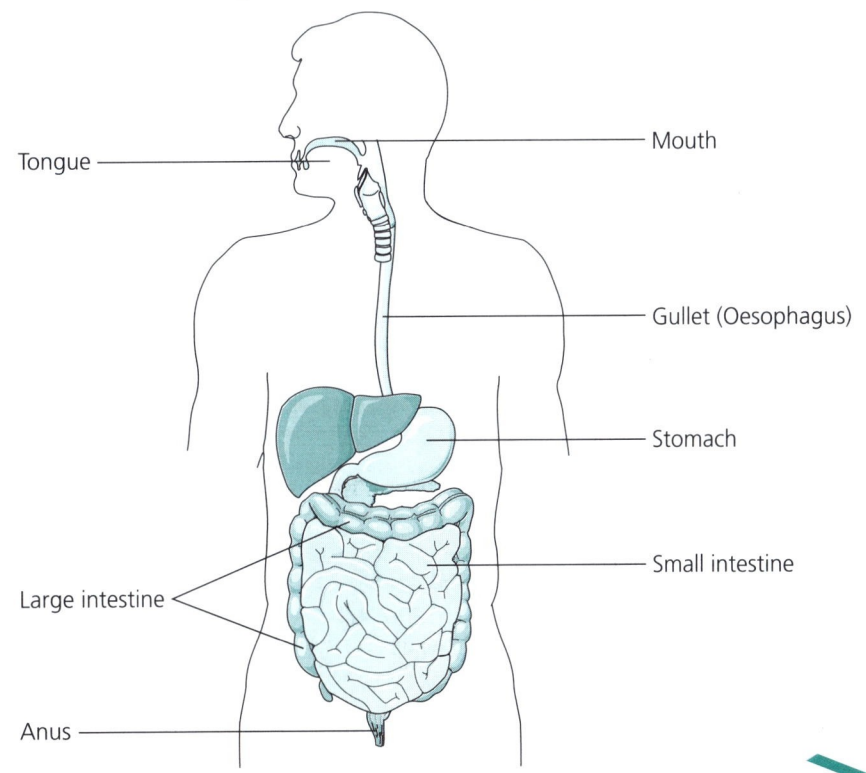

Labels: Tongue, Large intestine, Anus, Mouth, Gullet (Oesophagus), Stomach, Small intestine

Fig. 1.6 The digestive system

Chapter 2
The skeleton

2.1 Functions of the skeleton

The skeleton has four main functions:

❶ production of blood   Blood is produced in the marrow of the long bones. Bone marrow is a type of matter found in the centre of bones.

❷ protection   The skeleton protects the delicate parts of the body such as the brain, lungs and heart.

❸ support   The shape of the body is maintained by the skeleton and some organs are suspended from the bones.

❹ movement   This is made possible because the skeleton has many joints, and muscles pull on separate bones.

Examiner's tip

You should be able to name and place the major bones of the body and limbs. You should know their correct anatomical names as well as their common everyday names.

2.2 Skeletal system

The bones of the body make up the skeletal system (see Figs. 2.1 and 2.2). The skeletal system is divided into two main parts:

❶ The **axial** skeleton is made up of the *skull* and *thoracic vertebra*. These bones form the main support of the body.

The skull consists of over 20 bones, although many are fused together to form the *cranium* and upper jaw. There is no movement at these joints. The lower jaw is attached to the skull by *ligaments* (a type of connective tissue) to the cranium in front of and below the ear. The skull protects the brain, ears and eyes.

The thoracic vertebrae, including the ribs and *sternum* (or breast bone), are sometimes referred to as the **thoracic skeleton**. These combine to form a large compartment that contains the lungs and the heart. The movement allowed in this compartment is involved in the breathing mechanism of the body, explained more fully in Chapter 6. The vertebrae of the *sacrum* and *coccyx* regions of the spine or *vertebral column* are fused together and do not allow any movement.

❷ The **appendicular skeleton** includes the shoulder and hip girdle, and the arms and legs.

The shoulder and hip girdles form a strong rigid connection between the limbs and the axial skeleton. They also form good points of attachment for the muscles of the limbs which are also connected to the axial skeleton, thus allowing for movement.

The bones of the upper limbs are laid in a similar pattern to those of the lower limbs. Each is attached to the relevant girdle by a single long bone, the *humerus* in the upper arm and the *femur* in the upper leg. To each of these is attached two further long bones, the *radius* and *ulna* in the arm and the *tibia* and *fibula* in the leg. The hand is made up of 13 *carpals* and *metacarpals* and the fingers of 14 *phalanges*. The foot has 12 *tarsals* and *metatarsals* and the toes 14 *phalanges*. The leg has one further bone: the *patella* or kneecap. This overlaps the *femur* and *tibia*.

The skeleton

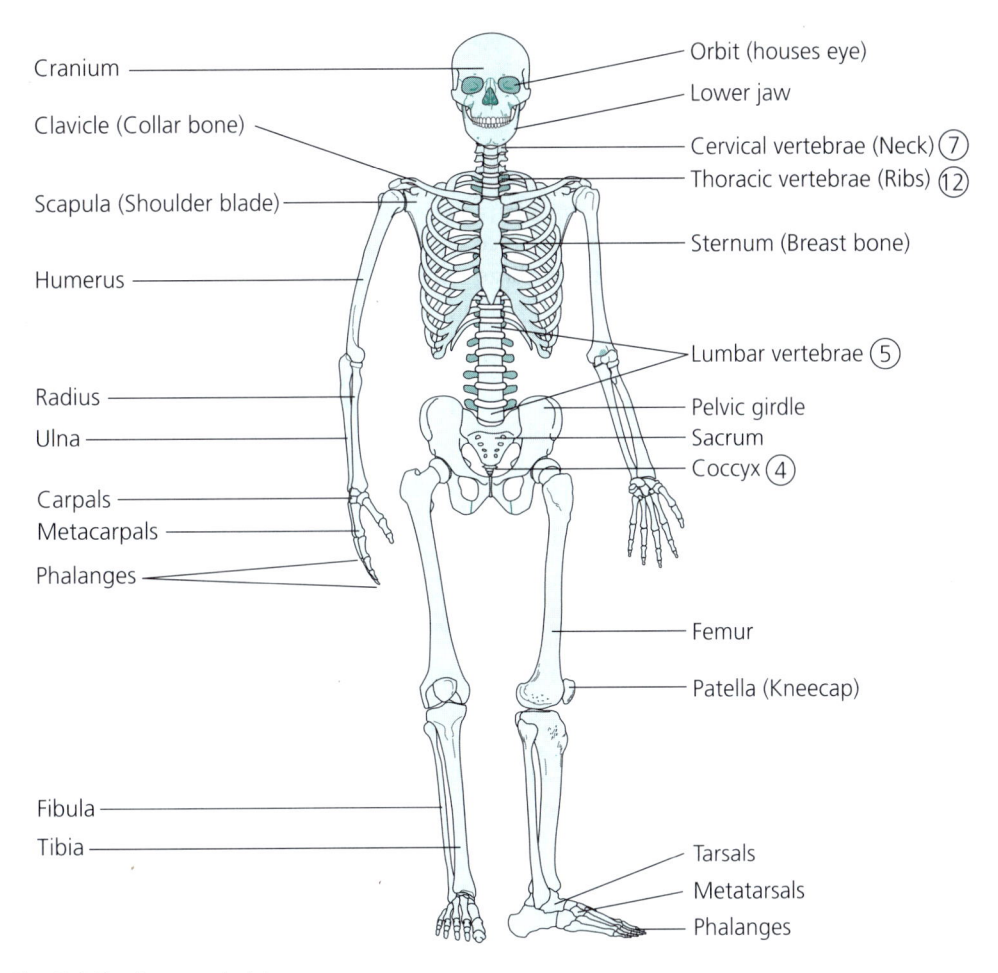

Fig. 2.1 The human skeleton

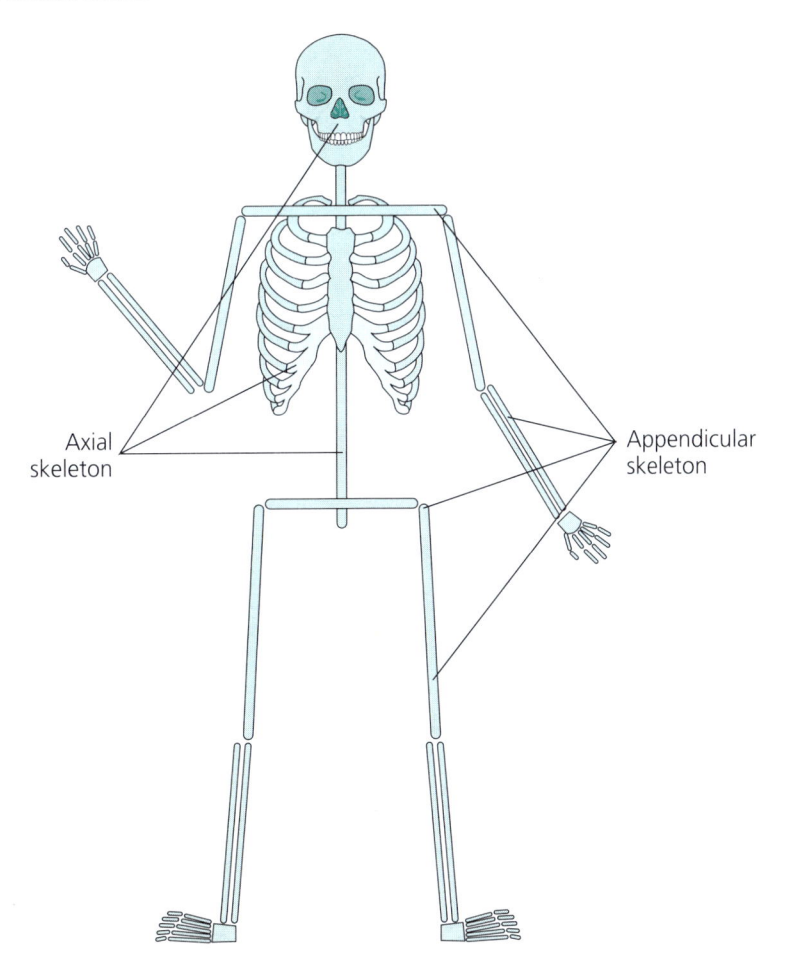

Fig. 2.2 The basic structure of the skeleton

The human body's make-up relating to movement

> **Examiner's tip**
>
> You should know the difference between spongy and compact bones and how to describe them. You should be able to describe the main shapes of bones, give examples and state their position in the body.

2.3 Bones

The skeleton consists of over 200 bones of many shapes and sizes. Bones are classified as being either **spongy** or **compact**.

Spongy bone has a honeycomb appearance and is found at the ends of bones. It is usually covered by **articular cartilage** which is a tough, durable substance that prevents wear.

Compact bone runs the length of the bone and consists of a central canal surrounded by concentric ring-shaped calcium-based plates, rather like the rings seen when you cut across a tree trunk. The whole of the length of a tubular or long bone is covered by a tough connecting tissue called the **periosteum**. This joins or connects muscle to bone, and contains many small blood vessels.

The main shapes of bones are:

1. **long** — Long bones are found in the arms and legs. They are also known as **tubular bones** (see Figs. 2.3 and 2.4).
2. **short** — Found in the wrist and ankle.
3. **flat** — Found in the skull or the *scapula* (shoulder blade).
4. **irregular** — Found in the spinal column (*vertebrae*) or the jaw bone.

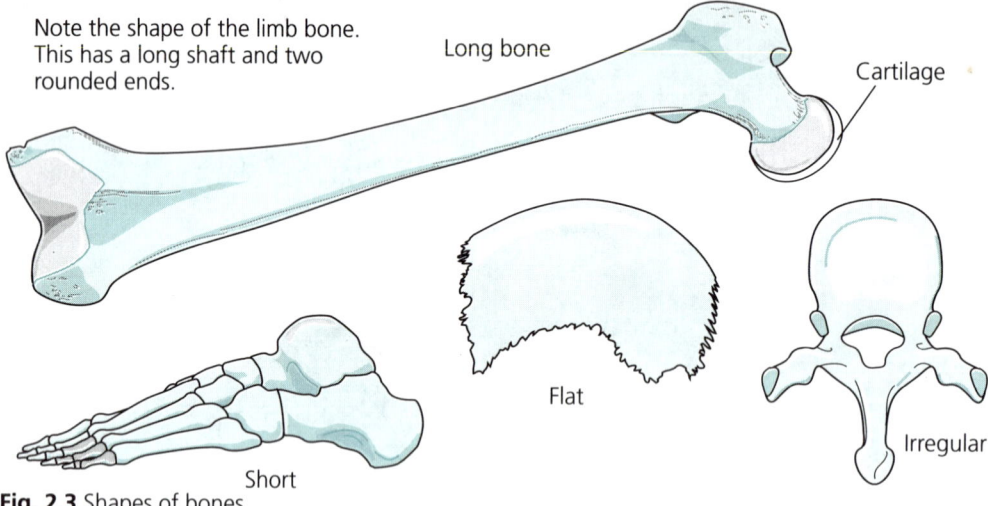

Note the shape of the limb bone. This has a long shaft and two rounded ends.

Fig. 2.3 Shapes of bones

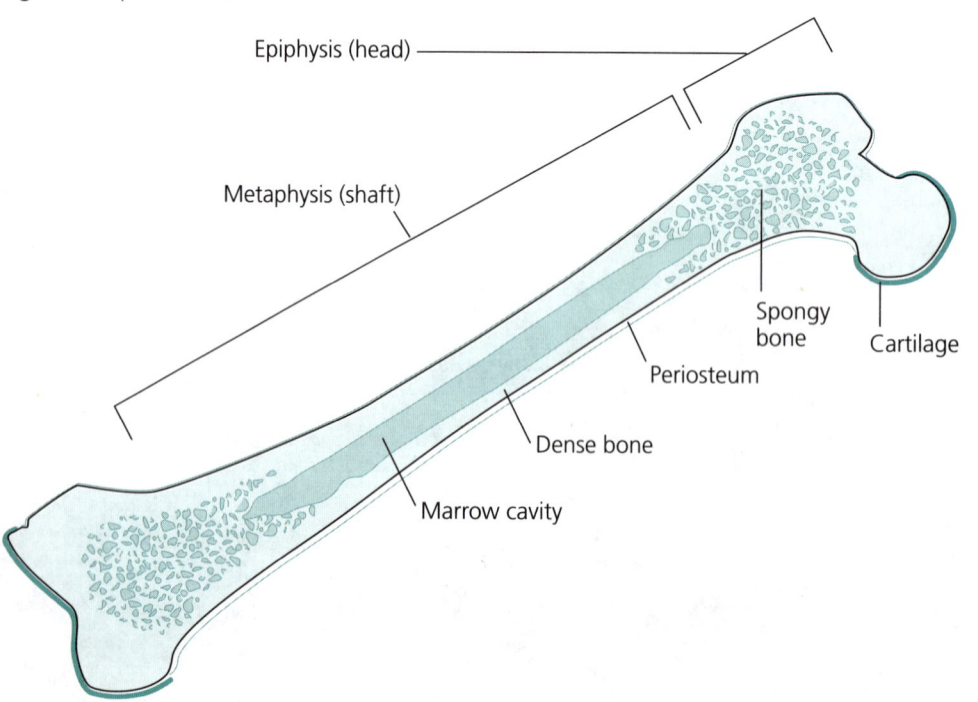

Fig. 2.4 The general structure of a long bone

The skeleton

Together, the bones of the skeleton form a strong structure. However, individual bones can be damaged. As they get older they become more brittle and can easily break or fracture.

Bones have the ability to repair themselves (see Fig. 2.5).

This bone has broken. Blood from the vessels that have burst in the bone form a clot round the jagged ends of the broken bone.

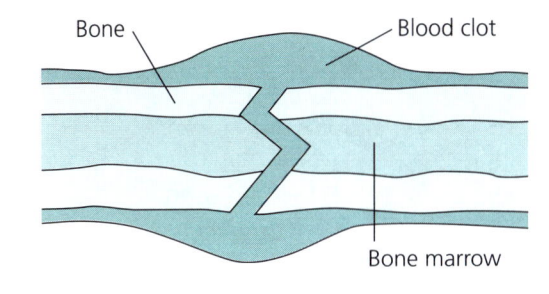

The ends of the broken bone become soft and a connective tissue forms a **callus** (soft bone) to hold both ends together. Special cells called **osteoblasts** strengthen the new bone tissue.

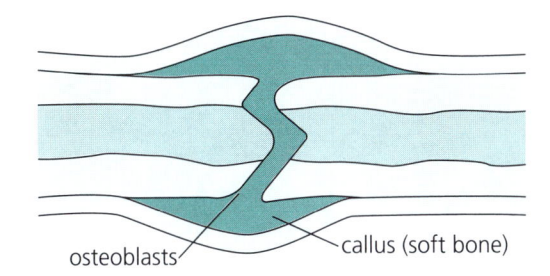

When the new soft bone (callus) hardens, the bone is almost fully repaired. The material round the injury site is absorbed back into the bone.

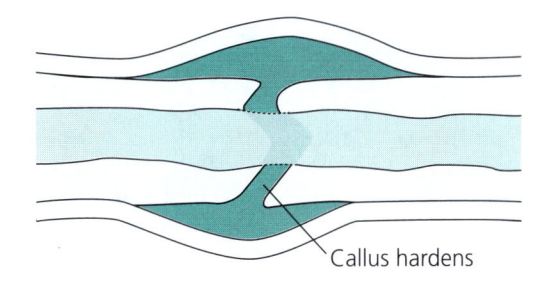

Fig 2.5 How a broken bone repairs itself

> **Examiner's tip**
>
> You should know the main types of joint, their strength and range of movement, and be able to give examples of each type.

2.4 Major types of joint

The places where two or more bones meet are called **joints** (see Table 2.1).

Table 2.1 Types of joint

	Type	How strong	Position in body	Range of movement
synovial joints (see Unit 2.5)	**i** ball and socket	very strong	hip/shoulder	full
	ii hinge	fairly strong	elbow	limited
	iii saddle	fairly weak	base of thumb	limited
	iv condyloid	weak	wrist	2 ways only
	v pivot	fairly strong	neck	rotation only
	vi slightly movable	weak	vertebrae (spine)	depends on position
	vii immovable *	–	skull	none
			sacrum	none

* These are the odd ones out as no movement occurs at these joints: the bones are fused together (see Fig. 2.8).

25

The human body's make-up relating to movement

i Ball and socket joint
The ball shaped end of the femur fits into a cup shaped socket in the pelvis and allows for movement in all directions.

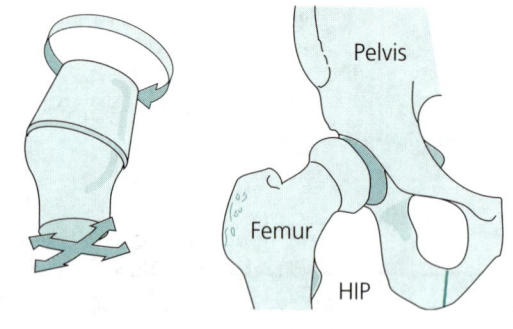

ii Hinge joint
Movement is allowed in one plane only.

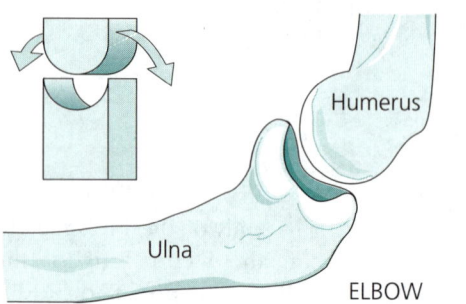

iii Saddle joint
The opposing convex and concave surfaces of the two bones allow movement in two directions.

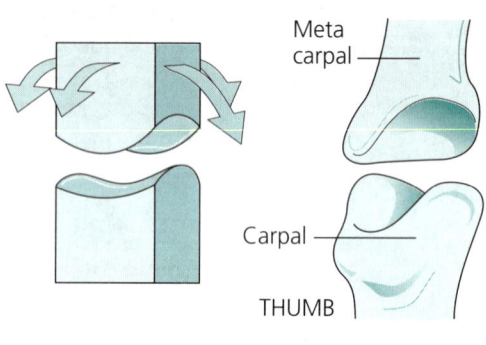

iv Condyloid joint
The full convex shape of one bone end fits into the full concave shape of an adjoining bone. This allows for movement in all directions, but ligaments prevent rotation.

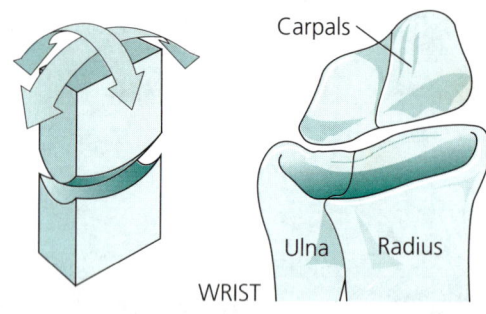

v Pivot joint
In the case of the atlas and axis vertebrae a circular section of the atlas sits on top of the peg shape of the axis. In the case of the radius and ulna, the radius is held within a fibrous ring attached to the ulna. Both these joints allow rotation to take place.

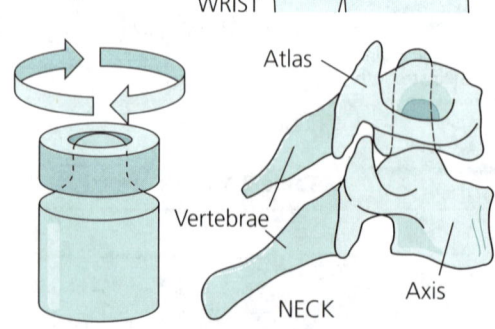

Fig. 2.6 Varieties of synovial joint

vi Slightly movable joint
When the back bends, the joint between two vertebrae moves only a small amount. The disc between the vertebrae is compressed on one side.

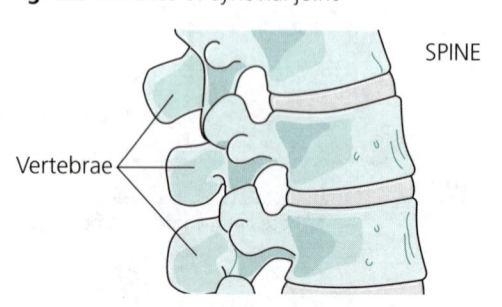

Fig. 2.7 Diagram of slightly movable joint

vii Immovable joint
The bones have fused together.

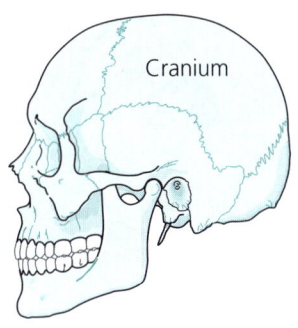

Fig. 2.8 Diagram of immovable joints in the cranium

2.5 Synovial joints

The first five joints listed in Table 2.1 are often referred to as **synovial joints**. This is because there is a liquid called **synovial fluid** between the bones which acts rather like the oil in a motor car engine. The synovial fluid lubricates the joint, helping it to move easily. The synovial fluid is produced in the **synovial membrane** which encloses the joint (see Fig. 2.9).

This diagram shows the structure of the knee joint.

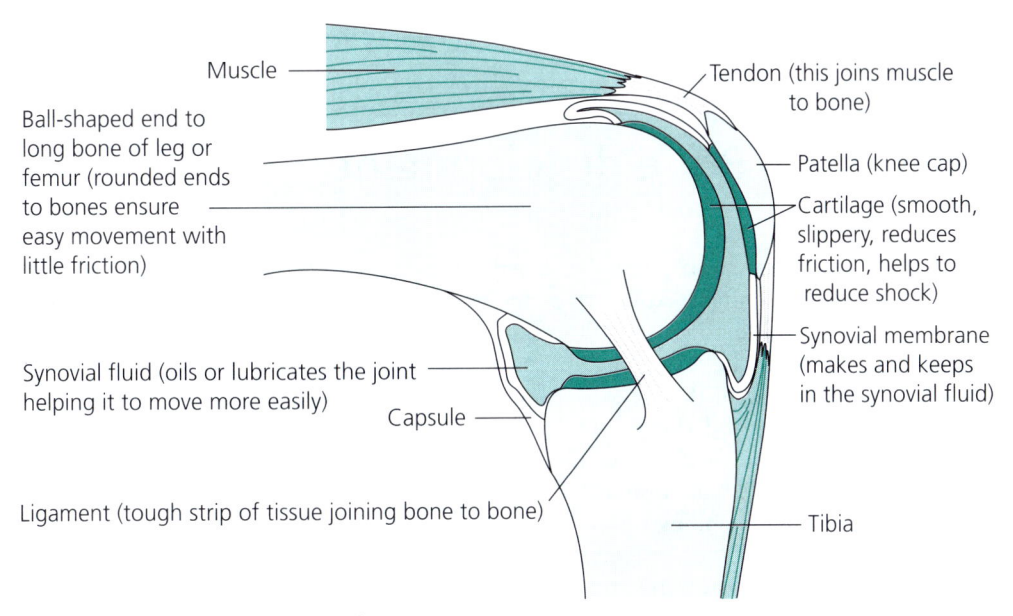

Fig. 2.9 The structure of a synovial joint

The range of movement at synovial joints varies according to the specific joint. However, the main movement patterns are:

1. **flexion** — The action of closing a joint.
2. **extension** — The action of opening a joint.
3. **adduction** — The action of moving an arm or a leg towards the centre line of the body.
4. **abduction** — The action of moving an arm or a leg away from the centre line of the body.
5. **rotation** — The action of turning a limb inwards or outwards.

The human body's make-up relating to movement

FLEXION   EXTENSION   ABDUCTION   ADDUCTION

The movements of the upper limb

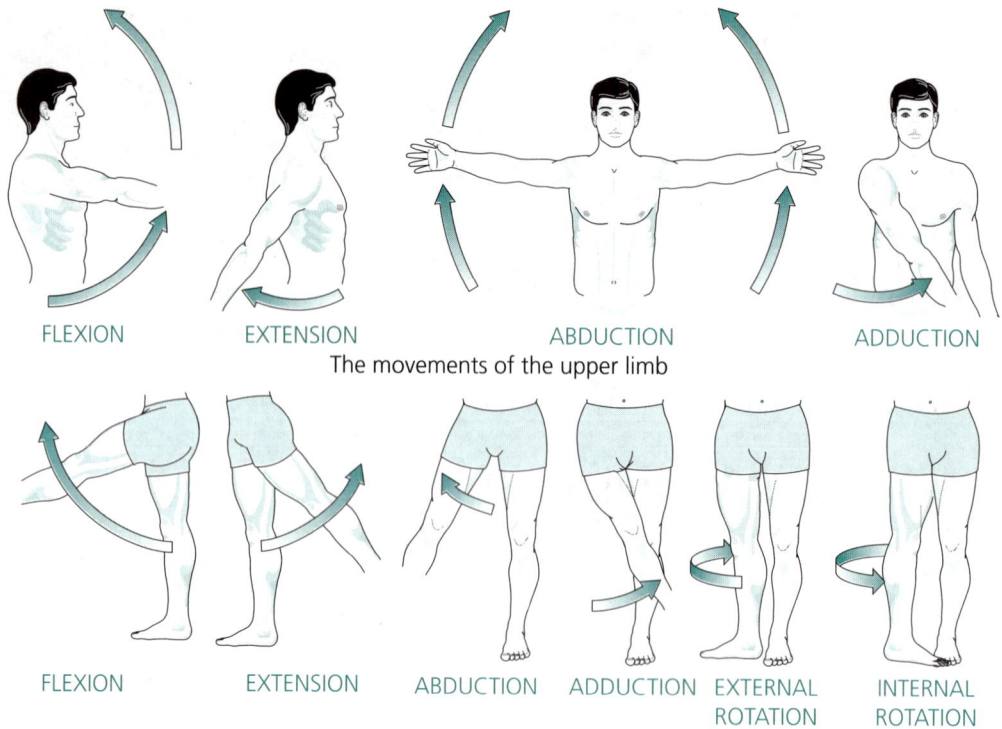

FLEXION   EXTENSION   ABDUCTION   ADDUCTION   EXTERNAL ROTATION   INTERNAL ROTATION

The movements of the hip joint

Fig. 2.10 Movement patterns at the shoulder and hip

2.6 Bone development

The initial shape of the skeleton is formed in the foetus within the first three months of development. At this stage the bones are made up of cartilage tissue and when the baby is born the bones are still soft. The bones become harder and stronger as the baby grows but are not fully developed until the end of the teenage period of life.

After birth, in the first few months of growth, the individual bones of the skull become harder and the joints fuse together to protect that most vital of organs, the brain. However, for the remaining bones of the body, the hardening process is a gradual one. The skeleton continues to grow in length and strength into the late teens of both boys and girls, depending upon the lifestyle adopted. The bones develop according to the quality of diet and the demand put upon them. The bones of very active sportspersons may well grow to suit the stress of the activity performed. For instance, weight-lifters' bones become very dense, to support the heavy masses they are called on to carry.

Bones act as attachment points for the muscles of the body so that movement can take place. Many of the internal organs of the body are attached to bones. In addition, the bones are used as storage points for calcium and other minerals within the bone marrow, where blood cells are also produced.

2.7 Ligaments

At all movable joints, the bones are fastened to each other by **ligaments**. These are made of tough fibrous tissue that has *some* elasticity.

Ligaments hold the bones together and allow movement.

They do not cause movement. Movement is achieved by muscle action on the bones.

The way the ligaments attach to the bones dictates the position of the ligaments across a joint. In this way, the ligaments allow for movement at the joint only in certain directions: they help to limit movement at a joint.

The skeleton

> **Examiner's tip**
> Remember the difference between ligaments and cartilage: it is a common error to mix them up.

2.8 Cartilage

Cartilage is a type of tissue which is present in all joints. There are two *main* types of cartilage:

1. **articular cartilage** — This is found at the end of the long bones. It is tough and hard-wearing, and protects the ends of the bones from rubbing together when they move.

2. **menisci** — These are crescent shaped pieces of cartilage found between two bones. They are strong, acting like shock absorbers between the two bones. The best examples are found between the bones of the knee. (See Fig. 2.11.)

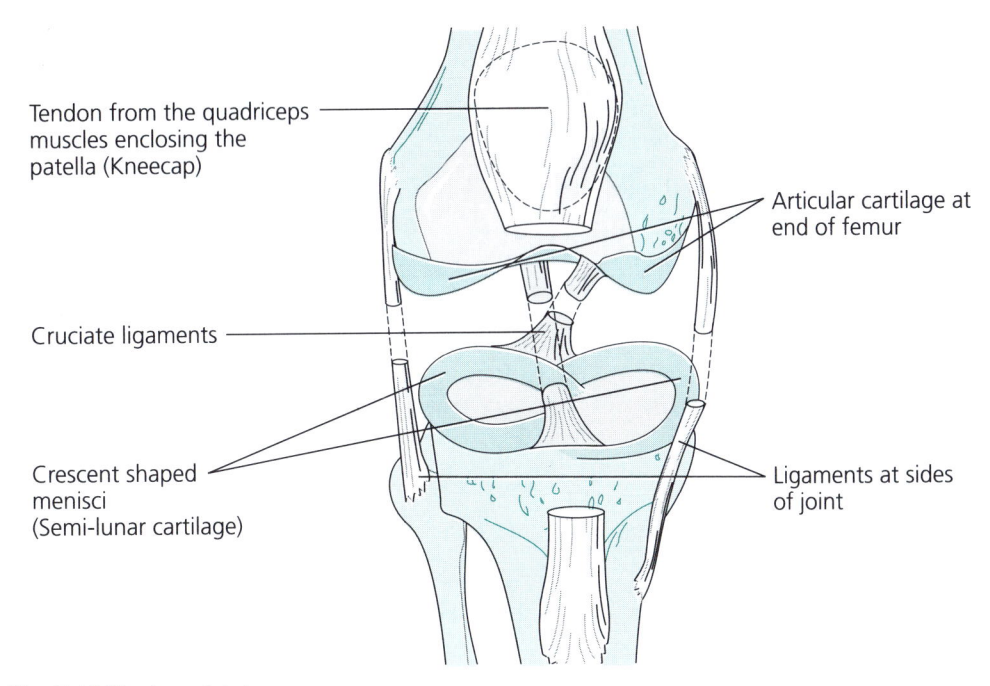

Fig. 2.11 The knee joint

The *cruciate ligaments* are attached to the tibia and femur inside the knee joint. As they cross each other from front to back they do not restrict the movement of the joint. They do stop the femur slipping forwards or backwards on the tibia.

PRINCIPAL TOPICS COVERED

1. The four main functions of the skeleton are: production of blood, protection, support and movement.

2. The main skeleton is divided into two main sections: the axial and the appendicular skeletons.

3. Bones are described as either spongy or compact and come in four main shapes: long, short, flat or irregular.

4. Bones meet at joints which are classified as: ball and socket, hinge, saddle, condyloid, pivot, slightly movable and immovable. The first five of these are all synovial joints.

5. Bones are connected to each other by ligaments which determine the range of movement of the joint.

6. The range of movement at a joint can include flexion, extension, adduction, abduction and rotation.

7. Bones harden as they grow older and have the ability to repair themselves.

The human body's make-up relating to movement

QUESTIONS ON THIS CHAPTER

1. Where in the body are the following found?

    (i) synovial fluid
    (ii) sternum
    (iii) ball and socket joint.

2. Give another name for each of the following:

    (i) shin bone
    (ii) collar bone
    (iii) spine.

3. List five types of movable joint, say how strong each is, where in the body they might be found and the range of movement each has.

    Examiner's tip: a simple list of the joints will earn few marks: more is asked for.

4. What joins bone to bone?

    Examiner's tip: a simple answer only is required for this type of question, not a long involved answer.

5. How do bones repair themselves?

    Examiner's tip: your answer needs to show the three main stages of bone repair. Diagrams can be useful.

Chapter 3
Muscles of the body

3.1 Muscle types

> **Examiner's tip**
> You should know the major differences between the three types of muscles.

There are three different types of muscle tissue in the body:

① cardiac muscle
This is found only in the *heart*. It relaxes and contracts continuously as the heart pumps blood around the body. The muscle fibres are laid in an interlocking network that gives the heart its strength and the ability to contract without pulling on a fixed point such as a bone. Each fibre has its own **nucleus**. The nucleus is the control centre of that muscle fibre. (See Fig. 3.1.)

② smooth muscle
This makes up the walls of certain soft organs in the body such as the *bladder*, the *intestines* and the *blood vessels*, where a sustained contraction is necessary. The fibres are laid in layers or sheets. These muscles do not need to be told when to contract or relax: they have the ability to work on their own as long as they have a satisfactory supply of blood. As such they are often called **involuntary** muscles. (See Fig. 3.2.)

Fig. 3.1 Cardiac muscle fibre

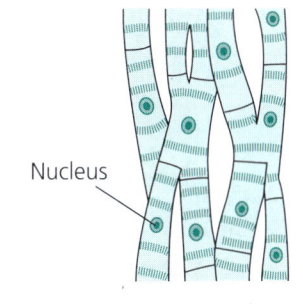

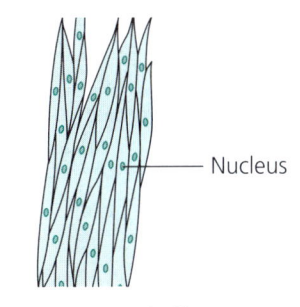

Fig. 3.2 Smooth muscle fibre

> **Examiner's tip**
> You should be able to name and place the major skeletal muscles of the body. You should know their correct anatomical names.

③ skeletal muscle
This makes up the geography or shape of the body. There are many hundreds of these muscles in the body, lying in layers over each other. Each group of skeletal muscles has its own name (see Fig. 3.3).

Skeletal muscles are all constructed in the same way. The whole of the muscle is contained within a membrane called the **epimysium**. Within this are many bundles of **fibres**, usually between 20 and 40 per bundle, that are each surrounded by a sheath called a **perimysium**. The individual fibres within the bundles all have their own blood supply and nerve attachment. Each fibre is made up of a large number of microscopic threads called **myofibrils** which in turn consist of two rows of protein molecules called **actin** and **myosin**.

It is the ability of the actin and myosin filaments to slide over each other that brings about the contraction and relaxation of these muscles (see Fig. 3.4).

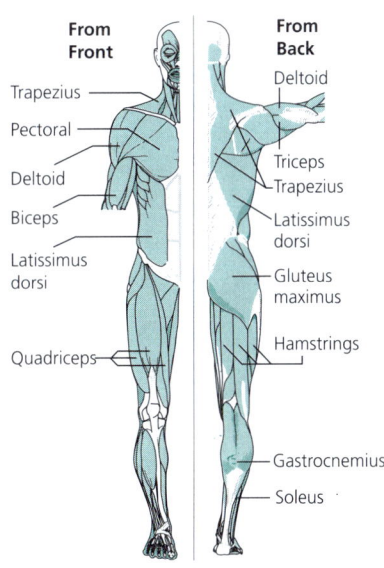

From Front: Trapezius, Pectoral, Deltoid, Biceps, Latissimus dorsi, Quadriceps

From Back: Deltoid, Triceps, Trapezius, Latissimus dorsi, Gluteus maximus, Hamstrings, Gastrocnemius, Soleus

Fig. 3.3 The muscular system

31

The human body's make-up relating to movement

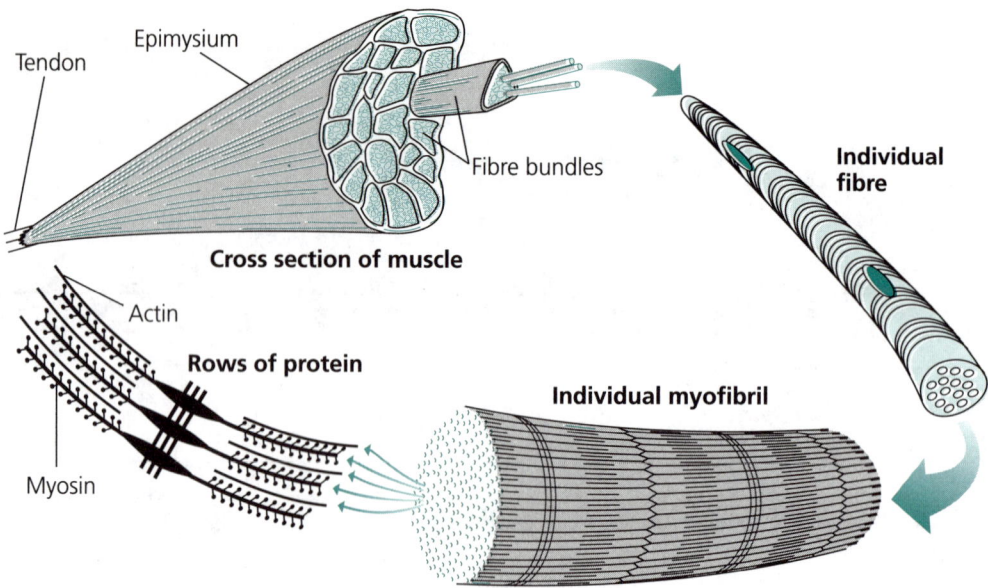

Fig. 3.4 Skeletal muscle fibre

As skeletal muscles have to be told when to contract and relax they are often referred to as **voluntary** muscles. As the fibres are striped in appearance they are often called **striped** or **striated** muscles.

3.2 Skeletal muscles at work

When a skeletal muscle contracts, not all of its fibres are used. The muscle uses only that number of fibres necessary for the task involved. The greater the demands of the job, the more muscle fibres are called into action. This allows us to pick up, in a controlled manner, a heavy object or a very light object, using the same muscles. Not all the fibres in a muscle may be prepared for work. In the sportsperson who does a lot of physical exercise many of the fibres are ready and prepared for work. In those people who rarely take part in physical activity many of the fibres are never used and thus are unprepared for work.

Skeletal muscle fibres are divided into two main types: **fast twitch** and **slow twitch** fibres.

Fast twitch fibres are generally larger than slow twitch fibres and have the ability to contract up to five times faster than slow twitch fibres. They develop a much higher force more quickly than slow twitch fibres. However, slow twitch fibres can resist fatigue much longer than fast twitch fibres. Fast twitch fibres appear whiter in colour compared to slow twitch fibres, which look more reddish in colour.

Although we all have the same number of muscle fibres as each other, we do not all have the same number of fast twitch and slow twitch fibres. The sportsperson who is more able in events which require explosive speed, such as the 100 metres sprint or the shot put, seem to have a greater number of fast twitch fibres. Those sportspersons who are more able in events which require considerable stamina, such as the 5000 metres, seem to have a greater number of slow twitch fibres.

Examiner's tip

You should know how muscles work together to produce movement.
You should be able to illustrate your answers by giving examples of muscles, by stating their correct places in the body, by using their correct anatomical names and by being able to identify correctly the bones to which they are attached.

3.3 Skeletal muscles and movement

In order to create movement, skeletal muscles have to be attached at *both ends* to bone. It is the fibres of the individual muscle, encased in the epimysium (the outer sheath) which are drawn together at each end to attach to the bone. The attachment is made by a connective tissue called a **tendon**. The tendon is strong but inelastic: *it will not stretch*. The tendon is attached to a membrane called the **periosteum** which covers the bone. (See Fig. 3.5.)

Muscles of the body

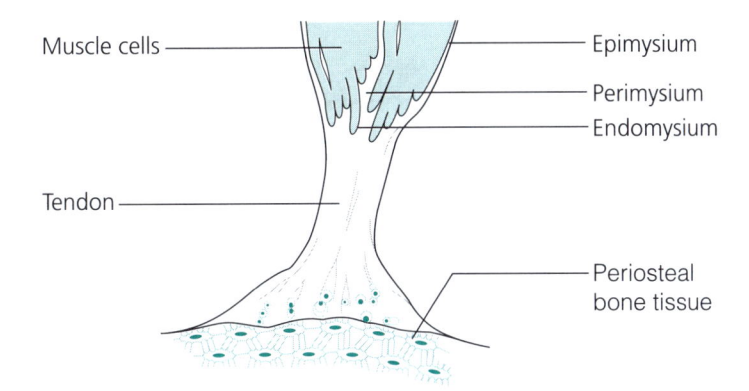

Fig. 3.5 How a tendon connects muscle to bone

In order to create movement, one muscle on one side of a joint must contract whilst the muscle in the same position on the opposite side of the joint relaxes (extends). This opposing action of two muscles (contraction and relaxation) is known as **agonistic muscle action** or **reciprocal innovation**. However, each muscle must have a point of attachment at both ends to different bones if movement is to take place.

Only *one* end of a muscle moves when it contracts:

- The point of attachment which does not move is called the **point of origin**.
- The point of attachment that does move is called the **point of insertion**. (See Fig. 3.6.)

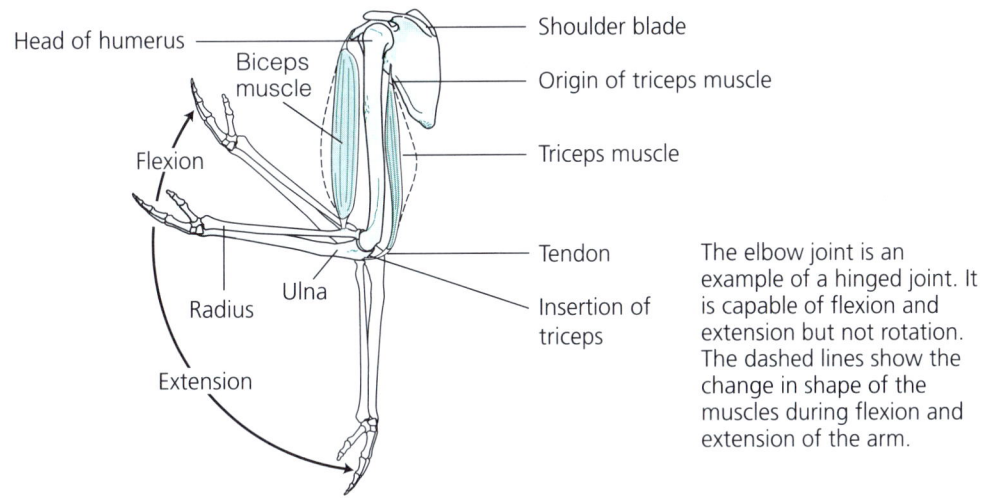

The elbow joint is an example of a hinged joint. It is capable of flexion and extension but not rotation. The dashed lines show the change in shape of the muscles during flexion and extension of the arm.

Fig. 3.6 How muscles work together to produce movement

A muscle that causes a joint to close is called a **flexor**, whilst a muscle that causes a joint to open is called an **extensor**.

A muscle which contracts is referred to as a **prime mover** or **agonist**. A muscle that relaxes in opposition to the agonist is called the **antagonist**.

For instance, when the arm bends at the elbow the *biceps* is the flexor muscle and, as it is initiating the movement, it is also the agonist. At the same time, the *triceps* must relax, and so the *triceps* is the antagonist muscle. When the arm straightens at the elbow, the *triceps* becomes the extensor muscle, and, as it is initiating the movement, it is also the agonist. In this action, the *biceps* is the antagonist muscle.

> **Examiner's tip**
> You should know the three ways that energy is produced within skeletal muscles.

3.4 Muscles and energy

When muscles contract they require energy. This energy comes from a substance called **adenosine triphosphate (ATP)** which is stored in small amounts in the muscle fibres. When the muscles contract the ATP is broken down into another substance, called **adenosine diphosphate (ADP)**. The store of ATP in the muscles is limited, so it has to be reformed from ADP if continued muscular contraction is to take place. This is done by using the following systems:

33

The human body's make-up relating to movement

❶ Aerobic system

The body uses the aerobic system to produce energy when muscles need to keep moving over a prolonged period of time.

This system is used when there is a plentiful supply of oxygen to the muscles whilst they are working. The oxygen is brought into the body through the normal action of breathing, with sufficient time for the oxygen to be transported by the blood from the lungs to the working muscles. The ADP formed during energy production is combined with *glycogen* (gained from the food we eat) to reform ATP. This chemical action also produces a by-product called **pyruvic acid**. When oxygen is added to pyruvic acid, the waste products carbon dioxide and water are created. (See Fig. 3.7.)

ATP <<<<<<<<<<<<<<>>>>>>> PYRUVIC ACID plus OXYGEN

↓

ENERGY FOR CONTRACTION

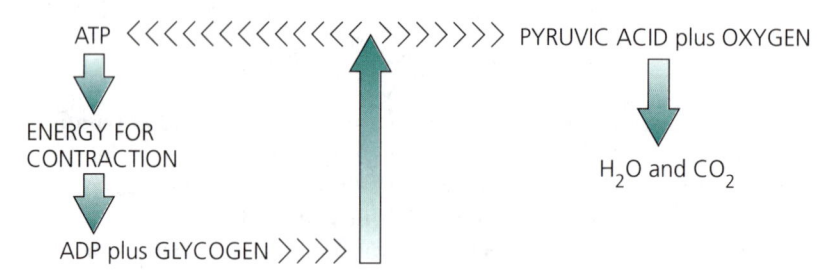

↓ H_2O and CO_2

ADP plus GLYCOGEN >>>>

Fig. 3.7 The aerobic energy system

As this system relies on a ready supply of oxygen the body can work in a steady state. The muscles are working below maximal effort and can often maintain this for long periods of time, for example, while jogging.

❷ Anaerobic system

The body uses this system to produce energy when muscles need to move suddenly, but don't need to keep going for very long.

In this system, as the name suggests, there is not a ready supply of oxygen. There are two anaerobic systems, known as the **CP system** and the **lactic acid** system.

- **The CP system**

  The CP system starts off in the same way as the aerobic system, but there is not enough time to continue a supply of oxygen to the muscle, so the oxygen runs out. The ADP is changed back to ATP by using a substance found in the muscles called **creatine phosphate (CP)**. (See Fig. 3.8) However, the amount of CP in the muscles is quite small and though ATP can be formed very quickly using this method it cannot be maintained for very long. The stores of CP are used up within 5 to 10 seconds, after which an alternative source of energy has to be found. The CP system of energy production is used in explosive events such as the shot put and 100 metres sprint.

ATP <<<<<<<<<<<<<<<<<<<<>>>>>>>>>>>> CREATINE

↓

ENERGY FOR CONTRACTION

↓

ADP plus CP (creatine phosphate) >>>>

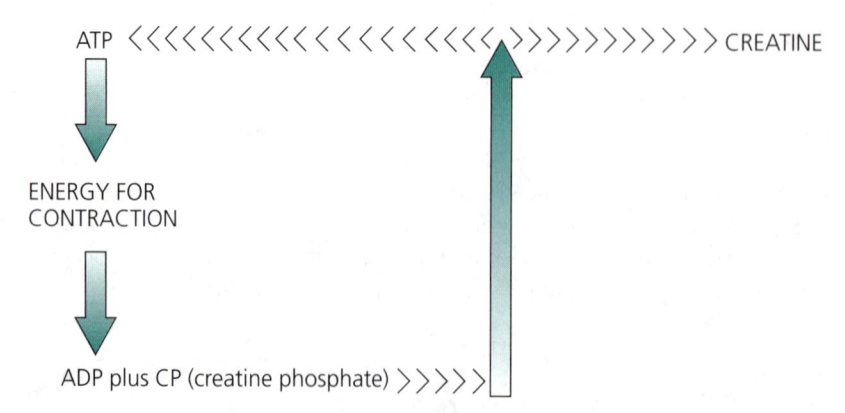

Fig. 3.8 The CP energy system

- **The lactic acid system**

  The lactic acid system of energy production is used by the body when oxygen is not available and the stores of CP have been used up. The ADP which has combined with glycogen to produce ATP has created the by-product pyruvic acid. If energy production continues without oxygen the pyruvic acid is turned into **lactic acid**. (See Fig. 3.9.)

Muscles of the body

As the lactic acid builds up in the muscle it makes muscular contraction more and more difficult. Lactic acid can be converted back to pyruvic acid and then disposed of only if there is a plentiful supply of oxygen. As there is a shortage of oxygen to convert the lactic acid back to pyruvic acid then the body is said to have developed an **oxygen debt**. This debt has to be repaid, or all muscular activity will stop. The lactic acid system is used to produce energy for events that require utmost effort for a period of up to two minutes, such as the 400 metres and 800 metres.

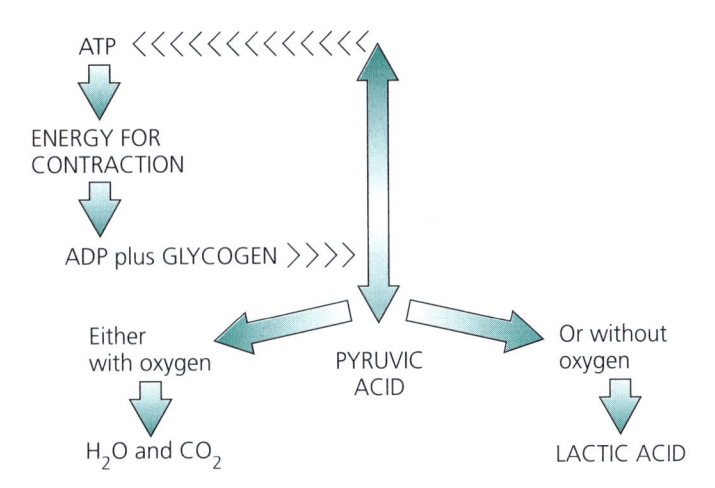

```
ATP <<<<<<<<<<<<
 ↓                    ↑
ENERGY FOR            |
CONTRACTION           |
 ↓                    |
ADP plus GLYCOGEN >>>>|
      ↙         PYRUVIC        ↘
Either           ACID          Or without
with oxygen                    oxygen
  ↓                              ↓
H₂O and CO₂                    LACTIC ACID
```

Fig. 3.9 The lactic acid energy system

Although the sportsperson may use one system more than the other two, there are many occasions when all three will be used in turn. Games such as soccer and hockey often require short sharp bursts of speed alternating with periods of less intensive effort. During the periods of less intensive activity any *oxygen debt* incurred can be repaid. In these situations the body uses whichever system of energy production is most suited to the effort required at any particular time.

3.5 Effects of exercise on muscles

Over time, the effects of regular exercise on skeletal muscle fibres are that:

- the individual fibres get shorter and fatter, increasing the thickness of the muscle
- more fibres are ready prepared for work, which also contributes to the size of the muscle
- as more fibres are prepared for work, the blood supply to the muscle is improved
- in this state of 'readiness for work' the muscle seems to react more quickly to stimuli.

PRINCIPAL TOPICS COVERED

1. There are three types of muscle tissue: cardiac, smooth and skeletal.
2. Skeletal muscle fibres are divided into two types: fast twitch fibres and slow twitch fibres.
3. Not all skeletal muscle fibres are prepared for work.
4. Not all skeletal muscle fibres are used on every occasion.
5. Muscles are attached to bones by tendons.
6. The points where muscles are attached to bones are called the points of origin and insertion. Only the insertion end moves when a muscle contracts.
7. Flexor muscles close joints: extensor muscles open them.

The human body's make-up relating to movement

8. Muscles work in pairs: in order for one to contract, an opposite one must relax.
9. Energy is produced in muscles by either aerobic or anaerobic methods.
10. Anaerobic methods of producing energy can bring about oxygen debt.
11. The size, shape and readiness for work of a muscle can be changed by exercise.

QUESTIONS ON THIS CHAPTER

1. Where in the body are the following found?
   (i) biceps
   (ii) hamstrings
   (iii) trapezius

   Examiner's tip: Be specific with regard to positioning on the front or back of the body.

2. Explain how muscles work together to produce movement.

   Examiner's tip: always try to use two named muscles at a joint to illustrate your answer.

3. Explain the difference between voluntary and involuntary muscles.

   Examiner's tip: you should be aware of the differing titles the muscle types are given.

4. State what changes might occur to skeletal muscles due to physical activity over a long period of time.

   Examiner's tip: it is sufficient to write your answer as a series of points.

5. Explain how lactic acid builds up and affects muscles during exercise.

   Examiner's tip: you should be able to place the main chemical components in order in your answer, i.e. ATP, ADP, O_2.

Chapter 4
The control of movement

The skeletal muscles of the body are controlled by the **nervous system**. This nervous system consists of four main parts:

1. the brain
2. the brain stem
3. the spinal cord
4. the nerves

4.1 The central nervous system (CNS)

The **CNS** is the decision-making part of the nervous system. It consists of the **brain, brain stem** and **spinal cord**. Decisions can be made in all of the three parts.

The CNS can be compared to a tower block of offices. The lower down the block you are, the less important are the decisions that can be made. The higher up the office block you go, the greater is the responsibility and the more important are the decisions. On the very top floor of the office block are the directors and they make the most important decisions of all.

Similarly, with the CNS, the less important decisions are made in the spinal cord. These will be actions relating to known and well-remembered situations. More important and more complex decisions are taken in the brain stem, and the most complex of decisions are taken at the top of the CNS in the brain.

> **Examiner's tip**
>
> Remember that nerves only carry information. Decisions are made in the central nervous system (CNS).

4.2 The nerves

The nerves, also known as **neurones**, spread throughout the body and are the pathway of all information to and from the CNS. (See Fig 4.1.)

The human body's make-up relating to movement

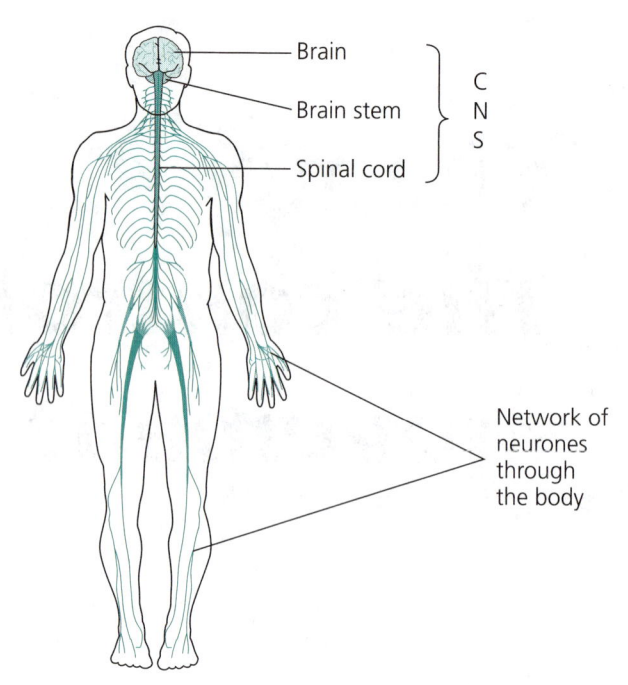

Fig. 4.1 The nervous system

Examiner's tip
You should be able to describe the actions of sensory, effector and connector nerves.

Examiner's tip
Know the difference between exteroceptors and proprioceptors.

Examiner's tip
Remember that nerves do not actually touch each other: where they meet is called a synapse.

Information can travel only one way along a nerve so the nerves are of two main types: those that carry information to the CNS and those that carry it away.

1. *Sensory nerves* carry information **to** the CNS.
   (Sensory nerves are also known as *afferent nerves*)

2. *Effector nerves* carry information **away** from the CNS.
   (Effector nerves are also known as *efferent nerves* and *motor nerves*)

Sensory nerves may obtain the information they pass to the CNS from a range of sources. If the information is received from outside the body then it is described as being received by **exteroceptors** such as the ears, eyes, nose and skin. However, if it is received from within the body then it is received by **proprioceptors** such as the stretch receptors in the muscles. It is the sensory input received from the proprioceptors that is telling you what position your legs or feet are in at this moment in time. You did not need to look to see what position they are in. A third type of nerve is called the **connector** nerve. This carries information from one nerve ending to another.

Although nerves are described as passing information from one to another they do not actually touch each other. Where they meet there is a minute gap and the information passes as an impulse from one nerve to another by bridging this gap. This place where two nerves meet is called a **synapse**. The gap between them is called the **synaptic cleft**. (See Fig. 4.2.)

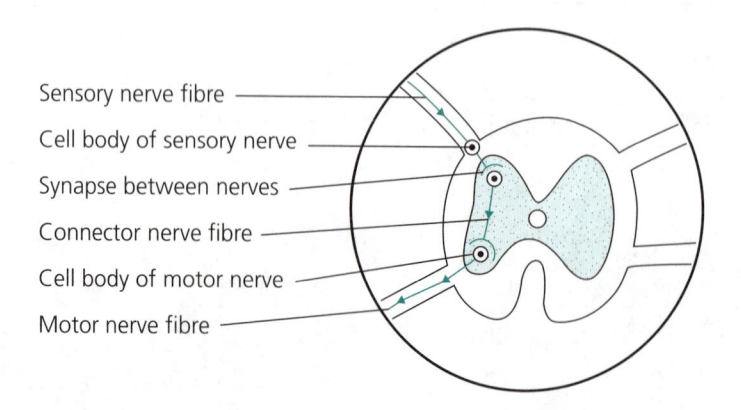

Fig. 4.2 Synapses (junctions) between nerve cells

4.3 Nervous co-ordination

The action that we take after a receptor receives information comes only after the impulses have travelled right along the network of neurones (nerves). They follow a clearly defined pathway in a set order, as follows:

The receptors receive information (**stimuli**), such as seeing a football being kicked towards them.

RECEPTOR

This is passed in the form of an impulse along a sensory nerve.

When the impulse reaches the CNS a decision is made on what action to take, such as receiving the football and kicking it towards the goal.

BRAIN
BRAIN STEM
SPINAL CORD

This is passed on in the form of an impulse along a motor nerve.

The muscle will react to the information received from the CNS.

MUSCLE
ACTION

Key: ----------------------▶ is the direction of travel of impulse.

The speed at which a decision is made is called the **reaction time**. The length of this time span stretches from the moment the *stimulus is detected* to the moment when the *response is initiated*.

Although a sensory nerve may only carry an impulse from a specific receptor, a single motor nerve may well control several muscle fibres within one muscle.

The single motor nerve and the group of muscle fibres it controls are called a **motor unit**.

Muscles that control delicate actions such as writing or the movement of the eyeball will be controlled by many nerves. Each nerve will control only a few fibres.

Muscles that control less delicate actions, such as running, will have a large number of fibres controlled by each motor nerve.

4.4 Reflex actions

Examiner's tip

Be able to describe and draw a reflex arc.

If you stab yourself in the finger with a pin or touch a very hot plate you will find that you withdraw your hand very quickly.

This type of seemingly 'automatic' reaction is called a **reflex action** and is very rapid indeed. The action is so fast because the nervous impulses that travel from the touch receptors to the CNS and back to the muscles travel by the fastest, shortest route possible. These short, fast routes are called **reflex arcs**. (See Fig. 4.3.)

The human body's make-up relating to movement

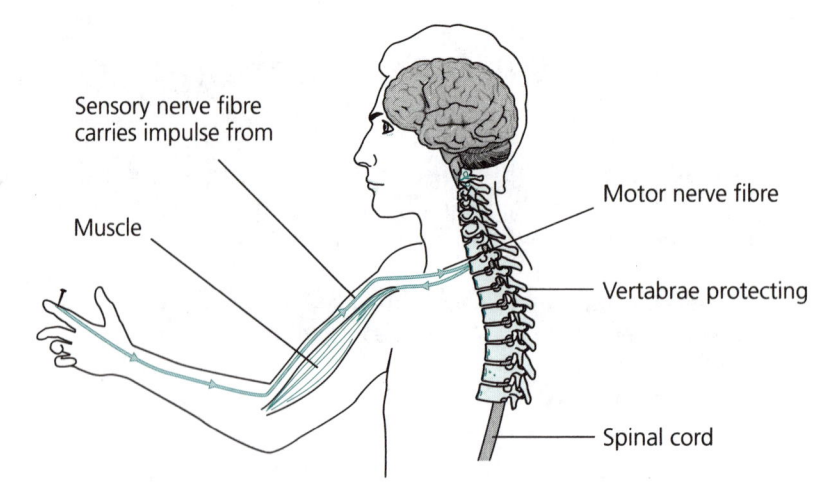

Fig. 4.3 Nervous impulses in a reflex arc

In this example, the decision to move the finger is being taken in the spinal cord. Although moving the finger from the source of pain could be described as an important decision to make, it is one that the body has met before on several occasions. Thus the decision is taken low down the CNS and can be made very quickly. If the information had been passed up the spinal cord to the brain for a decision to be made, then it would have taken longer for a reaction to be initiated. Therefore, you would have received pain for a much longer period of time. As it is, the decision made in the spinal cord is made so fast that you move your hand from the source of the pain 'without thinking about it'. The brain tends to deal with situations that you have not met before.

PRINCIPAL TOPICS COVERED

1. The place of the decision-making process (CNS) within the nervous system.
2. The receiving and sending of information to and from the CNS.
3. How information is received and acted upon.
4. How reflex actions take place.

QUESTIONS ON THIS CHAPTER

1. Describe what is meant by reaction time in sport.

   Examiner's tip: you must include the time it takes for stimulus recognition to take place as well as response time.

2. What is meant by the term 'motor unit'?

   Examiner's tip: do not forget that your answer must include muscle fibres as well as the motor nerve.

3. Where are low level decisions taken?

   Examiner's tip: think of the 'block of offices' and the amount of time available.

Chapter 5
The circulatory system

The three main parts of the circulatory system are:

① **the heart**

② **the blood vessels**

③ **the blood**

> **Examiner's tip**
> You should be able to describe the systemic and pulmonary blood circuits.

Blood travels around the body continuously in two distinct circuits. (See Fig. 5.1.)

The **pulmonary circuit** carries blood from the heart to the lungs and back to the heart.

The **systemic circuit** carries blood from the heart to the body and back to the heart.

BODY TISSUE ⇄ **HEART** ⇄ **LUNGS**

Systemic circuit Pulmonary circuit

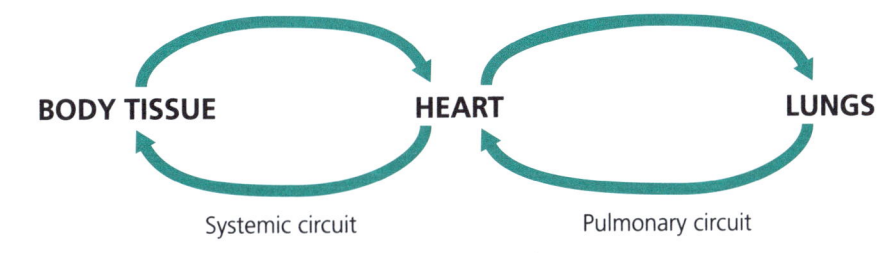

Fig. 5.1 The two blood circuits side by side

> **Examiner's tip**
> You should be able to explain why blood is directed away from some organs of the body to the muscles during exercise.

During exercise, the body has the ability to reduce the blood supply to some organs and concentrate it at the muscles which are working harder. (See Unit 7.5.)

5.1 The heart

LUNGS

High pressure — Low pressure

HEART — Right side | Left side

Deoxygenated — **Oxygenated**

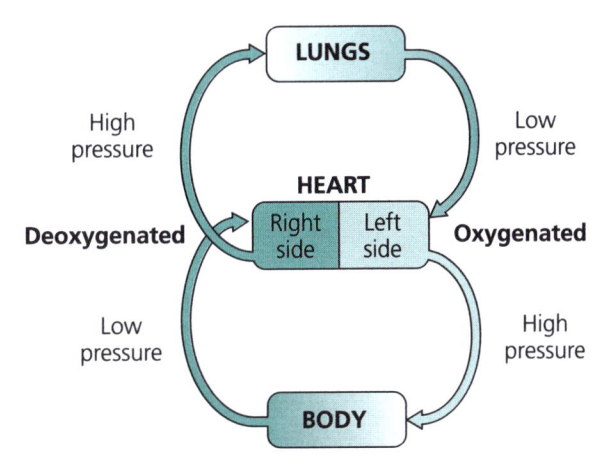

Low pressure — High pressure

BODY

Fig. 5.2 The double circulation of blood through the heart

The human body's make-up relating to movement

Examiner's tip

You should be able to describe the heart and how blood enters and leaves it.

The heart can be described as two muscular pumps that work continuously side by side. Each of the two pumps is divided into two chambers situated one above the other. The upper chambers receive blood from the body. The lower chambers force it round the body. (See Fig. 5.2.)

Each upper chamber is called an **atrium** whilst each lower chamber is called a **ventricle**. The blood that passes through the *right* atrium and ventricle is **deoxygenated** blood which has just returned from different parts of the body and is now being pumped to the lungs. The blood that passes through the *left* atrium and ventricle is **oxygenated** blood which has come directly from the lungs and is now being pumped to different parts of the body. (See Fig. 5.2.)

Superior vena cava the main vein taking back blood with little oxygen to the heart

Semi-lunar valve

Right atrium

Tricuspid valve

Tendons cords holding vein in place

Inferior vena cava a vein

Aorta main artery carrying oxygen around the body

Pulmonary artery takes blood with little oxygen to lungs

Pulmonary vein takes back blood with oxygen to lungs

Left atrium

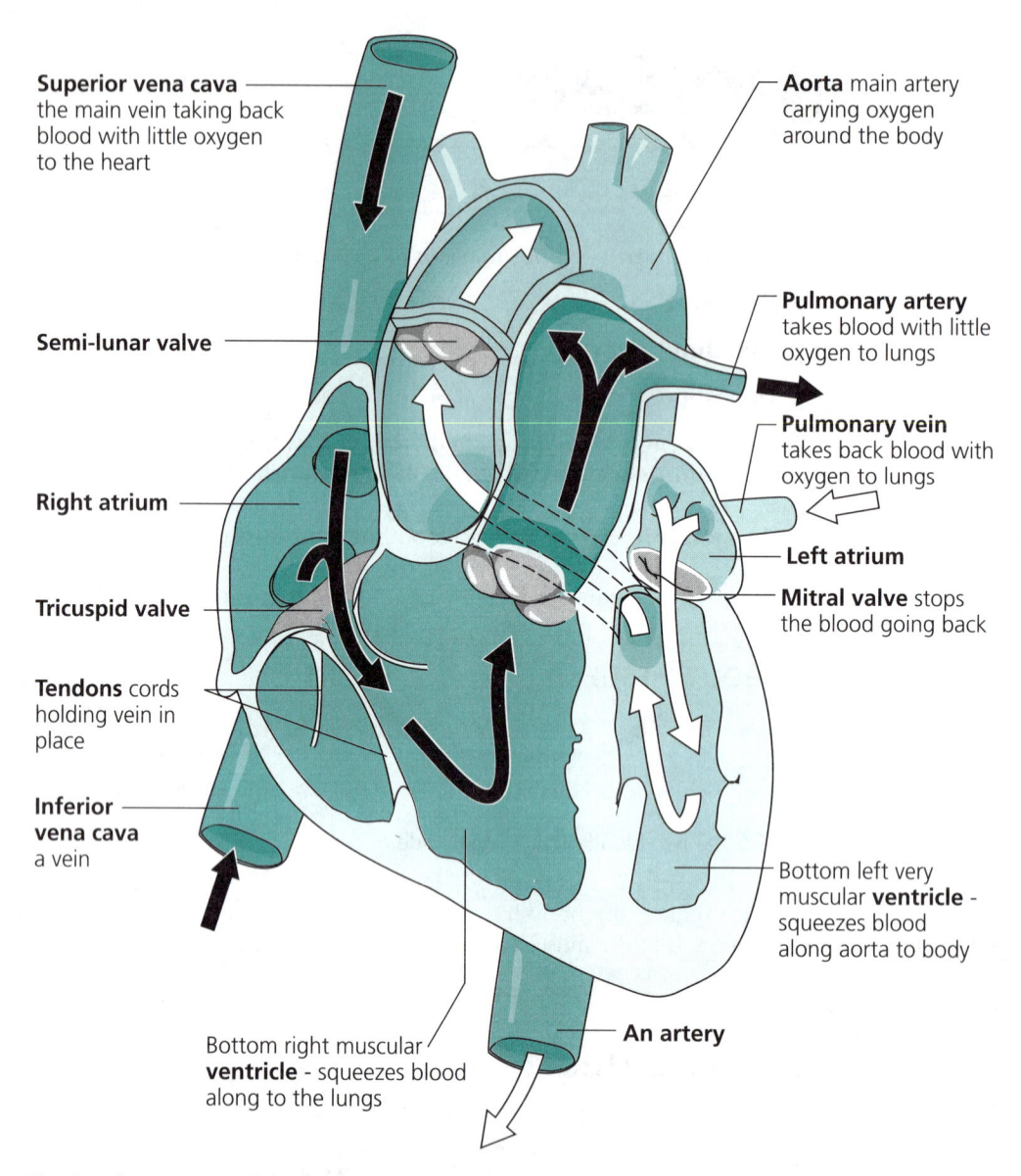

Mitral valve stops the blood going back

Bottom left very muscular **ventricle** - squeezes blood along aorta to body

Bottom right muscular **ventricle** - squeezes blood along to the lungs

An artery

Fig. 5.3 The structure of the heart.
The arrows show the direction of blood flow.

5.2 The pulse

Every time the *left ventricle* contracts it forces blood away from the heart and around the body, not in a continuous flow, but in a series of small surges. These surges of blood create a wave-like expansion in the arteries. This wave of expansion is called the **pulse** of the heart and can be felt at various points around the body such as the neck and the wrist. The pulse rate of a person is given in 'beats per minute', with the average adult having a resting rate of between 60 and 80 beats per minute. This rate can be increased considerably during exercise, illness or through sudden shock. (See Table 5.1.)

Table 5.1 Pulse rates in beats per minute

children 8/10 years	80 – 100 at rest
average adults	60 – 80
adults 20/30 years	180 – 200 maximum during hard physical exercise

5.3 The blood vessels

There are three main types of blood vessel: **arteries**, **capillaries** and **veins**. All are connected to each other. (See Fig. 5.4.)

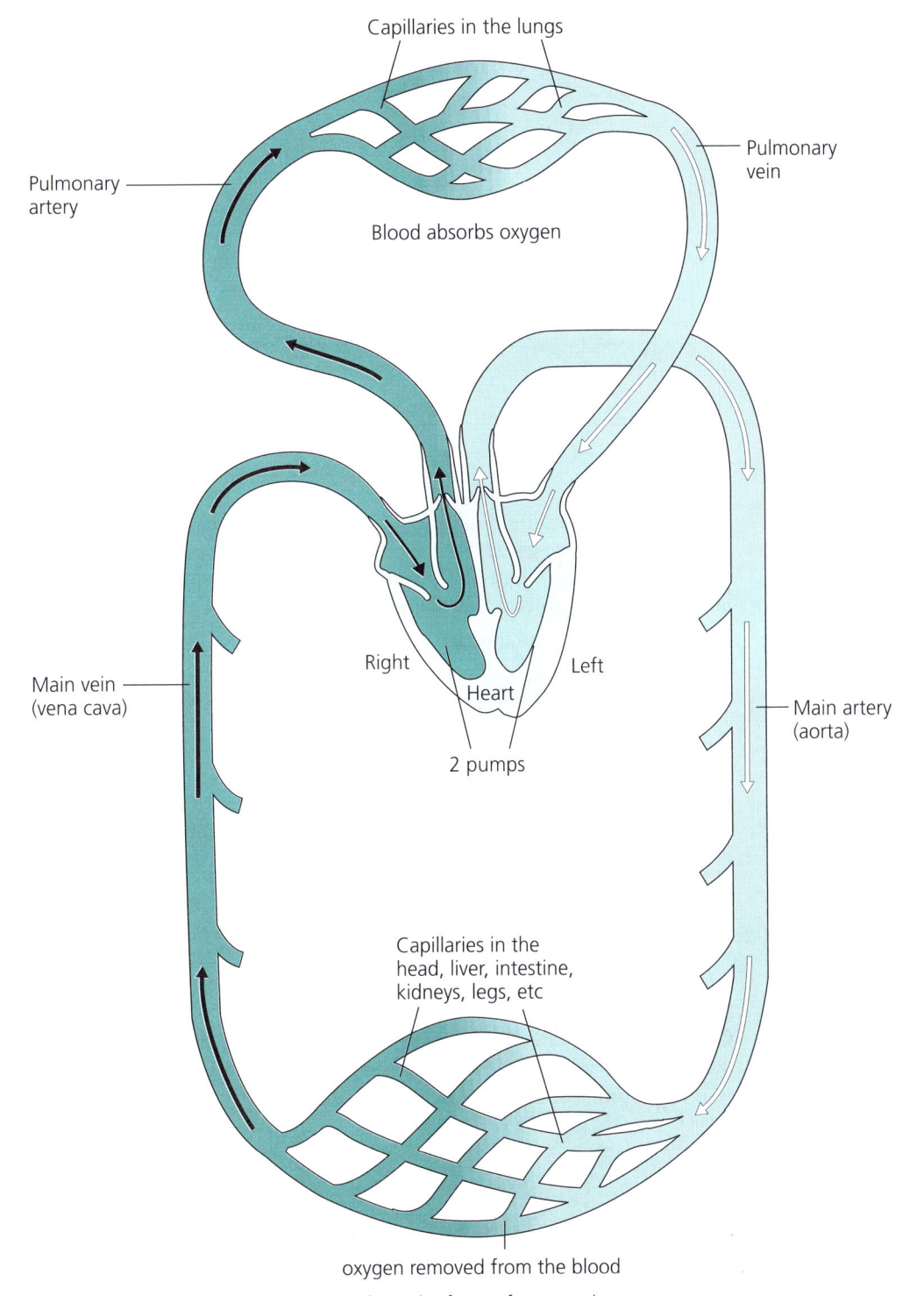

Fig. 5.4 The circulation of blood (seen from the front of a person)

The human body's make-up relating to movement

> **E**xaminer's tip
>
> It is important that you can describe the pathway of blood round the body.

The main features of each type of blood vessel are as follows:

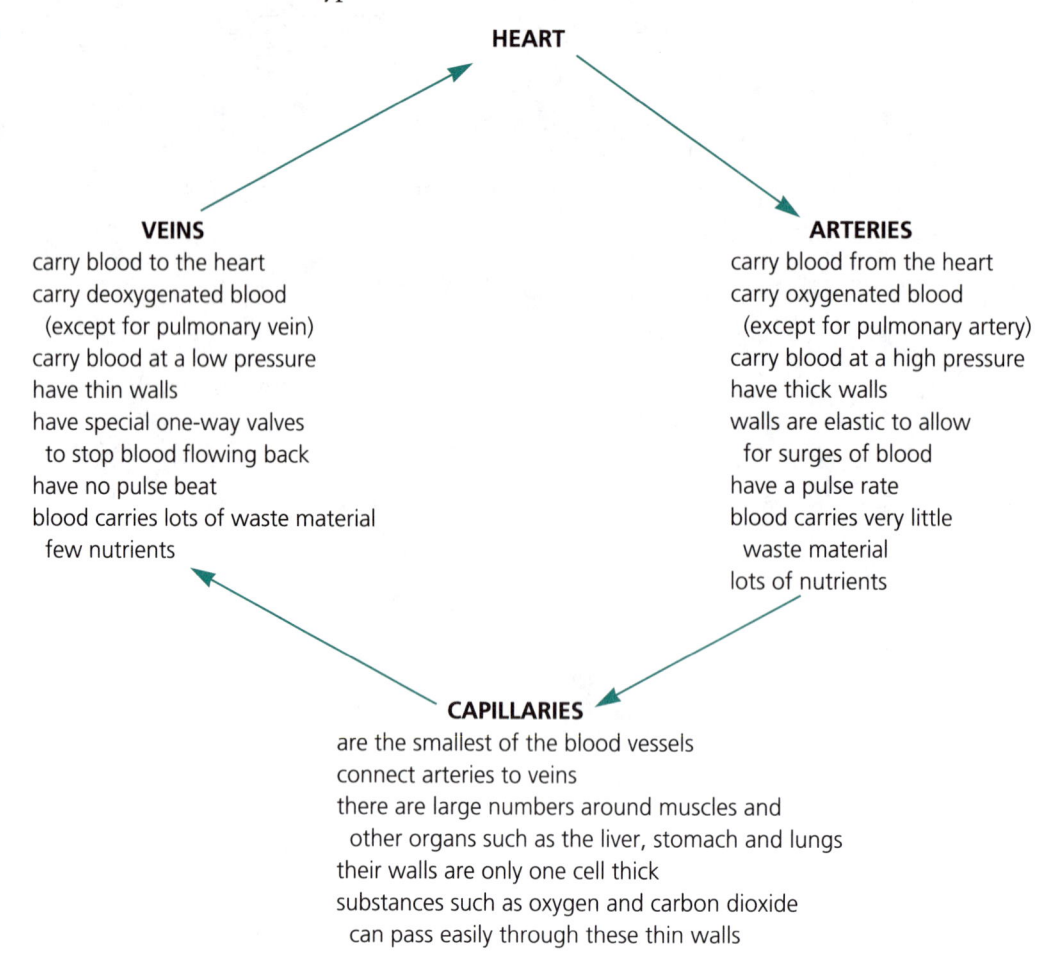

HEART

VEINS
carry blood to the heart
carry deoxygenated blood
 (except for pulmonary vein)
carry blood at a low pressure
have thin walls
have special one-way valves
 to stop blood flowing back
have no pulse beat
blood carries lots of waste material
 few nutrients

ARTERIES
carry blood from the heart
carry oxygenated blood
 (except for pulmonary artery)
carry blood at a high pressure
have thick walls
walls are elastic to allow
 for surges of blood
have a pulse rate
blood carries very little
 waste material
lots of nutrients

CAPILLARIES
are the smallest of the blood vessels
connect arteries to veins
there are large numbers around muscles and
 other organs such as the liver, stomach and lungs
their walls are only one cell thick
substances such as oxygen and carbon dioxide
 can pass easily through these thin walls

As with all arteries, the pulmonary artery carries blood away from the heart. However, as the pulmonary artery leads to the lungs, it carries deoxygenated blood.

As with all veins, the pulmonary vein carries blood back to the heart. However, as the pulmonary vein comes from the lungs, it carries oxygenated blood.

> The pulmonary vein and pulmonary artery are the only exceptions to the rule that veins carry deoxygenated blood and arteries carry oxygenated blood.

5.4 Watch pocket valves

It is the *high pressure* in the arteries that keeps the blood constantly flowing in them. However, *low pressure* in the veins means that the blood must be kept flowing back towards the heart by some other means.

Veins therefore contain special one-way valves called **watch pocket valves**. (These valves are named after the pocket of a gentleman's waistcoat in which a pocket watch was kept.) When the blood is flowing towards the heart the valves automatically open to allow the blood to flow freely. If for any reason the blood tries to flow backwards, away from the heart, the valves automatically close, stopping all blood flow. A slight swelling of the vein may occur when this happens. (See Fig. 5.5.)

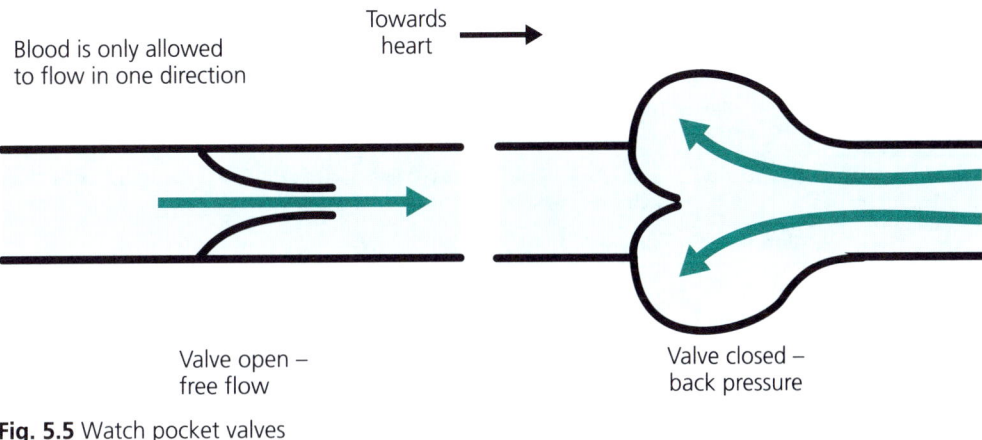

Fig. 5.5 Watch pocket valves

5.5 Blood structure

Whole blood is divided into **plasma**, **red cells**, **white cells** and **platelets**.

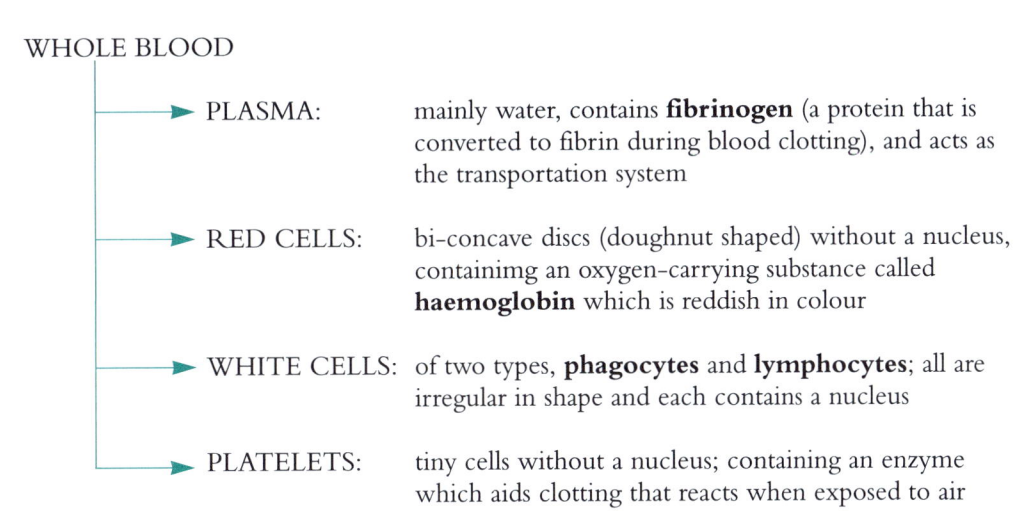

WHOLE BLOOD

- **PLASMA:** mainly water, contains **fibrinogen** (a protein that is converted to fibrin during blood clotting), and acts as the transportation system
- **RED CELLS:** bi-concave discs (doughnut shaped) without a nucleus, containimg an oxygen-carrying substance called **haemoglobin** which is reddish in colour
- **WHITE CELLS:** of two types, **phagocytes** and **lymphocytes**; all are irregular in shape and each contains a nucleus
- **PLATELETS:** tiny cells without a nucleus; containing an enzyme which aids clotting that reacts when exposed to air

5.6 Functions of the blood

The two main functions of blood are **transportation** and **protection**.

Examiner's tip

You should be able to describe the transportation function of blood.

Table 5.1 Materials transported by blood:

Oxygen	*From the lungs to all body tissue* The oxygen combines with the haemoglobin of the red cells of the blood where the capillaries meet the lungs. The haemoglobin gives up the oxygen to body tissue such as the stomach or muscles when required.
Carbon dioxide	*From all tissues to the lungs* The carbon dioxide forms a solution within the plasma which, when it reaches the lungs, gives up the carbon dioxide so that it can be breathed out.
Nutrients	*From the small intestine to all parts of the body* These are carried in solution form within the plasma.
Heat	*From the muscles to all parts of the body* When the muscles work they get hot. As the blood moves round the body it transports this heat to the cooler parts so that an even temperature can be maintained.
Waste products	*From all body tissues to the kidneys* Any waste product formed within the body is filtered through the kidneys so that it can be excreted.

The human body's make-up relating to movement

> **Examiner's tip**
> You should be able to describe the protective function of blood.

Table 5.2 Body protection by the blood

Antitoxins	These are produced by the lymphocytes to fight **toxins** (poisons) that might enter the body.
Antibodies	These are produced by the lymphocytes to fight disease and are kept in the blood stream. They give immunity to certain illnesses.
Destruction	This is done by phagocytes. When bacteria cause a threat to the body, the phagocytes attach themselves to and 'eat' the harmful organisms.
Clotting	This is activated by the platelets. When a blood vessel is cut the platelets combine together forming a temporary plug to stop immediate blood loss. The enzymes in the platelets react with the air and cause the fibrinogen from the plasma to change into thread-like fibres of fibrin. These form a mesh which seals the wound and prevents the entry of harmful bacteria. We see this mesh of fibre as a scab on a cut. (See Fig. 5.6.)
Repair	The blood acts as the transport system for nutrients and other materials that are needed to repair damaged tissue. This might be the repair of a cut on the body surface or the repair of broken capillaries that form a bruise under the surface of the skin.

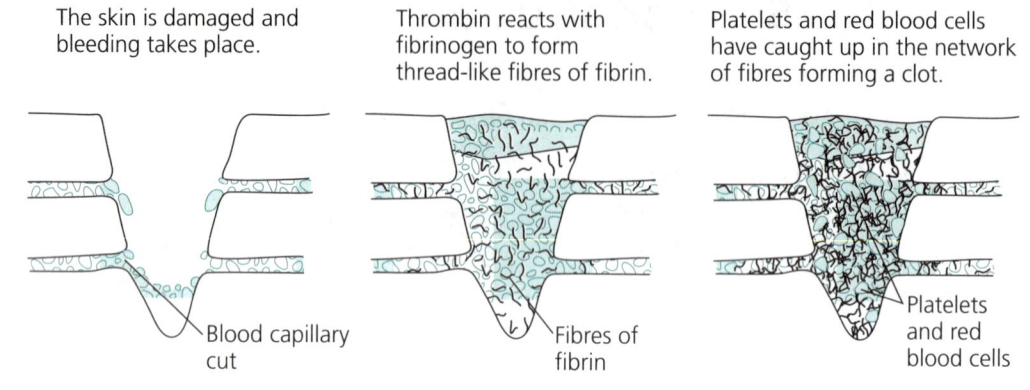

Fig. 5.6 Action of platelets at an open wound

5.7 Blood pressure

The heart pumps the blood under pressure. This pressure is calculated by measuring the pressure needed to stop the flow of blood through an artery. There are two readings:

- **systolic** pressure is the reading given as the heart contracts
- **diastolic** pressure is the reading given when the heart relaxes.

Blood pressure is always shown by these two figures e.g. 120 over 70. In this case the 120 refers to the *systolic* pressure and the 70 to the *diastolic* pressure.

There is no 'average' blood pressure reading. Blood pressure is lower in children than it is in adults. It increases in stress situations and especially when a sportsperson takes part in hard physical activity. Doctors become concerned if blood pressure remains high over a prolonged period of time. (See Table 5.4.)

Table 5.4 Range of acceptable blood pressure readings in mm Hg (mercury) related to age

systolic range	100/130	105/135	120/150	125/160
diastolic range	60/90	65/90	70/100	70/100
approximate age	15 years	20 years	40 years	60 years

If someone has high blood pressure when resting, it can be an indication that the walls of the arteries have fat deposits on them. These deposits partially block the arteries, making them narrower, and making it difficult for the blood to flow through. This is called **coronary artery disease**. In serious cases the heart may have to work too hard to force blood through the narrow arteries and this can cause a heart attack.

5.8 Effects of exercise

The effect that exercise has on the parts of the circulatory system depends on the type of physical activity performed, the intensity of the activity and the length of time spent on the activity. (See Table 5.5 and Table 5.6.)

Table 5.5 Main changes brought about during short-term physical activity on the circulatory system

Heart	increase in pulse rate
	increase in blood pressure
Blood	more brought into use
	diverted from soft organs (stomach) to muscles
	transports heat from muscles to surface of the body (skin goes red)

Table 5.6 Main effects of long-term high intensity activity training on the circulatory system

Heart	increase in size
	resting rate becomes lower
	stroke volume is increased (pumps more blood with each stroke)
	returns to resting rate faster after activity
	helps prevent onset of coronary artery disease
Blood	number of red cells is increased thus improving potential to transport oxygen
	supply to muscle fibres is improved
	return of deoxygenated blood to heart is improved

> **Examiner's tip**
> You should be able to describe effects that long-term physical activity has on the system.

PRINCIPAL TOPICS COVERED

1. The three main parts of the circulatory system are the heart, blood vessels and blood.
2. Blood travels around the body in two circuits.
3. Whole blood is divided into plasma, red cells, white cells and platelets. Its two main functions are transportation and protection.
4. The surges of blood away from the heart are known as the pulse. The heart pumps the blood under pressure.
5. Short-term and long-term exercise brings about changes on the circulatory system.

QUESTIONS ON THIS CHAPTER

1. State two changes that would occur in the circulatory system during strenuous exercise.

   Examiner's tip: do not confuse this with the long-term effects of exercise on the system.

2. How does the blood help to stop the body over-heating during exercise?

3. Explain the different roles of arteries and veins.

   Examiner's tip: remember that the pulmonary artery and pulmonary vein are exceptions.

4. Name the chambers of the heart.

   Examiner's tip: use a diagram, placing left and right as if you were looking out from the page.

5. Explain how blood prevents loss through an open wound.

Chapter 6
The respiratory system

The three main parts of the respiratory system are:

1. **nasal passages**
2. **windpipe**
3. **lungs**

The lungs are found within the **thoracic cavity** (chest) protected all round by the ribs and at the bottom by a strong elastic sheath called the **diaphragm**. (See Fig. 6.1.)

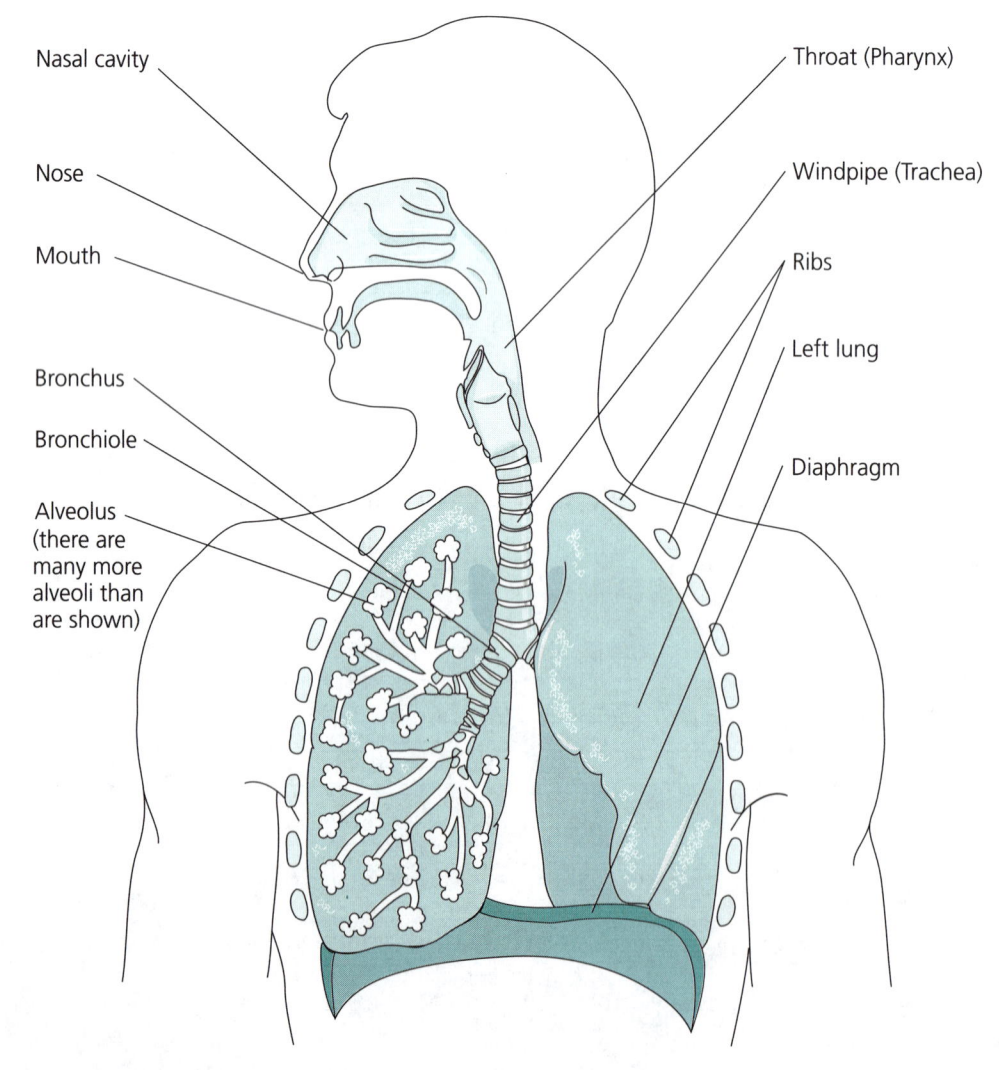

Fig. 6.1 The human respiratory system

The respiratory system

> **Examiner's tip**
> You should be able to describe the respiratory tract.

6.1 The respiratory tract

Air enters the body through the **nasal passages** down to the **alveoli** of the lungs, where the exchange of gases takes place. (See Table 6.1.)

Table 6.1 The respiratory pathway

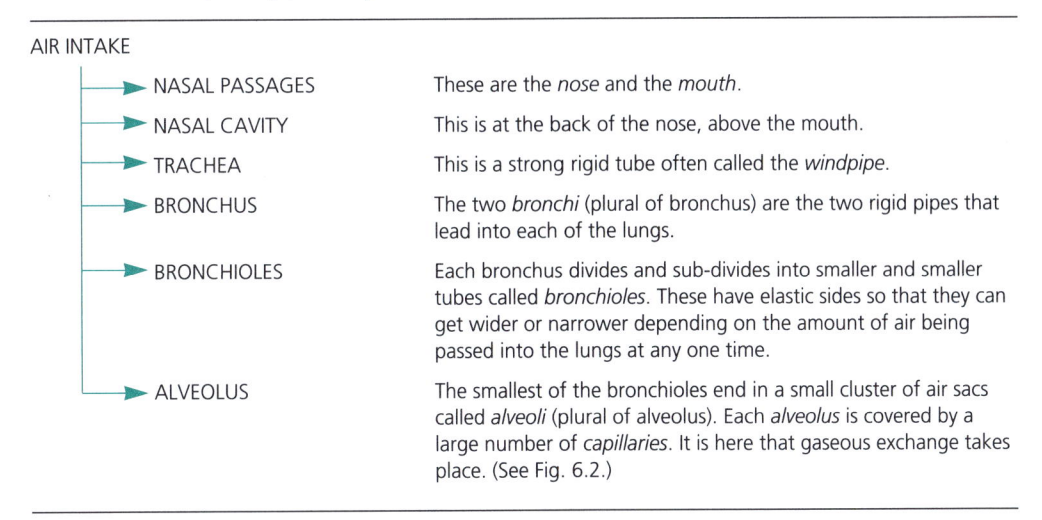

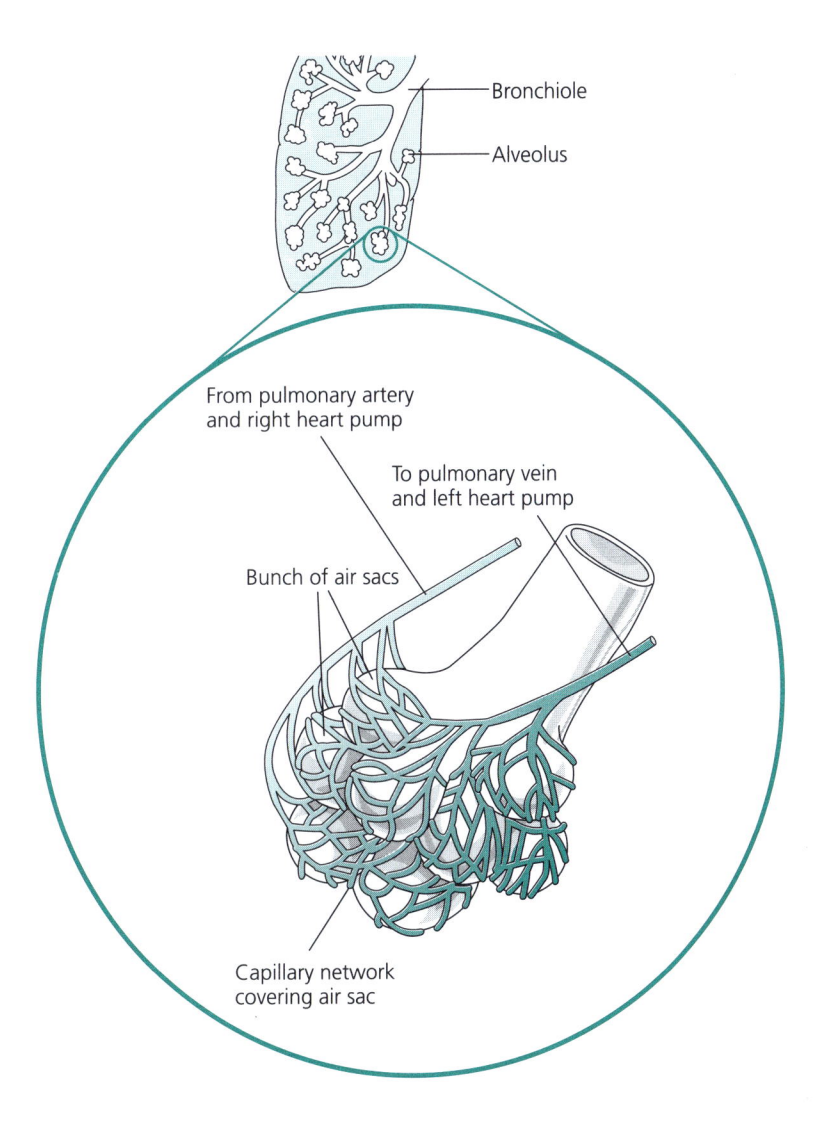

AIR INTAKE

NASAL PASSAGES	These are the *nose* and the *mouth*.
NASAL CAVITY	This is at the back of the nose, above the mouth.
TRACHEA	This is a strong rigid tube often called the *windpipe*.
BRONCHUS	The two *bronchi* (plural of bronchus) are the two rigid pipes that lead into each of the lungs.
BRONCHIOLES	Each bronchus divides and sub-divides into smaller and smaller tubes called *bronchioles*. These have elastic sides so that they can get wider or narrower depending on the amount of air being passed into the lungs at any one time.
ALVEOLUS	The smallest of the bronchioles end in a small cluster of air sacs called *alveoli* (plural of alveolus). Each *alveolus* is covered by a large number of *capillaries*. It is here that gaseous exchange takes place. (See Fig. 6.2.)

Fig. 6.2 The blood supply to air sacs

The human body's make-up relating to movement

6.2 Gaseous exchange

An exchange of gases takes place in the alveoli. When we breathe in, air is taken into the lungs and oxygen passes from the lungs through the walls of the alveoli and their surrounding capillaries into the blood. At the same time, carbon dioxide is passed from the blood into the alveoli. The walls of the alveoli, like the walls of the capillaries, are only one cell thick. This allows for the molecules to pass in each direction. (See Fig. 6.2.)

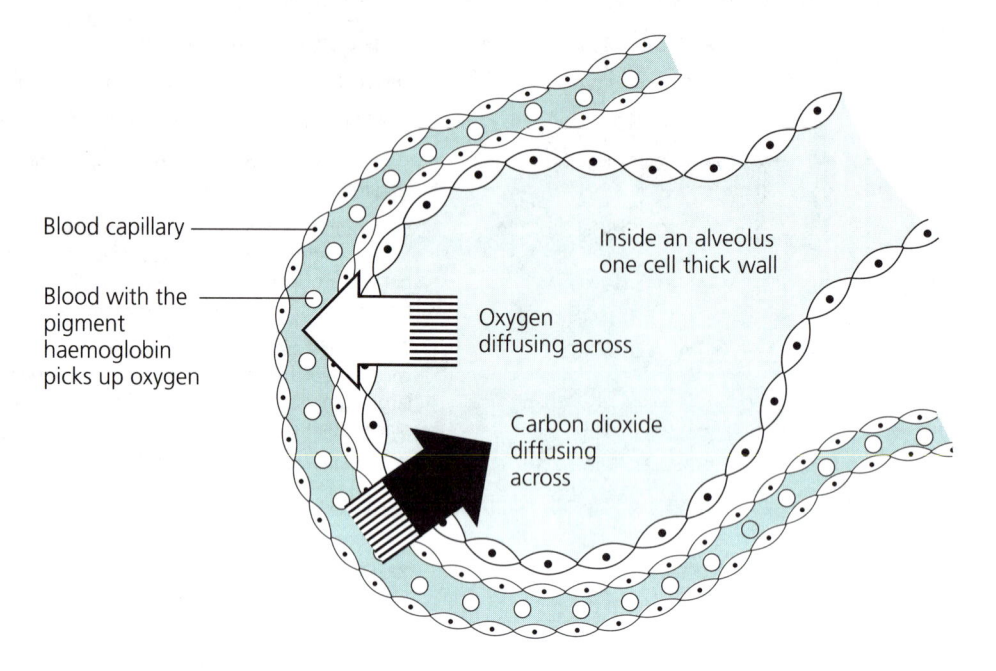

Fig. 6.2 Detailed section of one air sac

Not all the oxygen is removed from the air that we breathe in at any one time. This depends on the type of activity that we are doing. (See Table 6.3.)

Table 6.3 Amount of O_2 and CO_2 present in inspired and expired air

	INSPIRED AIR	EXPIRED AT REST	EXPIRED DURING EXERCISE
O_2	21%	17%	15%
CO_2	0.03%	3%	6%

As can be seen, we absorb a greater amount of oxygen from each breath during exercise. This is called **oxygen uptake**.

The amount of carbon dioxide that we breathe out goes up during exercise.

Examiner's tip

You should be able to describe the mechanism of inspiration and expiration.

6.3 Mechanism of breathing

In order to get air into the lungs, or **inspiration**, we have to make the chest cavity larger. This is done by lifting the ribs forward and upward and pulling the diaphragm downward. As the chest cavity is like an air-tight bag with only one opening, the action of the ribs and diaphragm create an empty space into which air is automatically sucked to make the air pressure equal inside and outside the body. (See Fig. 6.4.)

The respiratory system

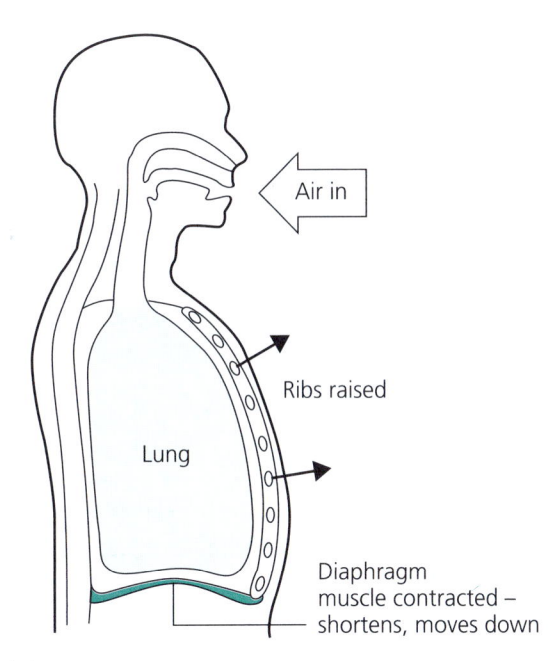

Fig. 6.4 Inspiration – taking air in

Breathing out, or **expiration**, is the opposite of inspiration. The ribs are pulled down and back and the diaphragm is pulled up. These actions squeeze the lungs and force the air out. (See Fig. 6.5.)

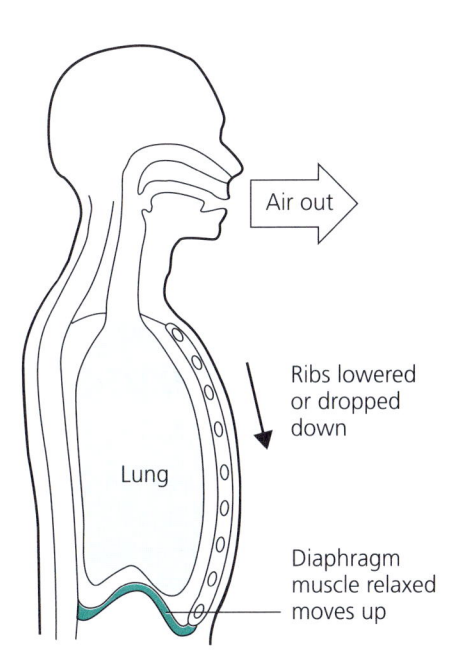

Fig. 6.5 Expiration – pushing air out

> **Examiner's tip**
> You should be able to identify the various parts of lung capacity.

6.4 Lung capacity

Each time we breathe in we do not fully inflate the lungs, and when we breathe out we do not fully empty the lungs. We can measure the amount of air that we breathe in and out by using a machine called a **spirometer**. This draws an ink line on a moving piece of paper and shows how much air is inspired and expired over a given period of time.

Whist sitting at rest we do not breathe in and out deeply. The amount of air breathed in and out in this way is called **tidal volume (TV)**.

It is possible to inhale an extra large breath and this extra amount of air is called the **inspiratory reserve volume (IRV)**.

The human body's make-up relating to movement

After breathing out normally, it is possible to exhale an extra amount of air. This extra amount is called the **expiratory reserve volume (ERV)**.

These three, TV + IRV + ERV , together make up a person's **vital capacity** (VC).

At no time are the lungs completely emptied of air. Even after breathing out the ERV there is still some air left in the lungs. This is called the **residual volume (RV)**. The air that makes up the RV is continually being changed each time we breathe in and out, so that it always contains oxygen.

Vital capacity plus RV together make up a person's **total lung capacity**. (See Fig. 6.6.)

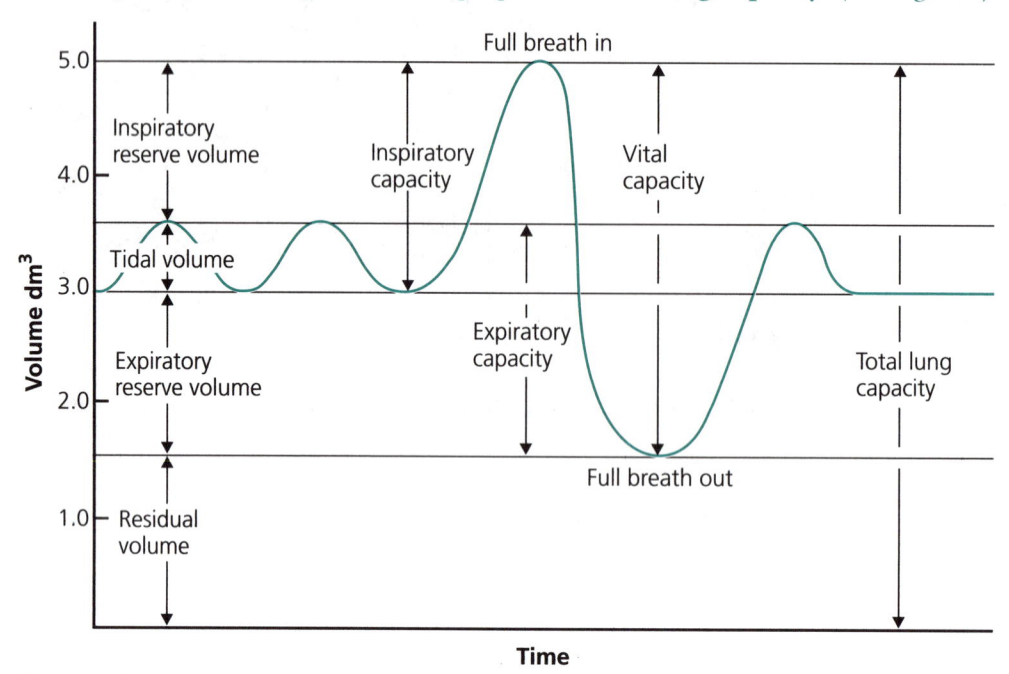

Fig. 6.6 Spirometer trace

Note: The values given are for a healthy male aged 20/30 years.
The equivalent for a healthy female aged 20/30 years would be around 20% less.

> **Examiner's tip**
>
> You should be able to explain the effect of exercise on the respiratory system

6.5 Effects of exercise

Although breathing becomes more rapid during exercise, the speed with which this occurs depends on the amount of physical activity the individual is used to. The following table lists the major effects that training has on the respiratory system. (See Table 6.7.)

Table 6.7 Effects of training on the respiratory system

1. the size of the chest increases
2. the amount the chest can expand increases
3. the breathing rate at rest is slower
4. the exchange of gases is improved
5. inspiratory and expiratory reserve volumes increase
6. tidal volume increases during exercise

After physical activity has taken place the sportsperson continues to breathe heavily until any oxygen debt that has built up is repaid. (See Unit 3.4.) However, the well trained sportsperson will revert to a normal breathing rate faster than an untrained person. This is because the well trained sportsperson will have produced more red blood cells than an untrained person and so will be able to take up more oxygen, transporting it round the body and using it more efficiently.

The respiratory system

PRINCIPAL TOPICS COVERED

1. The nasal passages, windpipe and lungs are the major parts of the respiratory system.
2. The respiratory pathway includes the nasal passages, trachea, bronchus, bronchioles and alveoli.
3. Gases are passed between the lungs and the blood stream through the one-cell thick walls of the alveoli.
4. During inspiration air is sucked into the lungs; during expiration it is forced out of the lungs.
5. Total lung capacity includes both the vital capacity and the residual volume.
6. The long-term effects of exercise on the respiratory system are increased chest size, increased chest expansion, a slower resting breathing rate and improved gaseous exchange.

QUESTIONS ON THIS CHAPTER

1. Describe the long-term effects of exercise on the respiratory system of a trained sportsperson.
2. Identify the main organs of the respiratory system.

   Examiner's tip: a simple table will do.
3. What is vital capacity?
4. Explain the term 'oxygen uptake'. What effect does exercise have on it?

Chapter 7
Digestion and diet

The main parts of the digestive system are:

1. **the mouth**
2. **the gullet** (*oesophagus*)
3. **the stomach**
4. **the small intestine**
5. **the large intestine**
6. **the anus**

These parts form a pathway that food follows through the body. This is called the **alimentary canal**. (See Fig. 7.1.)

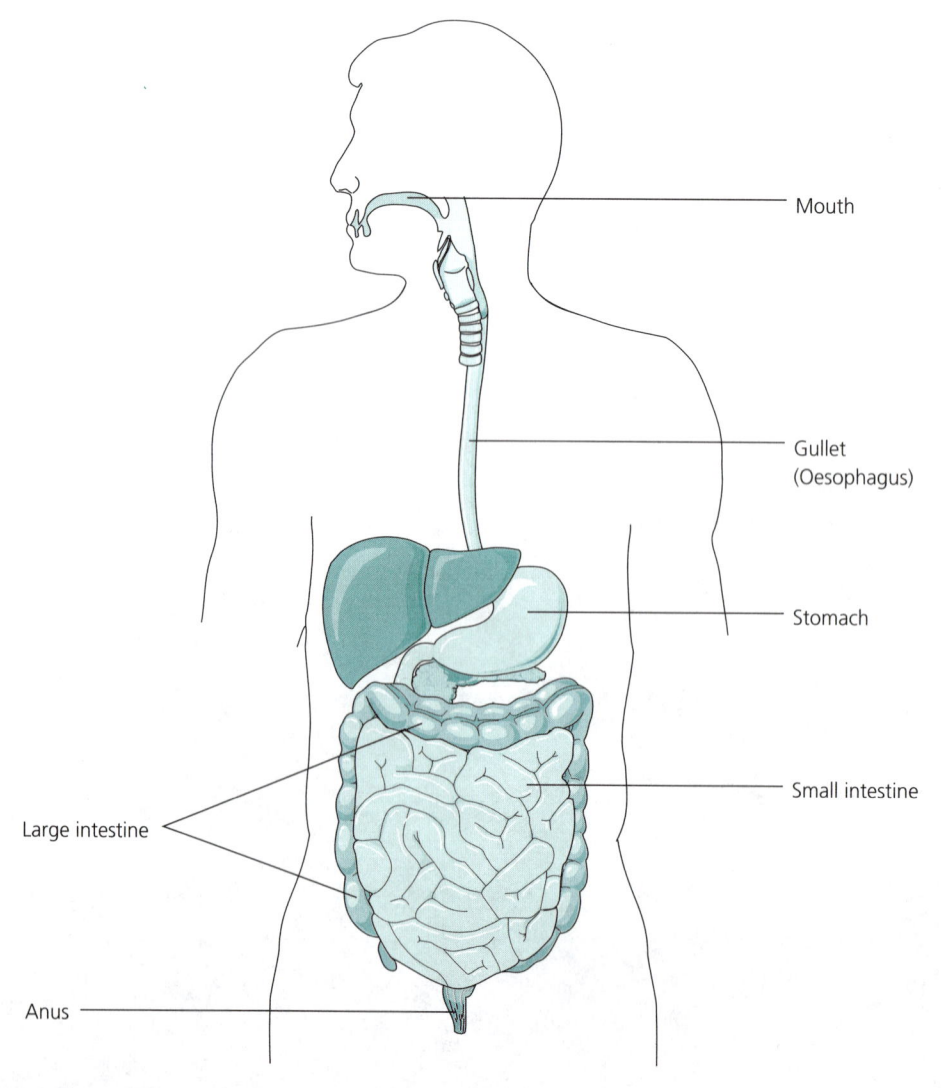

Fig. 7.1 The main parts of the human alimentary canal

Digestion and diet

Examiner's tip
You should be able to describe the alimentary canal.

7.1 The alimentary canal

Each part of the alimentary canal has a separate function.

Table 7.1 The functions of the alimentary canal

mouth	Takes in food and drink, chews and swallows food in small amounts. (A small amount is referred to as a **bolus** of food.)
oesophagus	Transports the food from the mouth to the stomach by a wave of muscular contraction called **peristalsis**. (See Unit 7.2 below.)
stomach	Holds food while digestion begins; the absorption of nutrients commences.
small intestine	Continues with the digestive process and the absorption of nutrients through its approximate length of 6 metres.
large intestine	Water and some salts are removed at this stage whilst solid waste is stored at the end of the intestine in the **bowel**.
anus	This is the end of the alimentary canal through which waste products are excreted from the body.

7.2 Peristalsis

When food is transported from the mouth to the stomach it does not just drop into the stomach by force of gravity. It has to be *forced* through the oesophagus.

The walls of the oesophagus are made of smooth muscle (see Unit 3.1) which is laid in long sheaths. These sheaths or long layers of muscle have the ability to contract and relax with a wave-like motion. This means that the bolus of food can be pushed down the oesophagus by the muscles. (See Fig. 7.2a.) This action is like pushing a marble through a tight rubber tube with your hand. (See Fig. 7.2b.)

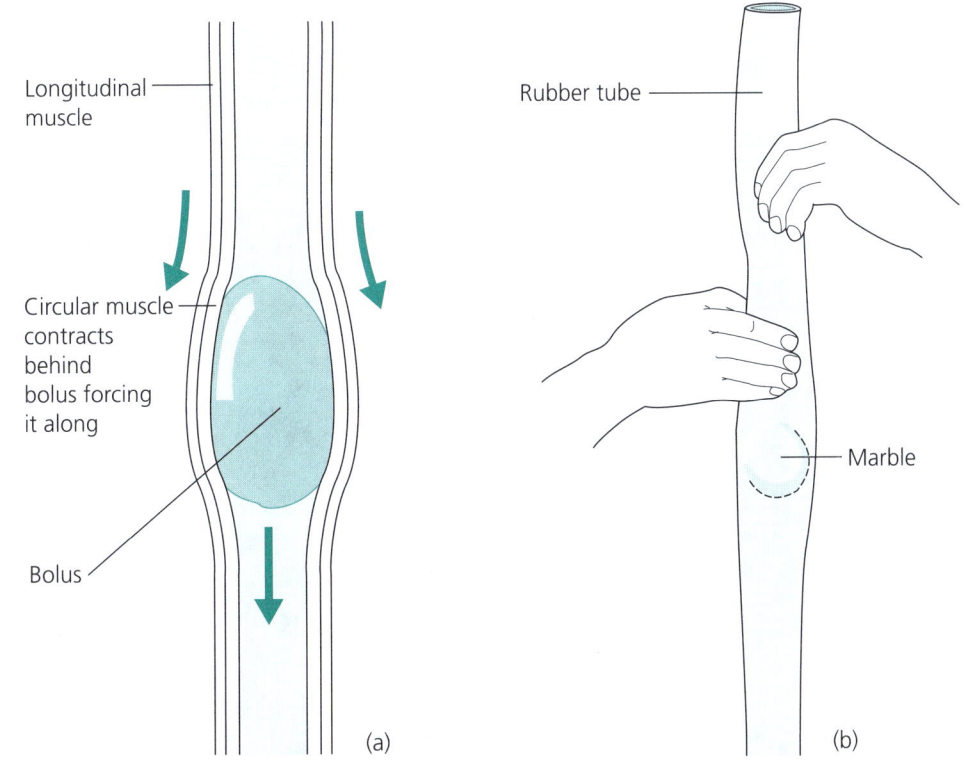

Fig. 7.2 (a) Peristalsis is the action of circular muscles of the gut in pushing the food along
(b) Demonstration of peristaltic movement; the marble is pushed along the rubber tube by hand

The human body's make-up relating to movement

It is because of this **peristaltic action** that a person standing on his or her head could still swallow a sandwich or a drink. This confirms the wave-like muscular movement through the oesophagus.

7.3 Diet

> **Examiner's tip**
> You should be able to describe the content of a balanced diet.

All people, whether actively involved in sport or not, need to have a balanced diet. This should include a daily intake from each of the following groups of food:

1. **fruit and vegetables**
2. **cereals and grain**
3. **eggs, cheese meat and fish**
4. **milk and other milk products**

Food from these groups should provide essential nutrients called **proteins**, **carbohydrates**, **fats**, **vitamins** and **minerals**, which our bodies need to function efficiently. (See Tables 7.2 and 7.3.)

Table 7.2 Sources of proteins, carbohydrates, fats, vitamins and minerals

proteins	found in meats, cheese, fish, eggs, soya, nuts
carbohydrates	found in flour foods (breads, cakes), sugar foods (jams), dried fruit
fats	found in milk products (butter, cream), lard, nuts, fish, meat
vitamins + minerals	found in the whole range of food: variety in diet should provide all those necessary

> **Examiner's tip**
> You should know the sources and functions of proteins, carbohydrates, fats, vitamins and minerals.

Table 7.3 Functions of protein, carbohydrates, fats, vitamins and minerals

proteins	needed for growth by building new cells in the body and repairing them
carbohydrates	provide energy
fats	provide energy and insulation; often stored under the skin, especially at the stomach, hips and bottom
vitamins	help in the formation of bodily tissues (such as hair, skin, nails, teeth) and are necessary for all chemical reactions in the body
minerals	are necessary for the efficient uptake of vitamins and also for the formation of bodily tissues and the carrying out of chemical reactions

Picture 7.1 Sources of protein and vitamins

The bulk of most fruits and vegetables is made up of fibre, which is essential to our diet. It provides a bulky mass for the intestine muscles to work on and this makes it easier for food to pass through the digestive tract. High fibre foods usually contain fewer calories than low fibre foods and make you feel fuller. This can help you to lose weight. (**Weight loss should always be carefully monitored.**)

7.4 Balanced diet

Food taken in daily is used to provide nutrients for body growth and energy for exercise.

- If more food is taken in than is needed for our daily requirements much of it is stored in the form of fats under the body's surface.
- If less food is taken in than is needed for our daily requirements the body will use up all its reserves and then begin to lose weight. (See Table 7.4.)

Table 7.4 Balanced diet

Daily Intake	EQUALS	Energy Expenditure	=	Stable Weight
Daily Intake	GREATER THAN	Energy Expenditure	=	Weight Gain
Daily Intake	LESS THAN	Energy Expenditure	=	Weight Loss

7.5 Diet and exercise

Involvement in physical exercise does not seem to have any long-term effects on the digestive system. However, exercise and the eating of large meals must be undertaken with care. During hard physical exercise, blood is diverted from the digestive system to the muscles so that immediate energy production can take place. This means that any food in the alimentary canal at this time will not be absorbed into the body. If a heavy meal is taken just prior to hard physical activity the sportsperson will feel uncomfortable and may well under-perform.

Diet is of major importance to the sportsperson. The balance of different types of foods in the diet should reflect the type of activity followed. For instance, it should take into account whether muscle bulk is to be developed for power activities or if stamina is to be improved for endurance activities, and should ensure that the necessary nutrients are provided in the right quantities to enable achievement of these things.

However, the objectives of diet may well change just prior to competition. The aims of a pre-competition diet may be to:

> **Examiner's tip**
> You should be able to explain the reasons for carbohydrate loading.

1. Attain a large store of carbohydrates in the body (**carbohydrate loading**) as this increases the muscle glycogen content and enables a longer supply of energy. (See Fig 7.3 and Picture 7.2.)

2. Enter competition with as little as possible in the stomach. This allows the diaphragm to descend as far as possible during inhalation.

3. Prevent gastric disturbances by avoiding gas-making foods such as onions, baked beans, cabbage and apples.

4. Achieve a positive psychological attitude by knowing that a beneficially correct, yet palatable, diet has been followed.

The human body's make-up relating to movement

days before competition								approx. rise in muscle glycogen
7	6	5	4	3	2	1		
>>>> normal training diet and activity >>>>>>>>>>>>>>							c o m p e t i t i o n	normal
hard session	low carbohydrate diet			high carbohydrate diet				140% increase
			hard session	high carbohydrate				
						high carbohydrate	d a y	50% increase

Fig. 7.3 Ways to achieve carbohydrate loading

Picture 7.2 Energy-giving foods are mostly carbohydrates. They include cereals, bread, potatoes and sugars.

PRINCIPAL TOPICS COVERED

1. The pathway that food follows through the body is called the alimentary canal.
2. Food is forced through the oesophagus by peristalsis.
3. The daily intake of food should include proteins, carbohydrates, fats, vitamins and minerals, in the right quantities for a person's body and for their level and type of activity.
4. In a balanced diet the daily intake of food should equal the daily expenditure of energy.
5. Diet should reflect the type of activity followed by the sportsperson.
6. Pre-competition diet should aim at carbohydrate loading but allow entry to competition with as little as possible in the stomach.

QUESTIONS ON THIS CHAPTER

1 Name three components of a balanced diet.
2 For what purpose does the body use carbohydrate?
3 Explain the disadvantages of eating a meal just prior to competition.
4 Name two sources of protein.
5 Explain the term 'peristalsis'.

Capabilities and limitations of the human body

Chapter 8
Fitness

8.1 What is fitness?

It is almost impossible to say what fitness is. It means different things to different people e.g. the person who wins the Olympic gold medal at weight lifting may well be said to be fit, but that same person could also be said to be totally unfit for running a marathon.

Perhaps the best definition of fitness is:

the ability to meet the daily physical demands of work and play without excessive fatigue and still have something in reserve.

If this definition is used it is possible to argue that one person is fit for a sedentary lifestyle while another may be fit to run the marathon.

When considering fitness you should always try to answer the question: 'Fit for what?' In trying to answer this question, you must take into account that fitness is divided into two main areas:

1. **physical fitness**
2. **motor fitness**

> **Examiner's tip**
> You should be able to distinguish between fitness, physical fitness and motor fitness.

8.2 Physical fitness

To the sportsperson, physical fitness can be described as:

the ability to meet the physical and physiological demands made by a particular sporting activity.

The effects of participation in any physical activity will alter the way various body systems work. (See Table 8.1.)

Table 8.1 Changes observed in body systems brought on by physical training

	AT REST	DURING ACTIVITY
Depth of breathing	8 lit/min	25 lit/min
Pulse rate	75 bts/min	190+ bts/min
Stroke volume	100 ml/beat	200 ml/beat
Cardiac output*	7 lit/min	35+ lit/min
O₂ used per minute	250 ml/min	4500+ ml/min
Size of O₂ debt developed	none	Up to 10 lit or more

★ **Cardiac output** is the volume of blood pumped by the left ventricle of the heart in one minute. It is measured in litres per minute. The sign for cardiac output is Q.

Whether the body can cope with these changes depends on how prepared it is for the demands that are being made upon it. If the demands of exercise are too great for someone's body systems, they will be unable to keep going.

The body adjusts to the demands that are regularly made upon it, e.g. someone who runs a little further each day will find it gradually easier to run for longer as their respiratory system becomes more efficient. When someone's body systems can meet the demands of exercise without undue stress then they are said to be in a **normal state**. However, the normal state for a person who runs 20 miles every day will be different from the normal state of a person who takes part in very little activity. Because the body is able to adjust, regular participation in physical activity will change the normal state of a person's body systems.

8.3 Components of physical fitness

> **Examiner's tip**
> You should be able to describe the major components of physical fitness: the four Ss.

Physical fitness is described as having four major components, **strength**, **stamina**, **speed** and **suppleness**, known as the four Ss. (See Fig. 8.1.)

```
        STRENGTH              STAMINA

                   PHYSICAL
                   FITNESS

         SPEED                SUPPLENESS
```

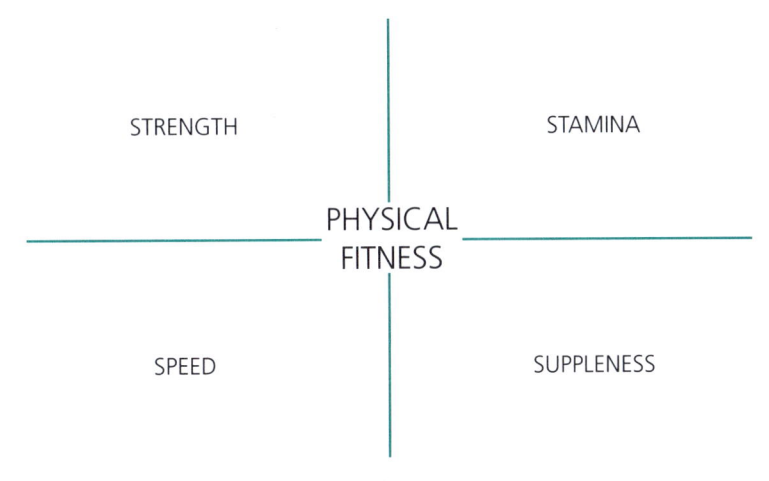

Fig. 8.1 The four main components of physical fitness.

The balance between each of these components may well vary according to the demands of a particular sport.

8.4 Strength

Strength is defined as:

> the ability to use the muscles to apply force to overcome a resistance.

There are three types of strength, each being best suited to different situations (see Table 8.2.):

1. static
2. explosive
3. dynamic

Capabilities and limitations of the human body

Table 8.2 Analysis of strength types

	STATIC	EXPLOSIVE	DYNAMIC
Body state	stays the same	moves fast	moves fast
Distance moved	little or none	little	can be considerable
Time taken	varies, but not long	small amount	can be considerable
Muscle state	stays the same	changes quickly	repeatedly changes quickly
Activity example	tug of war rugby scrum	shot put high jump	rowing 100 metres sprint

8.5 Speed

Speed is defined as:

> the shortest time taken to move the body or a body part over a specific distance.

The ability to move the body quickly is essential in many sports.

Speed may often be initiated by different body parts: e.g. the legs in running but the arms in swimming and gymnastics.

In some sports only one body part may be expected to move fast: e.g. in fencing an attack may be the straightening of the arm, in karate the moving of a foot.

In other sports such as archery, speed makes a negligible contribution to the accuracy demanded in competition.

8.6 Stamina

Stamina is defined as:

> the ability to perform strenuous activity over a long period of time.

Stamina is often referred to as **cardiovascular fitness**. In order to meet the requirements of cardiovascular fitness, there must be a continuous ready supply of O_2 to the muscles so that energy can be produced and waste matter removed (see Unit 3.4). If the body is worked too hard over a long period of time, then an oxygen debt will develop. This will eventually result in the build-up of lactic acid in the muscles which in turn brings on a feeling of fatigue and possible cramp in some muscles.

Many sports demand stamina, especially those such as rowing and long distance running.

8.7 Suppleness

Suppleness is defined as:

> the range of movement possible at a joint or joints.

Suppleness is often referred to as **flexibility** or **mobility**.

Suppleness is affected by the type of joint and the muscle attachments to it: e.g. some joints – such as that at the hip – move freely, giving a wide range of movement. This range of movement can be increased by training, for instance, to allow a person to do the splits.

Other joints have a very limited range of movement on their own, such as the joints between the vertebrae. However, these joints rarely act individually: several work together at the same time, giving a more extensive range of movement. Training can increase the flexibility at this type of joint only minimally. However, the sum of the small increases from several such joints together can increase the flexibility of the spine considerably.

A greater range of movement at specific joints can be of advantage to many competitors. The butterfly swimmer needs to be very supple at the shoulders and hips, whilst gymnasts and dancers want total body suppleness.

In those sports that place greater emphasis on strength, too much suppleness can be a disadvantage. The weight lifter requires only a limited range of movement at the shoulders and back in order to hold heavy weights above his head for a specified time. Despite this, it is generally agreed that suppleness allows the body to move easily and lessens the chance of sustaining an injury to the muscles, tendons or ligaments.

> **Examiner's tip**
>
> You should be able to identify a sporting activity to illustrate each of the components of physical fitness.

Table 8.3 Physical fitness components of some sporting activities

	STRENGTH	STAMINA	SPEED	SUPPLENESS
Rowing	✔	✔	some	some
Aerobics	some	✔	✗	✔
Skating	some	some	✔	some
Soccer	some	✔	✔	some
Archery	some	✗	✗	✗

8.8 Motor fitness

To the sportsperson, **motor fitness** can be defined as:

> the ability to perform successfully in a given sporting context.

Of course, to achieve success in any sporting context, all components of physical fitness are needed. But motor fitness will more directly affect the sportsperson's ability to perform the skills essential to the chosen physical activity.

The main components of motor fitness are:

1. **power** — The combination of strength and speed working together.
2. **agility** — The ability to change body position and direction quickly and with precision.
3. **co-ordination** — The ability to perform complex motor tasks involving several skills in sequence, such as in hurdling.
4. **balance** — An awareness of the body's position in a fast-changing physical situation, such as in gymnastic activity on the beam.
5. **reaction** — The time taken to respond to a given stimulus.
6. **attitude** — The psychological approach brought by the sportsperson to the sporting situation: often described as the 'will to win' factor. This element of motor fitness is often overlooked. A coach can have great influence in establishing the attitudes that the sportsperson has towards competition. Once an attitude is established it may be very difficult to change.

Capabilities and limitations of the human body

> **Examiner's tip**
> You should be able to describe the main components of motor fitness.

```
            ATTITUDE
                |
AGILITY ─ ─ ─ ─ ┼ ─ ─ ─ ─ CO-ORDINATION
                |
             MOTOR
            FITNESS
                |
REACTION ─ ─ ─ ─┼ ─ ─ ─ ─ POWER
                |
            BALANCE
```

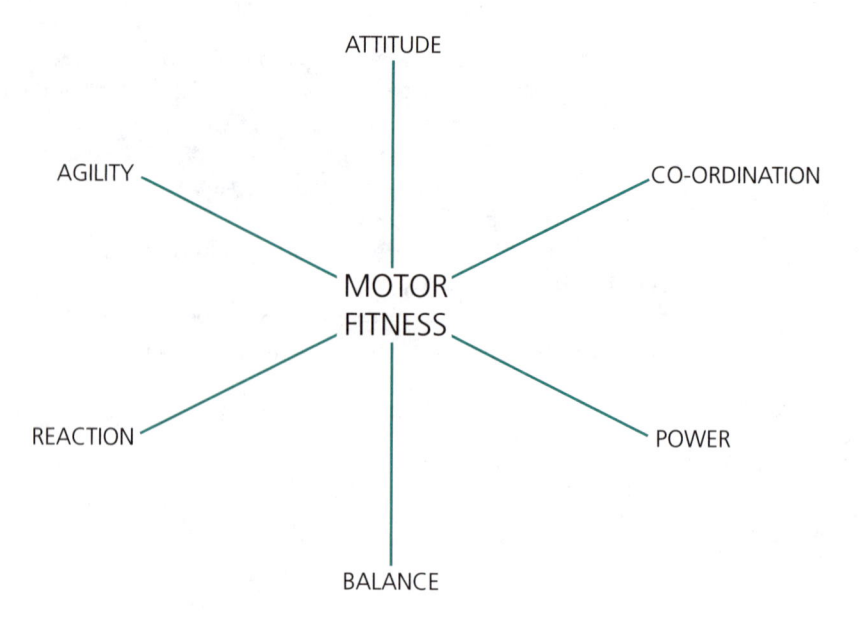

Fig. 8.2 The major components of motor fitness

8.9 Influences on fitness

There are a great many factors that can influence both physical and motor fitness. These include both *psychological* and *physiological* influences (influences affecting the brain and the body) and the way the body is prepared for physical activity. These are discussed in greater detail in succeeding chapters. (See especially Chapter 11.)

PRINCIPAL TOPICS COVERED

1. Fitness is the ability to meet the daily physical demands of work and play without excessive fatigue and still have something left in reserve.
2. Fitness is divided into two parts: physical fitness and motor fitness.
3. Physical fitness is the ability to meet the physical or physiological demands made by a particular sporting activity.
4. Motor fitness is the ability to perform successfully in a given sporting context.
5. The major components of physical fitness are strength, speed, stamina and suppleness.
6. The main components of motor fitness are attitude, agility, co-ordination, power, balance and reaction.

QUESTIONS ON THIS CHAPTER

1. Define the four components of physical fitness.

2. Describe the changes that occur in pulse rate, stroke volume and cardiac output during physical activity.

   Examiner's tip: if you can quote figures to illustrate the increase, more marks will be gained.

3. Describe the term 'explosive strength'. Give two examples of sports which include this.

4. Explain why suppleness would be an important factor for butterfly swimmers.

5. Explain why attitude is an important component of an individual's fitness.

Chapter 9
Improving fitness

The physical performance of the human body can always be improved. This is done by following a training programme which regularly places increasing demand upon it. Some programmes are more effective than others. There are four guiding principles which can help decide on an effective programme. These are:

1. overload
2. progression
3. specificity
4. reversibility

9.1 Overload

Overload is the term used to describe activities that impose demands on the body which are greater than usual.

The overload principle aims to put the body systems under stress: e.g. if excessive demand is put on a muscle, more muscle fibres become prepared to cope with the increased workload. If excessive demand is put on the body's aerobic system, it will produce more red blood cells so more oxygen can be taken up and so it can be used more efficiently.

It is possible to improve aerobic activity, muscular strength and flexibility by using the overload principle. This improvement can be attained in three ways:

1. by increasing the **intensity** of the activity. This means that you would have to run faster, lift heavier weights or stretch further than normal during training. These increases would be built up over a period of time.
2. by increasing the **frequency** of the activity. This means that there would be more training sessions with shorter rest periods between them.
3. by increasing the **duration** of the activity. This means that the length of each training session would be increased.

If all three methods of overload were to be used together then training sessions would take longer, be harder work and would happen more frequently.

> **Examiner's tip**
> You should be able to explain the terms 'intensity', 'frequency' and 'duration'.

9.2 Progression

It is essential that work done in a training session should be within the capabilities of the individual sportsperson. Although *stress* must be placed on the body systems for training to be effective, too much stress too soon can cause injury.

If the overload of the body systems is increased appropriately, then the improvements caused by training can easily be seen, especially in the early stages of the training programme.

However, as the body adapts and begins to find the harder programme less demanding, the overload must be continually increased, otherwise progression will stop. The stress factor should be increased gradually in a series of calculated progressively harder training sessions. If stress is not increased, then the training activity will become boring and stale.

9.3 Specificity

Training should be **specific**, which means that it should concentrate on the particular needs of the individual within the training programme. Lifting weights, for example, will increase muscular strength but will have little effect on the aerobic capacity of the individual.

Not only should the training be specific to the sport, it should also be specific to a particular part of the body. If upper body strength is required then exercises concentrating on the arms and chest will be needed. If both speed and endurance are needed then both types of activity must be included in training sessions.

Particular care must be taken if a person is returning to training after injury. Muscles that have recently recovered from a pull or a strain cannot be worked as hard as those that were not damaged. Lower levels of stress should be placed on recently repaired body tissue. However, carefully designed specific training focusing on an injured body part can help to rehabilitate that body part after injury.

9.4 Reversibility

Just as the body adapts to greater stress and gets bigger, stronger and faster through training, then it will also adapt to less stress should training cease.

It is not possible to keep to the peak of perfection reached through training unless physical work is maintained.

If training stops altogether then the body will adapt to the lower stress levels very quickly. Indeed it adapts to lower stress levels far more quickly than to higher stress levels.

Anaerobic activities are affected less than aerobic ones as they do not need vast amounts of oxygen. The aerobic capacity of muscles deteriorates very quickly. If the muscles are not used they begin to **atrophy** (waste away and get smaller and thinner). Weaker, smaller muscles are more prone to injury.

It is estimated that muscles lose strength three times more quickly than they gain it.

This means that as a general rule, it is suggested that a sportsperson has to do three weeks' training just to get back to the level he or she was at prior to stopping for one week.

9.5 Training threshold

Examiner's tip
You should be able to explain the terms 'overload', 'progression', 'specificity' and 'reversibility'.

As has already been indicated, for training to be effective, the body systems must be put under stress. What needs to be established is the correct level at which to start training so that it is both effective and safe.

There are several ways of establishing a safe level of stress and these usually relate to a person's pulse rate.

1 **The 180 method** – calculates the threshold level for training by deducting a person's age from 180. So a 40 year-old person should be safe to work at a pulse rate of 140 (180 – 40).

2 **The 60% method** – calculates the threshold level by adding 60% of the range of heart rate to the resting pulse rate.

If a person's resting pulse rate = 80
and his maximum rate = 180
then the range = 100   (180 – 80)
60% of the range = 60
so the threshold rate = 140   (80 + 60)

This method ignores a person's age and their maximum heart rate has to be established. **Maximum heart rate** is the most a person's heart is capable of beating per minute.

3 **The 70% to 80% method** – is based on a person working at 70% to 80% of a notional maximum heart rate that is related to a given age. For example:

Age	Max pulse/min	Safe working rate 70/80% of max
20	200	140/160
30	190	133/152
40	180	126/144
50	170	119/136

Examiner's tip
You should be able to work out the training threshold rate.

As you can see, any of these methods indicates a similar threshold rate. However, for strength work, only the 60% rule is usually used.

The strength exercises chosen, such as sit-ups, bench press and leg press, are each performed *for one minute* and the score recorded. The safe training level for the exercises is established at 60% of the *recorded scores* for each exercise. As training progresses and strength increases the 60% of maximum has to be recalculated at periodic intervals.

9.6 Training methods

Examiner's tip
You should be able to describe the following training methods:
a) interval
b) continuous
c) fartlek
d) circuit
e) weight

There are a wide range of different training programmes and each seems to place a different emphasis on the main components of fitness. (See Table 9.1.)

Interval training

This involves alternating work periods of high intensity with rest periods. The rest periods may be inactive, where the body stops moving, or may consist of a period where the body works at a low intensity.

Examples of interval training are:

- SWIMMING 10 by 50 metre sprints with 20 second rest between
- RUNNING   10 by 100 metre sprints with 300 metre jog between

Capabilities and limitations of the human body

With this training method there are four ways in which the stress level can be increased:

- increase the **speed** of the sprints
- increase the **number** of sprints
- increase the **distance** sprinted
- shorten the **rest** periods

Continuous training

This involves working for a prolonged period of time at a steady stress level but below maximum effort. The intensity of the work done is just below that where oxygen debt would begin to develop.

At the start of this type of programme the individual may work for only 20 to 30 minutes. However, over a number of sessions the time spent on training can be increased, though the workload stays the same. Swimming, jogging and cycling are most suited to this type of training.

Fartlek

This takes its name from the type of training carried out in Sweden, and the word means 'speed play'.

Fartlek is in fact very similar to continuous training but includes short, sharp bursts of effort of much higher intensity. These may be of only 5 to 10 seconds duration and recur every 2 to 3 minutes.

Circuit training

This has two basic variations, **fixed load** and **individual load**, but both follow a similar pattern. The individual completes a series of exercises in a set order, each exercise concentrating on a different part of the body.

- In **fixed load** circuits the individual attempts to perform each exercise continuously over a given time. When this is achieved the circuit is redesigned to increase the stress level by setting a new time target (e.g. by lengthening the work periods or shortening the rest periods).
- In **individual load** circuits the sportsperson establishes their own level of work for each exercise, i.e. the number of times that each exercise is to be done. This is usually about 50% to 60% of the maximum that they can do for each exercise in one minute. They are then timed for each completed circuit of exercises and aim to improve on the time of the previous circuit at successive training sessions.

Circuits are designed to build up strength and stamina, and one advantage of them is that they can be done indoors in all kinds of weather. (See Fig. 9.1.)

```
STEP-UPS  ─────────────▶  BENCH PRESS
(legs)                      (arms)
   ▲                          │
   │                          ▼
ARM CURLS                  SHUTTLE RUN
(arms)                      (legs)
   ▲                          │
   │                          ▼
SKIPPING  ◀─────────────   SIT-UPS
(legs)                     (stomach)
```

KEY: The main parts of the body being overloaded are written in brackets.
This type of circuit will help to improve both strength and stamina.

Fig. 9.1 Example of a simple six station circuit

Improving fitness

Weight training

This is similar to circuit training in that the individual completes a set of exercises in a specific order, each concentrating on a different part of the body. However, all the exercises include the raising of weights. As training progresses, the number of times the weights are lifted, called **reps** or **repetitions**, can be increased and the weight can be made a little heavier.

Also, as in circuit training, there are two main variations to weight training: **isometric** and **isotonic**. (See Fig.9.2.)

> **Examiner's tip**
> You should be able to explain the difference between isometric and isotonic contractions.

- **Isometric** weight training involves lifting the weight and holding the muscular contraction for up to 5 secs, then relaxing briefly before it is repeated. This means that the overload of the muscle is taking place while the contracted muscle fibres stay still, at the same length, over a given period of time. Isometric contractions develop strength more than endurance.
- **Isotonic** weight training involves raising and lowering the weights rapidly in a series of sustained repetitions. This ensures that the overload of the muscle is taking place as the shortening muscle fibres move. Isotonic contractions develop endurance and strength at approximately the same rate.

Fig 9.2 Example of a weight training programme

EXERCISE	MAIN MUSCLE GROUPS UNDER STRESS
Bench press (see pic 9.1)	chest, front of shoulder, back of upper arm
Front squat (see pic 9.2)	thigh, hip
Two hands curl (see pic 9.3)	front of upper arm
Deep knee bend (see pic 9.4)	legs, back, chest
Side to side bend (see pic 9.5)	sides of trunk, stomach
Heel lift (see pic 9.6)	lower leg, ankle

EACH EXERCISE TO BE COMPLETED FIVE TIMES
EACH SET OF EXERCISES TO BE COMPLETED TWICE.

To increase INTENSITY the size of the weights used in each activity would be increased.
To increase DURATION the number of sets of exercises would be increased.
To increase FREQUENCY the number of sessions would be increased.

In this type of activity the individual should start with easily manageable weights and progress to heavier weights gradually.

Picture 9.1 Bench press

Capabilities and limitations of the human body

Picture 9.2 Front squat

Picture 9.3 Two hands curl

Improving fitness

Picture 9.4 Deep knee bend

Picture 9.5 Side to side bend

71

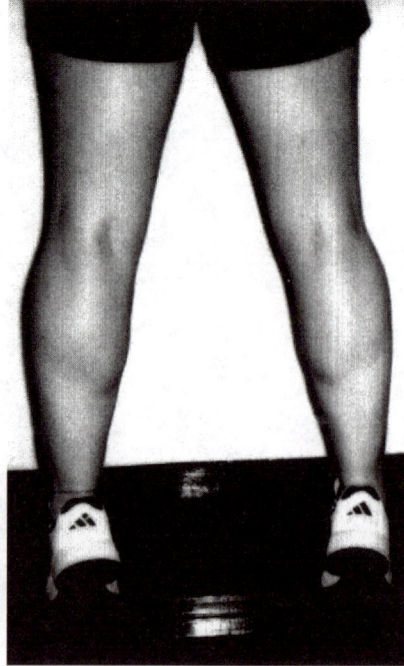

Capabilities and limitations of the human body

Picture 9.6 Heel lift

Table 9.7 Fitness components most affected by different training methods.

	INTERVAL	CONTINUOUS	FARTLEK	CIRCUIT	WEIGHT
Strength				✔	✔
Speed	✔		✔		
Stamina		✔	✔	✔	✔
Suppleness	✔				
Power	✔				
Agility				✔	✔
Aerobic capacity		✔	✔	✔	
Anaerobic capacity	✔		✔	✔	✔

9.7 Training sessions

All training sessions should be broken down into three main parts:

1. **warm up**
2. **training activity**
3. **cool down**

The bulk of the session, the training activities, may be subdivided to concentrate on specific aspects of the training schedule but these must not be attempted before a satisfactory warm up is completed.

Warm up exercises should develop gradually in a sustained manner, combining flexibility exercises with some cardiovascular work and some light resistance exercises.

A satisfactory warm up session will:

- increase the blood supply to the muscles so they can cope with extra work demands
- warm up the muscles so that they can stretch without causing injury
- prepare the joints to work over a greater range
- concentrate the mind on the physical work to be done.

The warm up should prepare both body and mind for work.

Cool down exercises at the end of a training session are of as much importance as warm up exercises. When a hard physical training session ends, a large supply of blood is retained in the muscles. This should be returned to the general circulation as soon as possible, otherwise it may *pool* in the veins. If this pooling does develop and the heart is still beating very fast, some organs of the body may be deprived of oxygen. The sudden stopping of hard physical exercise can bring about fainting or dizziness. Light exercise such as jogging will help to avoid **blood pooling** and help lower the heart rate to a more normal level in a controlled manner.

9.8 Rest periods

Resting periods are as important to training as hard physical exercise.

During intensive hard work the muscle fibres may become slightly damaged and also develop a shortage of glycogen. The inclusion of rest days in the training schedule when only very light physical work or none at all is done will allow the muscles to recover.

Rest days or light training days included up to seven days prior to competition in the training schedule have been shown to be of considerable value to the performer. The body is then better prepared for the stress of competition.

PRINCIPAL TOPICS COVERED

1. There are four guiding principles to be considered when improving fitness: overload, progression, specificity and reversibility.
2. There are a number of ways to calculate the training threshold for effective and safe stress levels in training.
3. Different training methods affect different fitness components.
4. Training methods include interval, continuous, fartlek, circuit and weight.
5. There is a difference between isometric and isotonic contraction.
6. Warm up and cool down are essential parts of a training session.
7. Light training and rest days are important in the training schedule.

QUESTIONS ON THIS CHAPTER

1. Name and briefly describe two training methods.

2. Explain how the principle of progression could be used to make training more effective.

   Examiner's tip: it is often best to answer this type of question by relating it to a specific training method.

3. Define the following terms and name an exercise or activity that would develop each of them:
   (i) strength
   (ii) suppleness

4. What is meant by the term 'isometric contraction'?

5. Give three reasons for a warm up before starting physical activity.

6. Choose one physical activity and describe a suitable training session.

   Examiner's tip: you should be able to list the main parts of a training session for a sport you know well.

Chapter 10
Acquisition of skill

What is skill? Skill is evident in all those who participate in sport at every level. Some people seem to be more skilful than others. Whilst performing a skilful act the sportsperson will include many of the components of fitness described earlier in Chapter 8.

> **Examiner's tip**
> You should be able to define the term 'skill'.

10.1 Skill defined

It is not easy to define skill as there are many different situations when skill can be used. The definition that is accepted by many people is that put forward by Barbara Knapp in 1963:

> skill is a learned ability to bring about pre-determined results with maximum certainty, often with the minimum outlay of time or energy, or both.

What is evident from this definition is:

- a skill is *something that is learned*: although some people may seem to perform a skill naturally, all physical skills have to be learned.
- a skill has a *result that is anticipated*: the outcome of a skilful action is known before it is carried out.
- skill is done with the *minimum of outlay*: it is an action that uses the components of fitness efficiently. There is control of physical movement.

10.2 Open and closed skills

Skills are usually described by the amount of control that the individual has over the timing of the performance of the skill, often called **pacing**.

In some situations the individual alone will decide when the skill will be performed, such as in the serve in tennis. In other situations it may well be that external forces will dictate when a skill has to be performed. An example of this would be a white water canoeist who has to consider water speed and the effects of rocks in the river before he or she decides how to paddle.

The performance of all skills is influenced to a greater or lesser extent by external factors.

> **Examiner's tip**
> You should be able to differentiate between open and closed skills.

Open skills

Open skills are those which are most influenced by external factors. Deciding when to carry out a tackle in hockey or football depends not only on the ability to perform the tackle but also on many other factors. The speed of the opponent, how close to goal you might be and how many supporting players there are will all influence when you will perform the skill of the tackle.

74

Acquisition of skill

Closed skills

Closed skills follow a pre-learned pattern of movement with little reference to external factors e.g. when shooting at archery, the performance of the skill follows a pattern which has been taught. (See Fig. 10.1.)

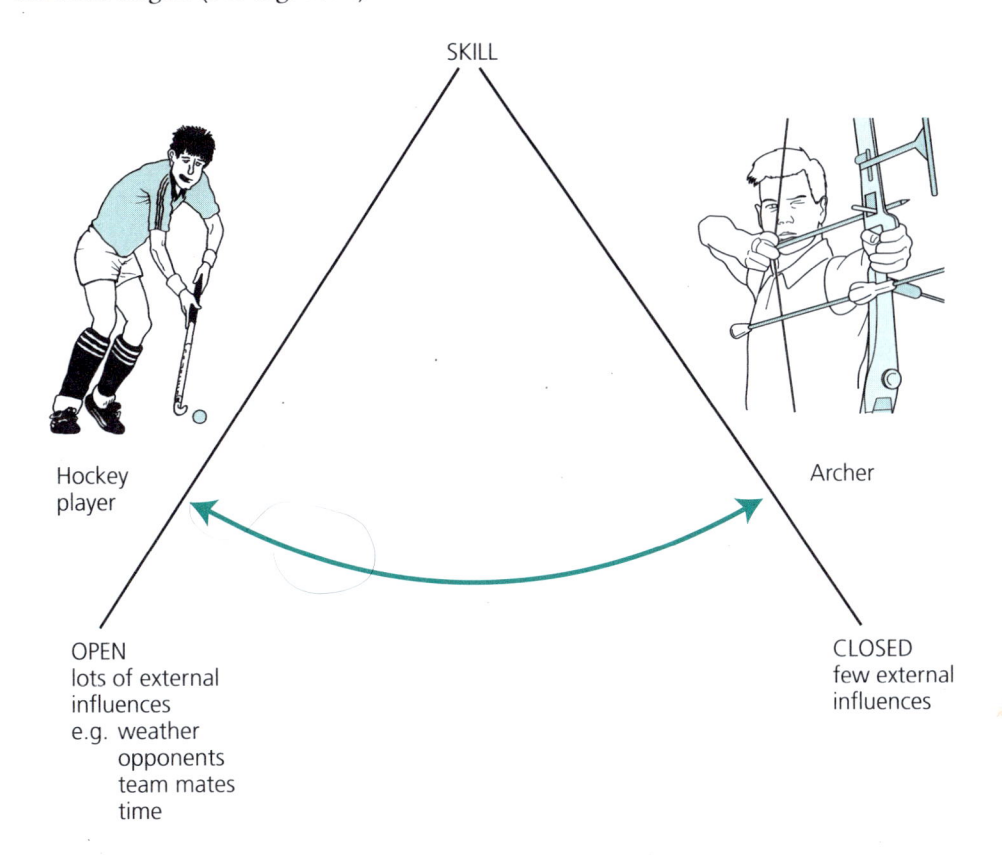

Fig. 10.1 The skill pendulum

- SKILL (top)
- Hockey player — OPEN: lots of external influences e.g. weather, opponents, team mates, time
- Archer — CLOSED: few external influences

10.3 Processing information

It is not only important to learn how to perform a skill, it is also important for the individual to know when to perform the skill e.g. the ability to make an excellent forehand return at tennis is one thing, but knowing when to do it is another.

As your opponent serves, you receive lots of information (stimuli) which is passed to the CNS. Information from exteroceptors such as the eyes and ears together with information from proprioceptors relating to body position all have to be passed to the CNS and acted upon. (See Unit 4.2.) All the information received (stimuli) is described as the **input**, and the action taken as the **output**. The receiving of this information and the decision-making process are shown in diagram form in Fig. 10.2.

INPUT → DECISION MAKING → OUTPUT

Fig. 10.2 A simplistic form of an information processing model

> **Examiner's tip**
> You should be aware of the importance of feed back in the information processing model.

The skilful performer will be able to adjust the output as it is actually being performed. Extra input is received as the output is being done so that it can be minutely adjusted to meet ever changing situations. This is called **feedback**. (See Fig 10.3.)

75

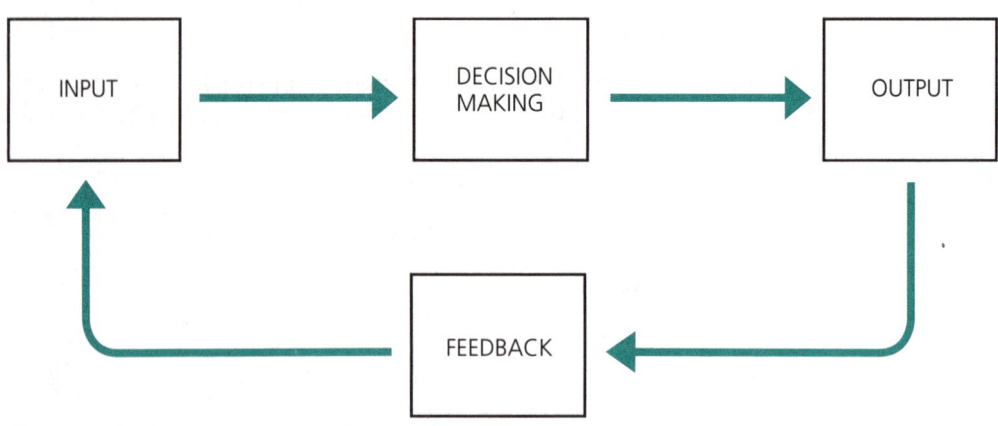

Capabilities and limitations of the human body

Fig. 10.3 The information processing model

> **Examiner's tip**
> You should be able to draw a flowchart diagram of the information processing model.

Stimuli received is interpreted: this is called **perception**. When perception occurs it is checked against known remembered patterns of stimuli before a decision is made relating to output. This checking is done very quickly in the memory stores of the CNS. (See Fig. 10.4.)

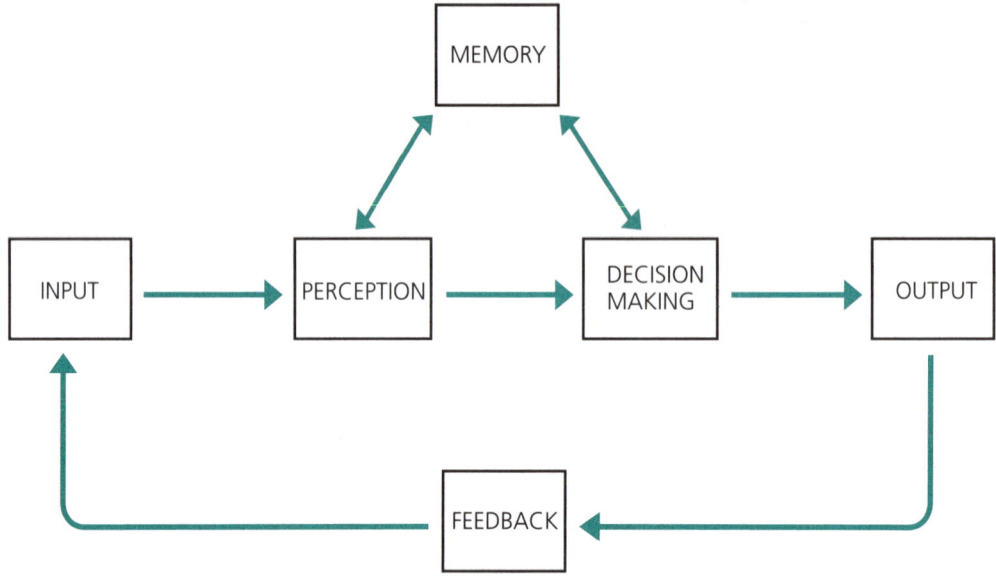

Fig. 10.4 An extended information processing model

10.4 Overloading the processing model

When our senses receive information, we often take in far more than is required. The footballer taking a penalty kick not only sees the position of the ball, goal and goalkeeper, he may also be aware of the noise of the watching crowd. In effect, the footballer is taking in more information than he wants or needs. His information processes are being overloaded.

However, the processes can deal with only a certain amount of information at any one time, so a selection process has to take place. All the information received is brought together in a narrow channel and what is thought to be the most important is allowed through. This part of the processing model is known as its **limited channel capacity**. (See Fig. 10.5.)

> **Examiner's tip**
> You should be able to explain the position of limited channel capacity within the information processing model.

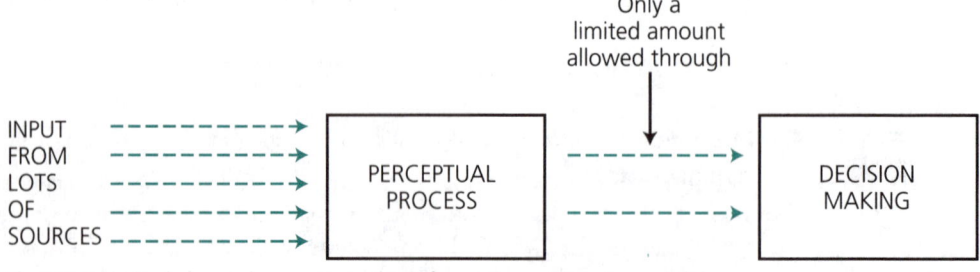

Fig. 10.5 Limited channel capacity in the information processing model

Acquisition of skill

10.5 Factors affecting performance

In a basic performance processing model it would seem logical that the output should always reflect the input. However, the output is often influenced by many factors.

1 Feedback

This is the information sent back to the input receptors saying how well the output is being performed.

> **Examiner's tip**
> You should be aware of the importance of feedback in the information processing model.

- Feedback can reinforce learning: a successful output is remembered

2 Motivation

Motivation is the amount of desire or enthusiasm that the inividual has for a given performance or activity. This can decide how well or badly an individual performs.

- Intrinsic motivation is when a person motivates him or herself to do well. The desire to pass an exam will motivate some people to revise hard.
- Extrinsic motivation is when a person works hard for gain or a reward that comes with success. Some individuals will compete in an event only if there is a prize for the winner. The bigger the prize, the harder they will compete. This type of motivation is often used by coaches to arouse competitors and make them try harder.

3 Arousal

> **Examiner's tip**
> You should be able to explain the Inverted U Theory.

Arousal can be described as how prepared the individual is to take part in an event. How keen they are to take part can influence how well they perform.

Unfortunately it is possible to over-arouse a competitor. Too much arousal will lead to anxiety and too much stress and this in turn can inhibit performance.

Fig. 10.6 represents what is called the **Inverted U Theory** of arousal. It is called the Inverted U Theory because the line graph looks like the letter U upside down.

At point A there is little arousal so the performance is not greatly affected.
At point B the arousal is just right and performance is affected so that it is at its best.

From point C onwards there is too much arousal and this brings on anxiety. The performer becomes 'psyched out' and performance gets progressively poorer.

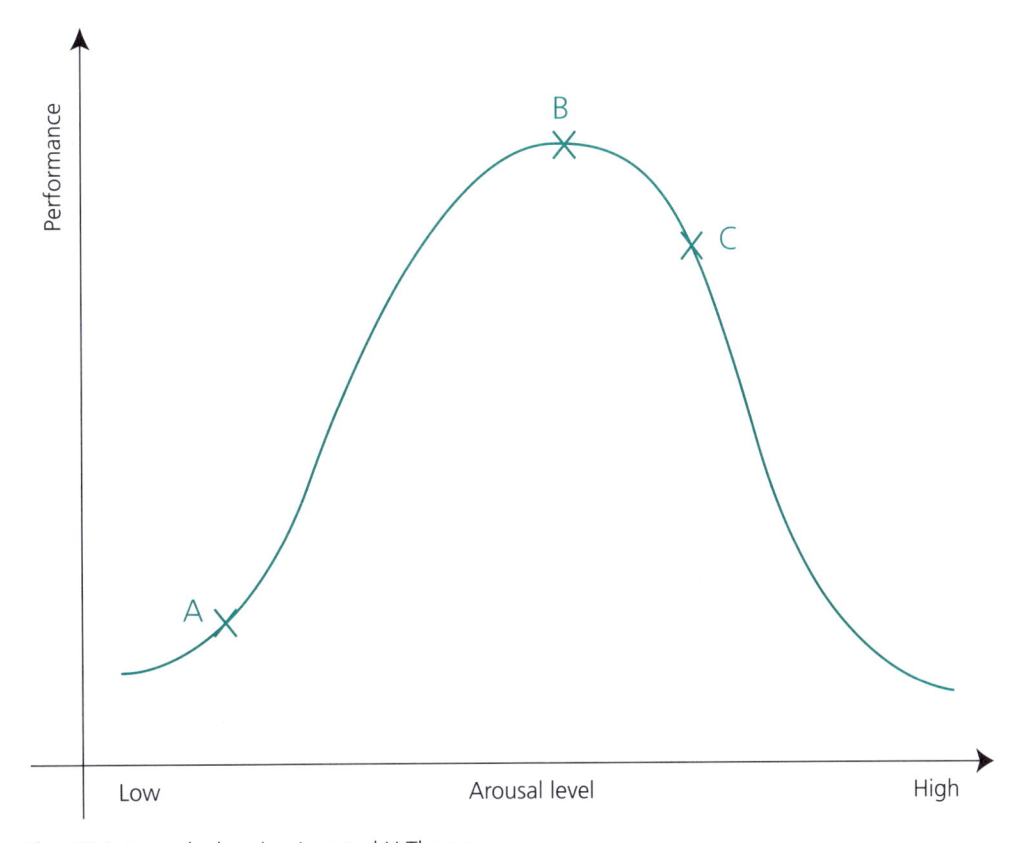

Fig. 10.6 A graph showing Inverted U Theory

Capabilities and limitations of the human body

> **Examiner's tip**
> You should be aware of the importance of motivation, arousal and goal-setting in performance.

④ Goal setting

Goal setting is the setting of attainable targets that often help in the training process. The targets or goals are designed to lead to an ultimate long-term goal such as winning an Olympic Gold Medal. The long-term goal is broken down into short- and medium-term goals where the individual can see success being easily attainable. These goals are like stepping stones towards the ultimate long-term goal. You can remember the way the goals should be set by using the mnemonic SMARTER:

S – specific to the long-term target
M – measurable, so that progress can be seen
A – agreed between coach and individual
R – realistic i.e. be attainable
T – timephased to fit into the long-term goal
E – exciting, just like the ultimate goal
R – recorded so that progress can be seen

PRINCIPAL TOPICS COVERED

① Skill is defined as a learned ability to bring about pre-determined results with maximum certainty and often with the minimum outlay of time and energy.

② Open skills are most influenced by external factors.

③ Closed skills are least influenced by external factors.

④ The information processing model has four main parts: input, decision-making, output and feedback.

⑤ The processing of input from the sensory organs is subject to the limited channel capacity of the person.

⑥ Feedback, motivation, arousal and goal-setting are all factors that influence performance.

QUESTIONS ON THIS CHAPTER

1 Define skill.

2 Give one example of an open skill and one example of a closed skill.

3 Explain the term 'extrinsic motivation'.

4 List the main parts of the information processing model and show their relationship to each other.

   Examiner's tip: the use of a flow chart diagram helps give a clear answer.

5 Explain how arousal might influence performance in competition.

   Examiner's tip: your answer should include both positive and negative aspects.

Chapter 11
Effects on fitness

All the training in the world cannot always produce a world-class performance from an individual. The final performance might well be influenced by one or more other factors that can add to or detract from it. These factors are often grouped together to form the mnemonic FLIPPED:

- **F** ood and diet
- **L** ifestyle
- **I** llness and injury
- **P** hysical make-up
- **P** ersonal history
- **E** nvironmental conditions
- **D** rug use and abuse

11.1 Food and diet

> **Examiner's tip**
> Know that the contents of a balanced diet must include proteins, carbohydrates, fats, vitamins and minerals.

The body needs fuel to provide the energy for all its actions. A suitable balanced diet should provide all the protein, carbohydrates, fats, vitamins and minerals needed by a sportsperson. (See Unit 7.3.)

Diet needs to reflect the type of activity being performed, the type of training being followed and the competition calendar. An inappropriate or inadequate diet might well be reflected in the fitness levels of the performer.

11.2 Lifestyle

Training for fitness not only includes the correct form of physical work, but also makes demands upon the way the individual lives his or her life: e.g. it is not possible to complete hard daily training sessions and still expect to be able to go dancing until all hours every night of the week. This 'burning the candle at both ends' can lead to a feeling of continuous fatigue and lack of motivation for training. Sleep is an important factor in all training programmes. It provides great physical restoration. If the correct attitude towards training is adopted, an enjoyable lifestyle can be followed alongside a successful competitive career.

11.3 Illness and injury

Illness cannot necessarily be avoided just because you are fit. It is true that the individual who trains hard and maintains a high level of fitness may be more resistant to contracting some infections, but catching a common cold is not unusual for the trained performer.

Capabilities and limitations of the human body

What is evident, however, is that the physically fit person tends to recover from many infections more quickly than the average person. They often seem to find illness less debilitating. Perhaps the biggest problem for athletes is that they try to return to a heavy training programme before a full recovery from illness has taken place.

Injuries are perhaps one of the biggest problems that any individual meets throughout their sporting careers. Injury seems to be the single most limiting factor to performance. A great many injuries can be prevented.

Prevention of injury can be achieved by:

> **E**xaminer's tip
>
> Be aware of the preventative measures that can be taken to avoid injury.

- **correct training**, aimed not only at developing fitness but also to strengthen those areas of physical deficiency which have been defined earlier.
- **the adequate use of warm up and flexibility exercises** before any form of physical work is performed.
- **the use of protective equipment** such as mouthguards, shin pads and helmets. These are not designed for fashion but to give protection and to enhance performance. (See Picture 11.1.)
- **the wearing of the correct clothing for the sport concerned,** e.g. ill-fitting shorts can cause serious chafing of the skin and poorly fitting footwear can lead to a host of leg and foot injuries.
- **playing to the rules of the sport.** These have been established not only for the sake of fair play but also with safety in mind: e.g. illegal tackles in soccer can injure both the opponent and the perpetrator. It is important that referees and umpires should enforce all the rules for the safety and welfare of all competitors.

Picture 11.1 Without the correct protective clothing ice hockey could not be played in safety

Effects on fitness

Examiner's tip
Know that injuries are often caused by an opponent, an implement or a surface.

Injuries caused by violence are common in both contact and non-contact sports. These include broken bones, cuts, bruises and sprains. Most occur during contact with:

- **an opponent** – such as during a tackle in soccer
- **an implement** – such as finger injuries caused by striking a volleyball incorrectly
- **the playing surface** – such as playing rugby on frozen ground.

The treatment of injuries is considered more closely in Chapter 13, Sports related injuries.

11.4 Physical make-up

Examiner's tip
Know what the word somatotype means and be able to describe the three body types of endomorph, mesomorph and ectomorph.

Successful competitors in different sports tend to have different body types: e.g. while it is true that not all basketball players are over 2 metres tall, there is no denying the fact that height does contribute significantly to the game as a whole. It is also true that sumo wrestlers tend to be very heavy and that gymnasts tend to be short in stature.

In 1940 an American, William Sheldon, developed a system to classify body type called **somatotyping**. In this system individuals are measured on three scales with scores ranging from 1 to 7, the scales being known as **endomorph, mesomorph and ectomorph**.

- A person rating 7 as an endomorph has a large amount of body fat.
- A person rating 7 as a mesomorph is broad-shouldered and muscular.
- A person rating 7 as an ectomorph is tall and very thin.

(See Fig. 11.1.)

Extreme endomorph
(7,1,1)

Extreme mesomorph
(1,7,1)

Extreme ectomorph
(1,1,7)

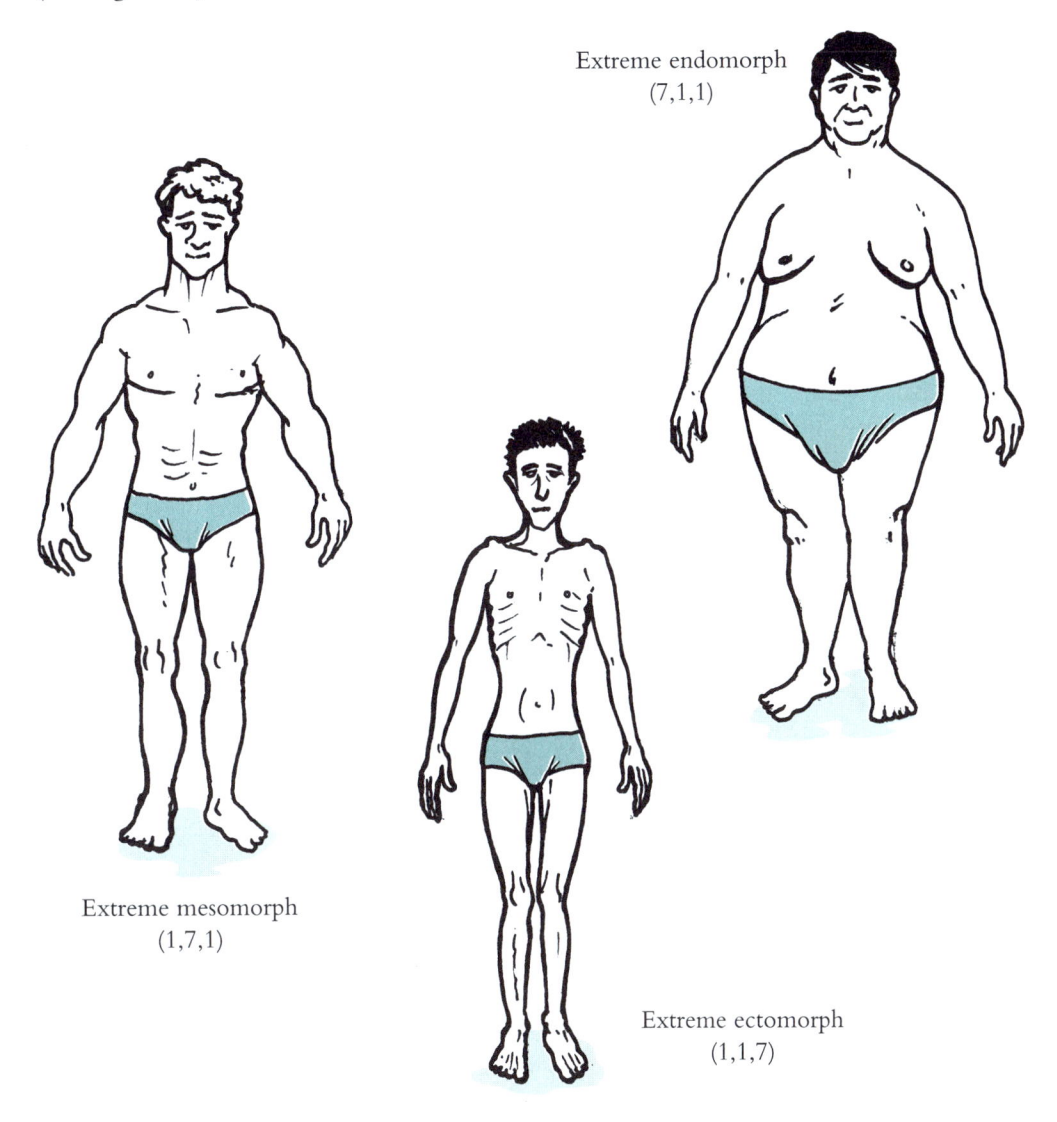

Fig. 11.1 Somatotypes (body types)

Capabilities and limitations of the human body

We all have some parts of each of the three body types in our physical make-up and it is rare to find an extreme endomorph, mesomorph or ectomorph.

The most common somatotype rating would be 4:4:4. This would be an average score on each of the three scales. Top level sport tends to be played by those towards the extremes of each scale, as extreme characteristics of body type help to produce extraordinary achievements in physical performance. (See Fig. 11.2.)

Examiner's tip

Be able to give examples of sporting activities related to each of the three body types.

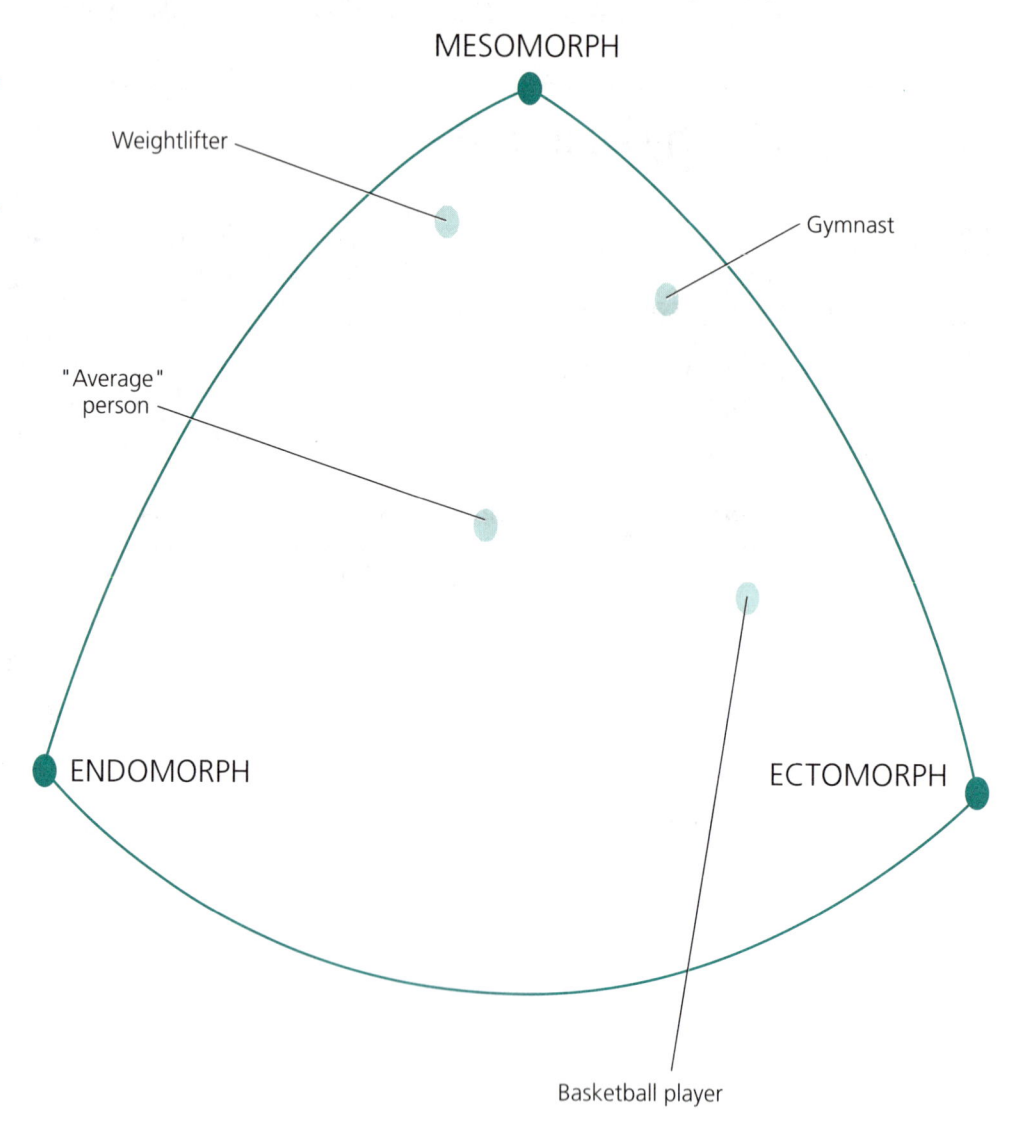

Fig. 11.2 The Somatotype Triangle

It is also important to remember that sex can influence body shape and size. Up to the approximate age of 10 boys and girls are very similar in size and build. However, the onset of puberty, usually earlier for girls than boys, can bring about many changes. Girls usually attain physical maturity at 16 or 17: for boys this often does not occur until 20 or 21. This leads to a smaller ratio of muscle size to fat in women than men. After puberty men develop a greater strength to weight factor than women.

Males tend to have a bone structure that is longer and heavier than that of females, while the child-bearing nature of the female means that her pelvis tends to be broader and flatter than that of the male. This contributes to increased flexibility in females.

Female athletes also have to contend with the menstrual cycle and this can affect performance. Although there is evidence of women achieving success at all stages of the menstrual cycle, it would seem that each month there is an optimum performance period when the woman is at her lightest and least stressed. (See Fig. 11.3.)

Effects on fitness

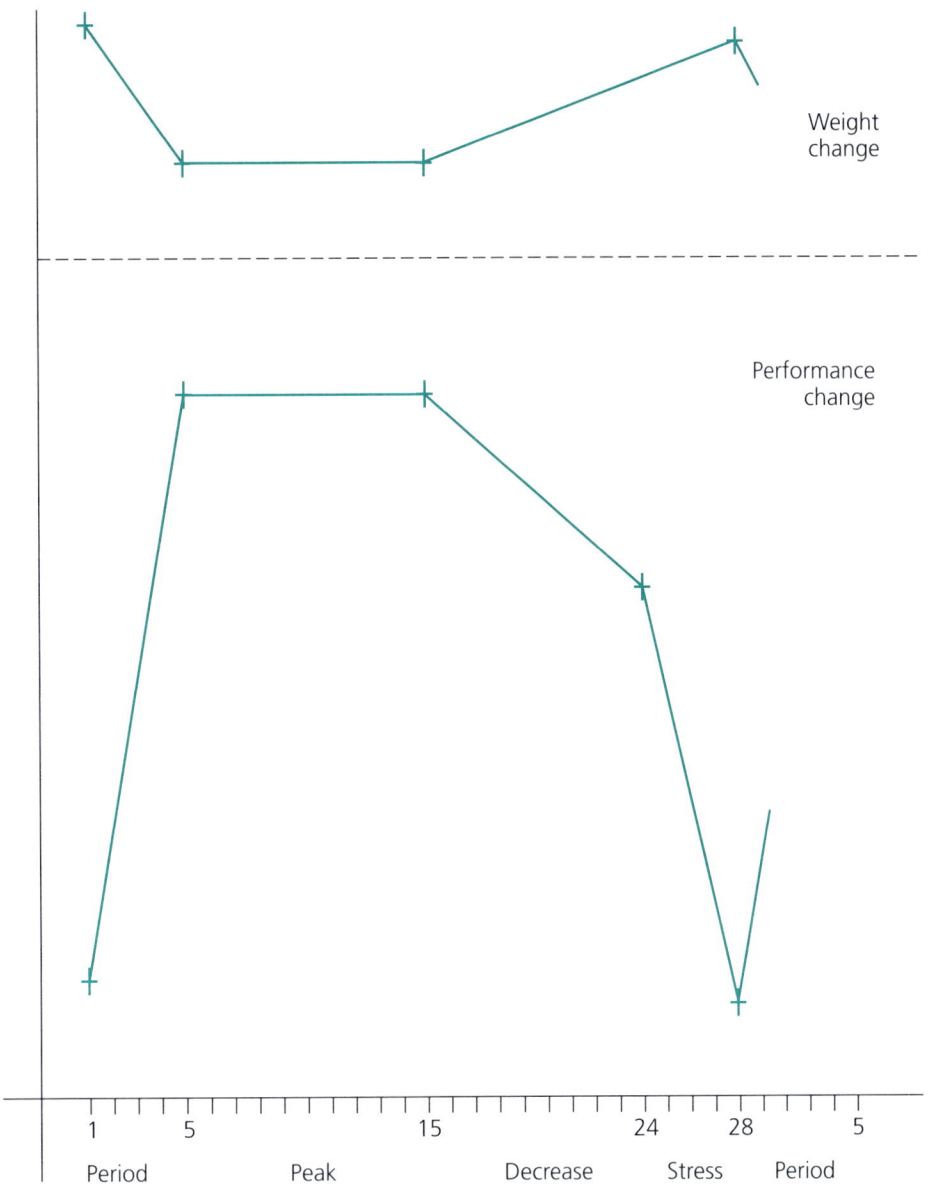

Fig. 11.3 Influence of menstrual cycle on performance

11.5 Personal history

> **Examiner's tip**
> Be able to describe the background information needed before starting a fitness programme.

No fitness programme will be effective if it does not build on what has gone before. The background of the individual is of vital importance. *Age*, *size* and *weight* must all be considered before a programme can be devised, as should *past experience* and *expertise*. The *physical and medical history* of the individual needs to be fully taken into account so that a safe and satisfactory programme can be established.

11.6 Environmental conditions

Training should acclimatise the individual for known competitive conditions.

83

Capabilities and limitations of the human body

- **The weather** can be too hot, cold, humid or windy to perform physical activity comfortably. Few athletes put in their best performances if it is raining or they have to compete with the elements as well as their opponents. This means that a training programme should also try to take into account the environmental conditions in which competition will take place: e.g. winter training for competitions held in summer is perhaps best done in a country with a warm climate.
- **The state of the sports arena,** such as the track or sports field, can also have some influence on performance. Pitches with too much or too little grass can affect the movement of a ball in hockey, soccer and cricket. Dusty or wet floors in gymnasia and dance studios can be dangerous as they can cause slipping.
- **The venue** for competition should also be related in the training programme, especially if altitude could have some bearing on the outcome. The Olympic Games in Mexico City in 1968 took place at an altitude of 7350 feet above sea level. At this altitude the air is 25% thinner than that at sea level. This means that oxygen intake to the lungs is reduced and less can be transported around the body in a given time. Long periods of high altitude training can increase the red cell content of the blood, thus improving the uptake of oxygen. It can also enlarge the lung volume, allowing for more air to be breathed in at each breath. Both of these serve to compensate for the lack of oxygen in the atmosphere at high altitudes.

> **Examiner's tip**
> Know the effects and problems of competing at high altitude.

11.7 Drug use and abuse

Drugs are used by many individuals when they play sport. There are many times when this can be referred to as *use* not *abuse*.

The use of some drugs is quite acceptable in sport: e.g. asthmatics and hayfever sufferers are allowed to take suitably approved drugs to help them overcome their medical condition. The use of prescribed drugs to overcome illness or injury is also considered to be quite acceptable.

What is considered to be unacceptable is the *abuse* or *misuse* of drugs to enhance performance. Not only is it considered unfair, it is also illegal.

Drugs are often divided into the following types:

1. **Analgesics** – are pain killers
2. **Antidepressants** – relieve anxiety
3. **Stimulants** – increase reactions
4. **Hallucinogens** – distort perception
5. **Cannabis** – relaxants
6. **Solvents** – intoxicate
7. **Miscellaneous** – drugs which do not easily fit into the above groups including **anabolic steroids** (see below), mild **opiates** and **laxatives**. Opiates, including the painkillers codeine and morphine, are derived from a herbal substance called opium. Laxatives, if over-used, can lead to a condition of excessive weight loss known as *anorexia nervosa*. **Diuretics** increase urination, which acts as a masking agent for other drugs in the body.

Not all those drugs listed above are used readily in sport but drugs have been known to be misused in sport for at least the last 50 years. In 1967 the International Olympic Committee (IOC) first banned some types of drugs from sport and over the years the list has steadily grown. It now numbers some 4000 different types of drug and variants of them. The main groups of drugs banned in sport are:

> **Examiner's tip**
> Have a sound knowledge of the types of banned drugs used to enhance performance in a range of sporting activities.

1. **Analgesics** – used to decrease the amount of pain from injury, or to increase the pain threshold during competition.
2. **Stimulants** – used to increase alertness, reduce fatigue and increase competitiveness and aggression.

3 **Beta-blockers** – used in sports where a steady hand is needed, such as shooting and archery. The drugs reduce tremor that is brought on by tension, anxiety and nervousness.

4 **Diuretics** – used to remove fluids by excessive urination to help bring about weight loss. The effects of increased urination make them a good masking agent for other drugs as evidence of banned substance can be washed out of the body by repeated visits to the toilet.

5 **Anabolic steroids** – used to develop muscle size and thus strength, and to aid recovery from physical stress and injury. They also produce a more competitive and aggressive nature.

6 **Polypeptide hormones** – have a similar effect to anabolic steroids.

It is also important to remember that both *alcohol* and *nicotine* are drugs, despite the fact that they are found in easily and legally obtained substances. Their use can affect performance. In the short-term, alcohol acts as a depressant. It is quickly absorbed into the blood stream, reaction time becomes slower and muscular co-ordination less efficient. Judgement and balance become increasingly affected. While alcohol also acts as a disinhibitor, improving morale and the so-called 'feel good' factor, it also inhibits the absorbtion of vitamins and raises heart rate and body temperature.

Nicotine found in tobacco products can, when inhaled, increase heart rate and blood pressure. The accumulations of tar substances on the lungs restricts the exchange of gases between the lungs and the blood and thus reduces the individual's capacity to transport oxygen round the body.

PRINCIPAL TOPICS COVERED

1 The main groups of factors that can affect fitness are: food and diet; lifestyle; illness and injury; physical make-up; personal history; environmental conditions; drug use and abuse. These groups are remembered by the mnemonic FLIPPED.

2 Diet needs to reflect the type of activity being performed.

3 Sleep is an important part of any training programme.

4 Fitness can speed recovery from illness and injury. Many injuries can be prevented.

5 The three main body types are endomorph, mesomorph and ectomorph.

6 Competitors in different sports have different body types.

7 Training should acclimatise the individual for competition.

8 Some drugs can be used in sport but many are banned in sport because of their abuse.

QUESTIONS ON THIS CHAPTER

1 Describe fully the effects that smoking could have on the physical fitness of a performer.

2 Explain how injuries can be avoided in sporting activities.

3 Describe the body somatotype that a successful weight lifter might have.

4 What factors would you take into account when preparing a training programme?

5 Explain how body shape and size affect performance in physical exercise. Give examples to illustrate your answer.

6 Describe the effects that anabolic steroids have on athletes.

Chapter 12
Measurement in sport

It can be argued that measurement is taking place in sport at all times. At the most simplistic level this includes counting the score in a game of football and badminton, or timing individuals over a given distance.

On a more complex level it is possible to measure the effects that specific types of training have on the individual. It is possible to establish how fit they are, how strong they are and how supple they are.

By testing the individual before he or she starts a training programme it is possible to identify those physical deficiencies that need to be improved to attain fitness.

Repeated testing can indicate levels of progression during a training programme. In all tests it is important to ensure that the test measures what it sets out to measure. This is called its **validity**: e.g. tests that include a high degree of skill should measure skill not strength. A test of arm strength should not include the use of the leg muscles.

WARNING   No test should be attempted unless:

- a suitable, qualified person is present
- a good warm up has taken place.

The following rating tables given are for guidance only.

12.1 Tests for suppleness

Shoulder lift

Aim	to measure suppleness at the shoulders
Resources	one stick, approximately 50cm long, one metre rule
Method	subject lies on floor face down, grasps shorter stick in each hand with hands shoulder width apart
	stick is raised with arms straight and the chin is kept on the floor
Measurement	is the height the stick has been raised from the floor

(See Picture 12.1 and Table 12.1.)

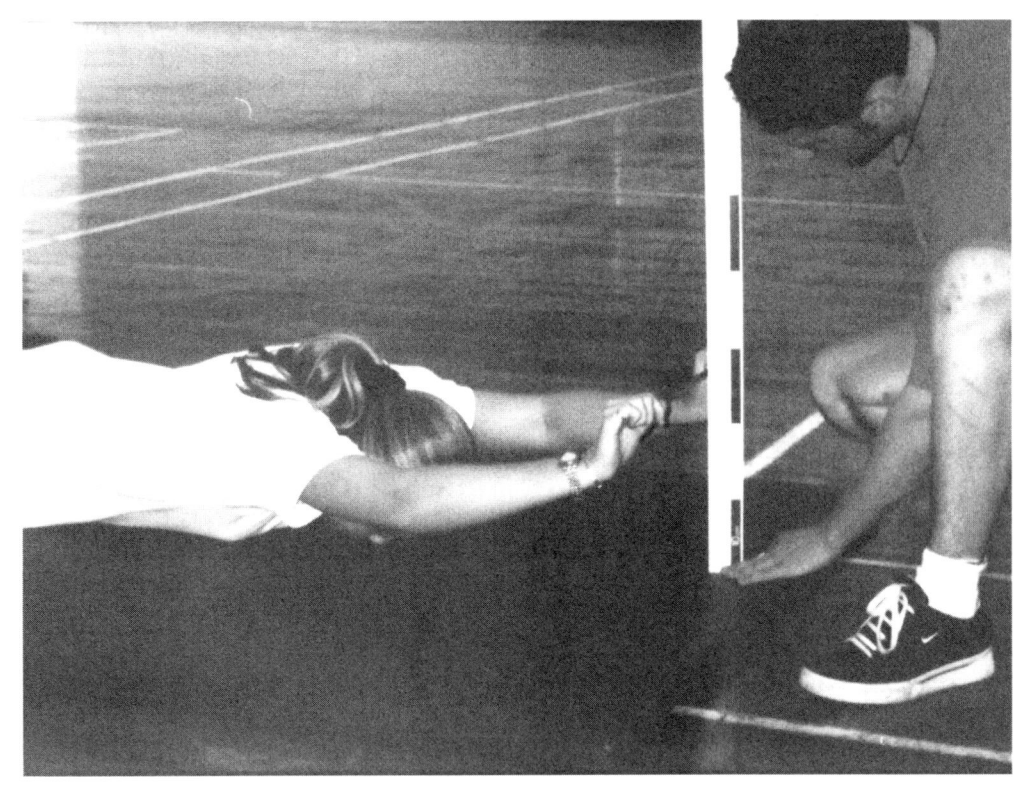

Measurement in sport

Picture 12.1 The shoulder lift

Sit and reach

Aim	to measure the suppleness of the back and the hamstrings
Resources	a ruler
Method	subject sits on floor with legs extended and feet flexed
	subject stretches forward, keeping legs straight and slides palms of hands along legs
Measurement	is the distance that the finger tips reach beyond the toes. If the subject cannot reach beyond the toes, then the distance to the toes is recorded as a negative score

(See Picture 12.2 and Table 12.1.)

Picture 12.2 Sit and reach

Trunk extension

Aim	to measure the suppleness of the back
Resources	a metre rule
Method	subject lies face down on the floor with both hands clasped behind the head
	head and shoulders are raised as high as possible whilst the feet remain in contact with the ground
	a partner holds down the ankles
Measurement	is the distance from the floor to the point of the chin

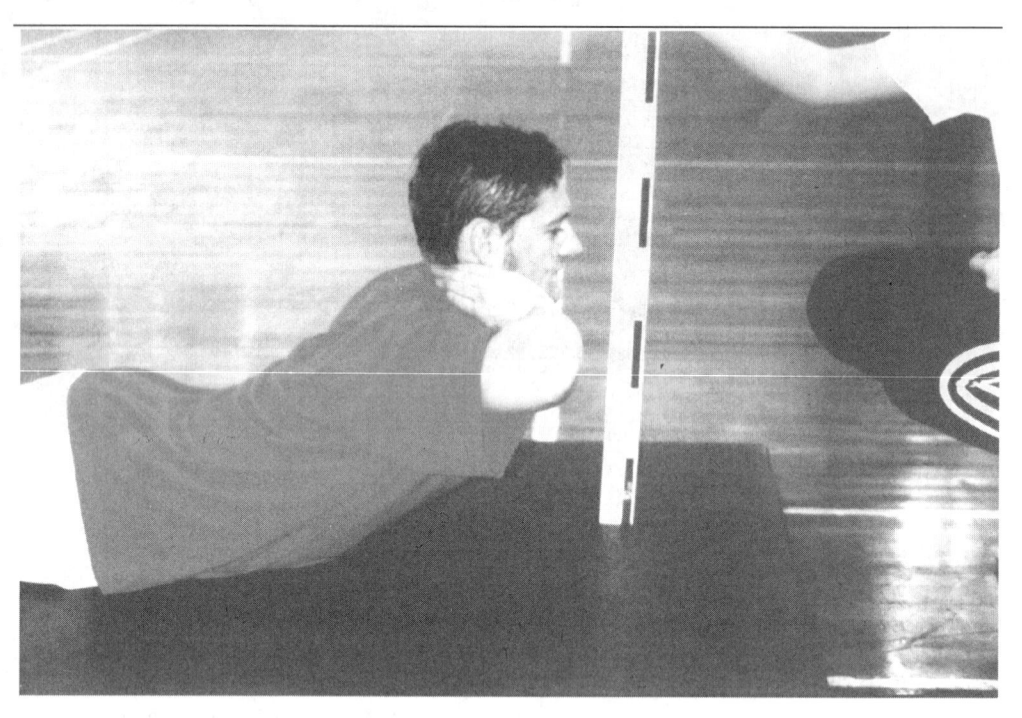

Fig. 12.3 Trunk extension

(See Picture 12.3 and Table 12.1.)

Table 12.1 Rating table for suppleness

RATING	SHOULDER LIFT	SIT AND REACH	TRUNK EXTENSION
VERY GOOD	36+	10+	50+
GOOD	25+	5+	40+
FAIR	20+	0+	30+
POOR	15+	-5	20+

All scores are in cm

Factors affecting suppleness:

- Individuals who regularly take part in physical activities tend to be more supple than non-participants.
- Girls tend to be more supple than boys.
- Research indicates that children have a greater degree of suppleness up to the age of 10 or 11 years. After this age they seem to lose flexibility.
- Suppleness can be improved by the local warming of a joint over and above the normal warm up as it is then more prepared for work.

12.2 Tests of strength

Standing long jump (SLJ)

Aim	to measure explosive leg strength
Resources	non-slip surface marked with a straight line, usually a gymnastic mat
Method	subject stands with both feet together with toes behind the start line
	subject performs a two-footed jump along the mat
	subject may swing the arms as desired
Measurement	is taken from the start line to the back of the rearmost heel

(See Fig. 12.4 and Table 12.2.)

Fig. 12.4 Standing long jump

Standing high jump (SHJ)

Aim	to measure explosive leg strength
Resources	suitable board attached to wall
Method	subject faces wall and stretches both arms above head with hands side by side so that fingertip level can be marked
	subject then turns sideways to wall and with both feet together jumps as high as possible to touch board with fingertips of the outstretched hand
	subject may swing arms as desired
Measurement	is the distance between the two recorded marks on the board

(See Fig 12.5 and Table 12.2.)

Capabilities and limitations of the human body

Fig. 12.5 Standing high jump

Sit-ups

Aim	to measure the strength and endurance of the abdominal muscles
Resources	suitable mat on a flat surface a stopwatch
Method	subject lies on back on mat with hands clasped behind the head, knees at right angles, both feet flat on floor and slightly apart
	subject sits up to touch knees with elbows and then returns to starting position
	partner holds subject's ankles to ensure his/her feet stay on the floor
Measurement	total number of sit-ups completed in 30 secs

(See Fig 12.6 and Table 12.2.)

Fig. 12.6 Sit-ups

Table 12.2 Rating table for strength

RATING	SLJ	SHJ	SIT UPS
VERY GOOD	190+	65+	25+
GOOD	170+	60+	20+
FAIR	150+	50+	16+
POOR	130+	40+	14+

Scores for SLJ and SHJ in cm

Arm strength

Overall arm strength can be measured by the number of pull-ups (see Fig 12.7), press-ups (see Fig 12.8) or dips (see Fig 12.9) which an individual can perform. A *grip dynamometer* (as shown in Picture 12.4) measures the strength specifically in the hand and forearm.

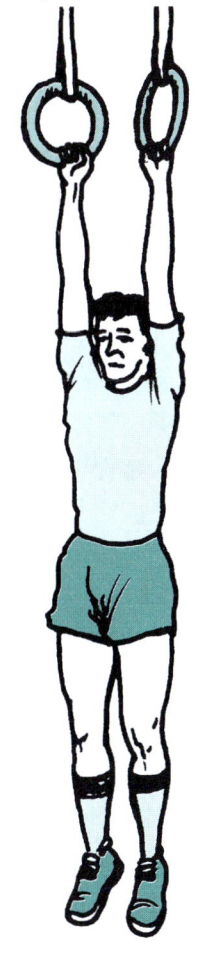

Fig 12.7 Pull-ups

Fig. 12.8 Press-ups

Capabilities and limitations of the human body

Fig. 12.9 Dips

Picture 12.4 A grip dynamometer, used for measuring strength in the hand and forearm

Leg and back strength can be measured by using a *tensiometer* (see Picture 12.5).

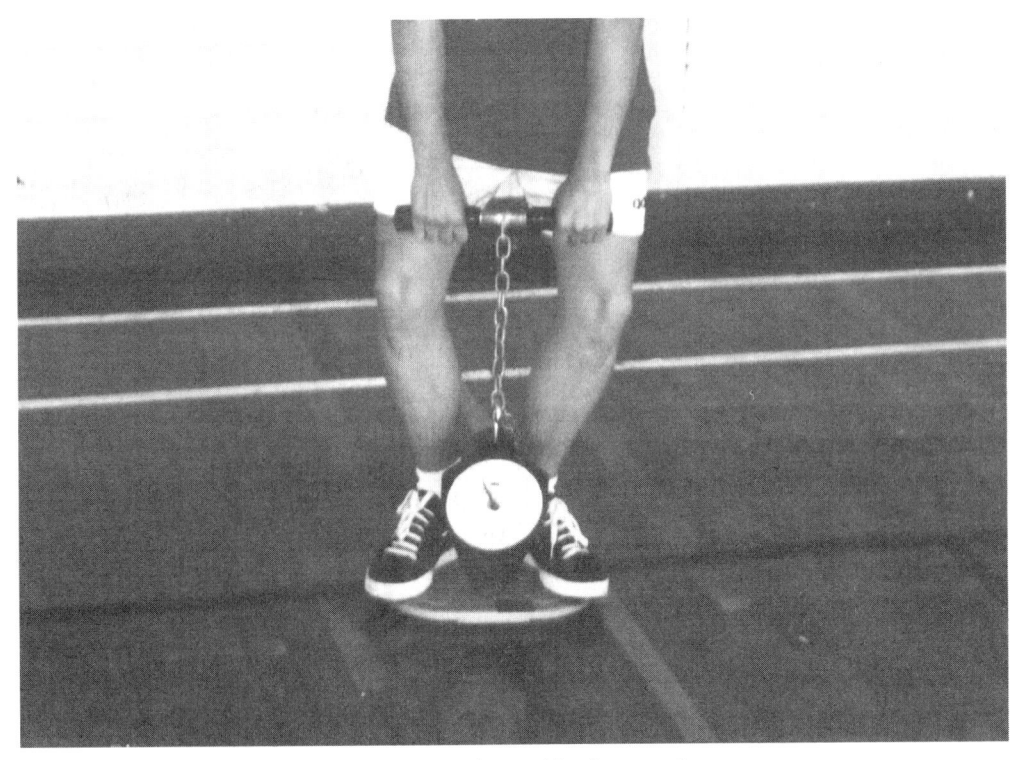

Picture 12.5 Using a tensiometer to measure leg and back strength

Factors affecting strength:

- Strength seems to increase in proportion with age up to approximately 30 years.
- Males usually have larger muscles than females and this contributes to their greater strength.
- Results obtained from tests that involve jumping should be considered along with the subject's weight.

12.3 Tests of endurance

Step test

Aim	to measure cardiovascular endurance
Resources	bench or sturdy box 45 cm high stop watch
Method	subject steps fully on to and off the bench for 5 min at a rate of 30 steps per min, at the end of the exercise the pulse rate is counted for 30 secs after a 1 min rest
Measurement	a Fitness Rating is obtained by using the following formula: $$\frac{100 \times 300 \text{ (length of exercise in secs)}}{5.5 \times \text{no. of heartbeats per min}}$$

N.B. Only a simple formula is used to obtain the fitness rating in the step test. There is a range of other, more complex formulae that can be used but each requires many more readings.

(See Fig 12.10 and Table 12.3.)

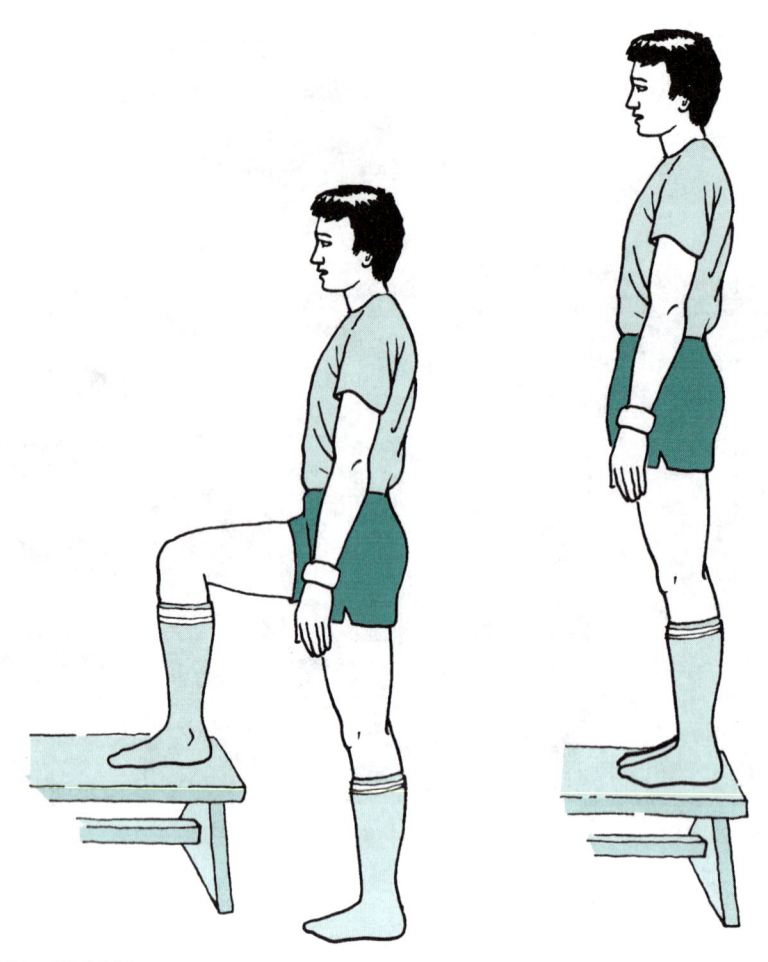

Capabilities and limitations of the human body

Fig. 12.10 The step test

12 min run test

Aim	to measure cardiovascular endurance
Resources	suitable running surface of known distance, usually an athletics track, stopwatch
Method	subject runs as far as possible in 12 mins
Measurement	the distance ran in 12 mins

(See Table 12.3.)

Table 12.3 Rating table for cardiovascular endurance

RATING	STEP TEST	12min RUN	
		male	female
VERY GOOD	90+	2600+	2200+
GOOD	80+	2400+	2000+
FAIR	65+	2200+	1800+
POOR	50+	2000+	1700+

Scores for 12 min run in metres

Factors affecting cardiovascular endurance

- As both the tests described each take several minutes to perform, the attitude of the subject can influence the outcome. In both cases the time period may not be completed.
- The results of the 12 min run test can be affected by different weather conditions.
- If the subjects are tested in a group, then they may compete with each other and inflate their scores, whereas those tested individually can compete only with themselves.

Measurement in sport

Examiner's tip

You should be able to describe at least one test for each of the following: suppleness, strength and endurance.

Examiner's tip

You should be aware of any factors that might influence the results of any tests carried out.

PRINCIPAL TOPICS COVERED

1. Testing can measure anything in sport: strength, suppleness, endurance, speed, height, weight, skill, etc.

2. 3 tests of suppleness are:
   Shoulder lift
   Sit and reach
   Trunk extension

3. 3 tests of strength are:
   Standing long jump
   Standing high jump
   Sit-ups

4. 2 tests of endurance are:
   Step test
   12 min run test

QUESTIONS ON THIS CHAPTER

1. Give the name of a test that will measure each of the following:
   (i) cardiovascular stamina
   (ii) suppleness.

2. Explain how testing can show that a fitness training programme is being effective.

3. Explain the effect that age might have on the suppleness of the average person.

4. Explain how an individual's score for the 12 min run test might be affected by external factors.

5. Explain how testing might help in the preparation of a training programme.

Chapter 13
Sports related injuries

The body is designed to provide movement. However, unfortunately the requirements of sport can put excessive demands on the way that we move. A high level of intensity of physical action can result in great stress on the physical body. Regrettably this stress can lead to a range of injuries that can be related to sport.

13.1 Safe practice

Injuries, and the after-effects of injuries, directly related to sport are perhaps the single most limiting factor to physical performance.

With care, a great many sports injuries can be avoided. As we have seen in Chapter 11 Unit 3, the main criteria for safe practice in sport are:

> **Examiner's tip**
> You should be able to explain the main criteria for safe practice in sporting activities.

1. **correct training**
2. **the correct use of warm up and cool down**
3. **the use of protective equipment**
4. **the use of appropriate clothing**
5. **the playing of the game according to the rules**

Should an injury unfortunately occur, there is likely to be some kind of pain. Remember that pain is the body's way of informing you that something is wrong. It should never be ignored.

It is important that all sportspersons should be able to recognise when an injury has occurred and have some knowledge of how it should be treated. It must be emphasised that this knowledge will not make an individual an expert.

The aims of First Aid treatment are to preserve life, to prevent a condition worsening and to promote recovery.

On no account should anyone attempt to treat an injury without medical knowledge or advice.

13.2 What to do in the event of an injury

> **Examiner's tip**
> You should be able to describe what to do when first confronted with a possible injury situation.

Should any injury occur in training or competition it is advisable to:

- **stop** the game or the activity at once
- **look** at the affected area, note any colour change, swelling or abnormal shape
- **listen** to the injured person, as they can best tell you where there is pain or restricted movement

Sports related injuries

- **feel** very gently round the affected area to detect any swelling or abnormality. *Do not prod* an injured area. Change the injured person's body position with extreme care otherwise you may cause further damage.
- **apply** first aid procedures *if you know what you are doing*
- **seek** medical advice

For injuries where a fracture (broken bone) is not suspected, then treatment usually follows the **RICE** formula. (See Fig 13.1.)

REST   Stop using the injured part of the body as soon as localised pain is felt.

ICE   The application of ice to the injured area can reduce swelling and any muscle spasm. It will also restrict the flow of blood to the painful area. Ice treatment should continue for periods of 20 minutes with breaks of 20 minutes between applications.

COMPRESSION   The use of elastic bandages around the painful area can help to limit swelling. However, the bandage should not be applied so tightly that it completely restricts the flow of blood.

ELEVATION   If movement does not cause pain, the injured area should be raised above the level of the heart. This not only helps to reduce the blood flow to the injured area but also aids waste fluid to drain from it.

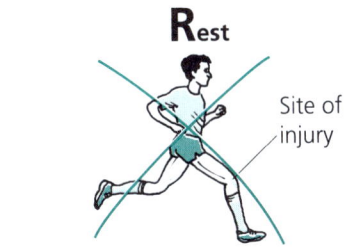

Rest

Stop using the injured body part. You could cause permanent damage.

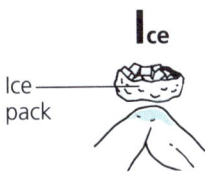

Ice

Apply ice to the injured area. Ice will cause injured blood vessels and surrounding tissues to contract. This will reduce blood flow to the area. Apply ice through a towel or gauze. Remove ice pack after 10–12 minutes. Repeat every 3 hours if necessary.

Compression

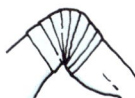

Keep swelling to a minimum by wrapping an elastic bandage firmly around the area, even over the ice pack. Do not wrap bandage so tightly that the blood supply is cut off. Remove ice pack and bandage after 10–12 minutes to allow skin to warm up and blood flow to return.

Elevation

Raise the injured body part above the level of the heart. The force of gravity will help to drain excess fluid from the damaged area.

Fig. 13.1 The RICE formula

Capabilities and limitations of the human body

Examiner's tip

You should be able to explain the RICE formula and the ABC of First Aid.

Remember that the RICE procedure is for minor injuries only. Should a more serious accident occur when a person may appear to have lost consciousness and is not breathing, then the **ABC of First Aid** should be followed.

A = open **airway**. It is possible that the air passage could be blocked. If so, it must be cleared at once. Mouth guards and other obstructions should be removed. A slight tilting of the head backwards will remove the tongue from the air passage. If the airway is open, then check for signs of breathing (movement of the chest or the feeling of breath on your cheek). If there is no sign of breathing then mouth-to-mouth ventilation may be required.

B = **breathing** for the casualty. The most efficient way to do this is to blow air from your own lungs into the casualty's by mouth to mouth ventilation. This should not be attempted unless you have followed a course of instruction. However, continued mouth-to-mouth ventilation is pointless if there is no blood circulation.

C = the **circulation** of the blood. This is best checked by feeling for a pulse at the neck. If you cannot feel a pulse, then there may well be no circulation and external chest compression can help the heart to start working again. External chest compression should not be attempted unless you have followed a course of instruction and should *never be practised on a person who is conscious*. External chest compression should always be preceded and accompanied by mouth-to-mouth ventilation.

(See Fig 13.2.)

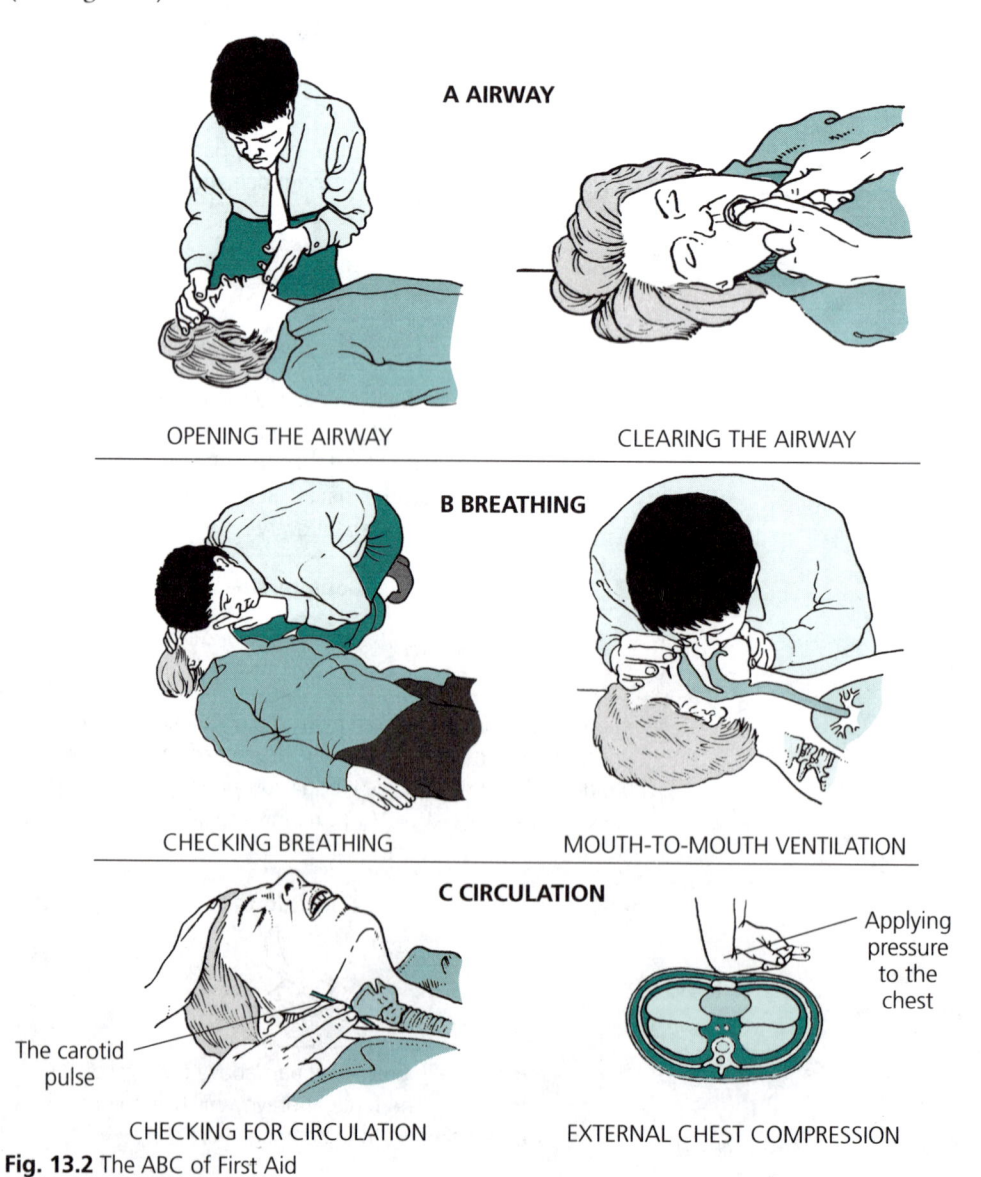

A AIRWAY

OPENING THE AIRWAY CLEARING THE AIRWAY

B BREATHING

CHECKING BREATHING MOUTH-TO-MOUTH VENTILATION

C CIRCULATION

The carotid pulse

Applying pressure to the chest

CHECKING FOR CIRCULATION EXTERNAL CHEST COMPRESSION

Fig. 13.2 The ABC of First Aid

When the casualty is breathing unaided, then they should be placed in the **recovery position** until specialist help is obtained. (See Picture 13.1.)

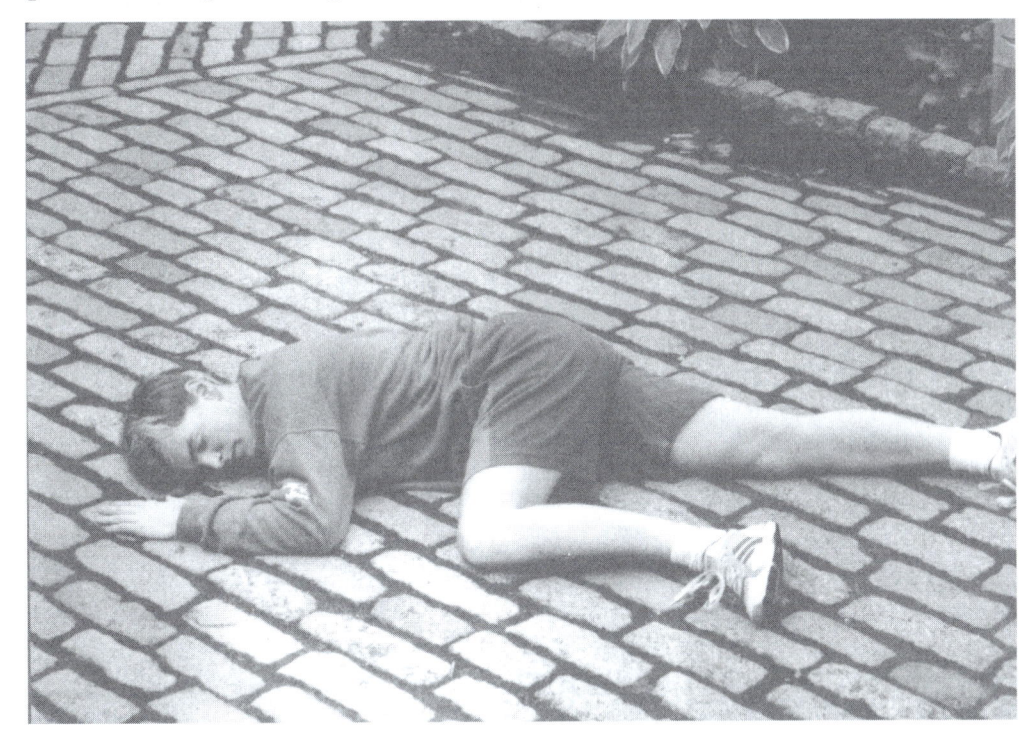

Picture 13.1 The recovery position

As a general rule, players should never be allowed to continue in a game after recovering from a loss of consciousness. In rugby they are not allowed to play again for a further 14 days.

13.3 Soft tissue injuries

These are injuries to any body tissue other than bone. **Soft tissue injuries** account for over 90% of all sports injuries. There are two types of soft tissue injury:

❶ **Open wounds** are those which allow blood to escape. They include cuts, grazes, blisters and chafing.

Table 13.1 Open wounds

TYPE	CAUSES	TREATMENT
cuts and grazes	contact with hard objects or surfaces	application of pressure raising affected area
blisters	repeated rubbing of skin	clean and apply antiseptic cover with sterile dressing
chafing	ill-fitting clothing	remove source of irritation apply antiseptic cream

❷ **Closed wounds** are those where there is no external bleeding. They include bruising, muscle strain and damage to ligaments, tendons and cartilage.

E **xaminer's tip**

You should know the difference between open and closed wounds.

Capabilities and limitations of the human body

Table 13.2 Closed wounds

TYPE	CAUSES	SYMPTOMS	TREATMENT
bruising	impact with hard object	pain swelling discoloration	RICE
strained muscle	stretching of 'cold' muscle	pain tenderness	RICE
torn muscle	poor warm up over-stretching sudden movement	sharp pain discolouration	RICE medical advice
tendonitis	repeated stress of tendon	pain swelling inflammation	rest followed by slow, gentle exercise
sprained ligament	sudden forcing of joint beyond normal range	pain swelling loss of movement	RICE
meniscal tears*	violent impact sudden twisting	pain loss of movement	surgical repair

*Meniscal cartilage are wedge-shaped and found in mobile joints such as the knee. (See Chapter 2.8 Fig 2.9.)

> **Examiner's tip**
> You should know how to treat open and closed wounds.

> **Examiner's tip**
> You should know the difference between hard and soft tissue injuries.

13.4 Hard tissue injuries

Hard tissue injuries are injuries to bone tissue and, fortunately for the sportsperson, occur far less frequently than soft tissue injuries. They are most common in contact sports and are usually caused by:

- contact with an opponent – such as during a tackle
- contact with an implement – such as a hard ball hitting the hand
- contact with a surface   – such as falling on hard ground

The four main types of fracture are **closed**, **open**, **compound** and **stress**.

1. **Closed fracture** – the bone is broken but the skin is not
2. **Open fracture** – the ends of the broken bones appear through the surface of the skin
3. **Compound fracture** – the broken bone has caused another injury

The general symptoms of these fractures are:

- the break of the bone may be felt and heard
- pain and tenderness
- swelling and a possibly abnormal shape in the painful area

Treatment should always be provided by a medical expert. (See Fig 13.4.)

Closed fracture

Open fracture

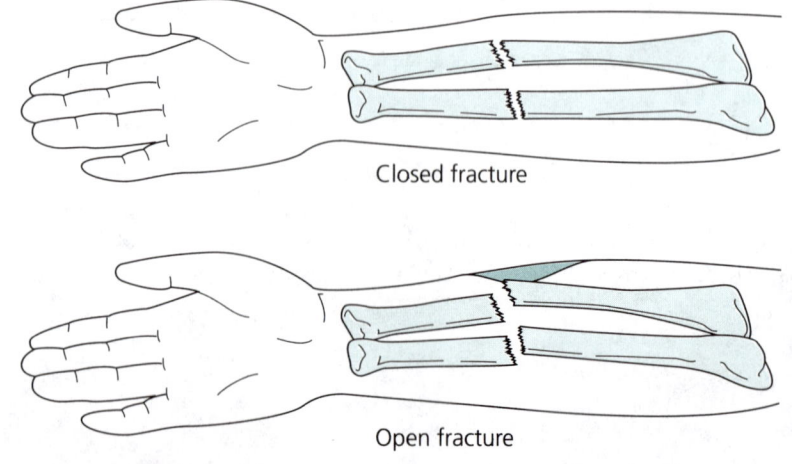

Fig. 13.4 Types of fracture

NOTE
Both closed and open fractures may be complicated by injury to blood vessels, nerves or adjacent organs by fractured bone ends or fragments.

④ Stress fractures – are cracks that appear along the length of the bone and are caused by repeated stress applied to the bone over a long period of time. In long distance runners these fractures are often called **shin soreness** or **shin splints**. The accepted treatment is to stop exercise and seek medical advice.

13.5 Miscellaneous injuries

- **Winding** – caused by a blow to the concentration of nerves in the upper abdomen called the **solar plexus**. This causes the diaphragm to go into spasm. This is often referred to as being *winded*. The loosening of clothing, sitting in a relaxed position and taking long breaths out are the recommended treatments.

- **Hypothermia** – is the lowering of the body temperature below 35 °C. When this happens, the nervous system is affected, muscular rigidity can develop and the heart beats irregularly. Unconsciousness may then follow. Treatment is to bring the patient's body temperature back to normal (36/37 °C) in a steady, sustained manner. Hypothermia may occur in sports such as canoeing and hill-walking.

- **Hyperthermia** – often referred to as *heat exhaustion*, is when the body temperature rises above normal owing to excessive effort and dehydration. The individual begins to lose co-ordination and may go into shock. Marathon runners and long distance cyclists have been known to suffer from this. Treatment is to place the individual in a cool place, provide liquids and seek medical help.

- **Stitch** – a pain in the side of the abdomen or in the lower chest brought on by physical activity. It is best described as a form of cramp of the diaphragm and restricts deep breathing. It is often caused by jolting movements such as running, and eating before participation. The treatment recommended is to breathe in deeply and out shallowly, and to keep bending up and down.

- **Cramp** – is an instantaneous contraction of a skeletal muscle that cannot be relaxed. It can last for a few seconds or several minutes. Its precise cause is unknown as muscle cramps can occur during hard physical activity or during complete relaxation. Causes are thought to be a lack of minerals and salt in the diet, or a temporary restriction of blood to the affected muscle. The recommended treatment is to stretch the affected muscle manually and then massage it. (See Fig 13.5.)

Examiner's tip
You should know what the causes and recommended treatments are for cramp, winding and stitch.

Capabilities and limitations of the human body

FOR CRAMP IN CALF MUSCLES

FOR CRAMP IN THIGH MUSCLES

Fig. 13.5 Treatment for cramp

13.6 Injuries associated with specific sports

> **Examiner's tip**
>
> You should be aware that players of specific sports are more prone to certain types of injury in particular.

Whilst any individual participating in sport may pick up an injury, it is true to say that some injuries tend to be closely associated with certain sports in particular: e.g. a body contact sport such as rugby is more likely to produce hard tissue injuries than the game of badminton, as each sport puts different demands upon the body.

Some injuries will also reflect the position in which a person plays in a team. It is to be expected that a goalkeeper in soccer will suffer from different injuries from those of his outfield colleagues.

Participants in more recreational activities such as aerobics and keep fit can still pick up an injury, but of a different type from that of the games player. (See Fig 13.6.)

Sports related injuries

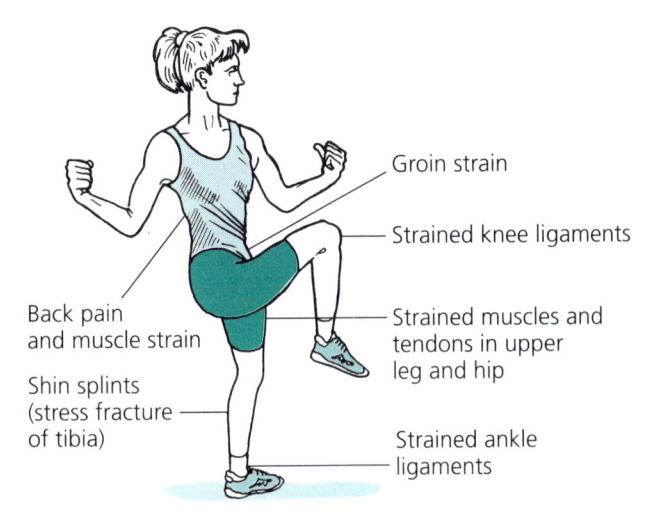

Sports injuries associated with aerobics

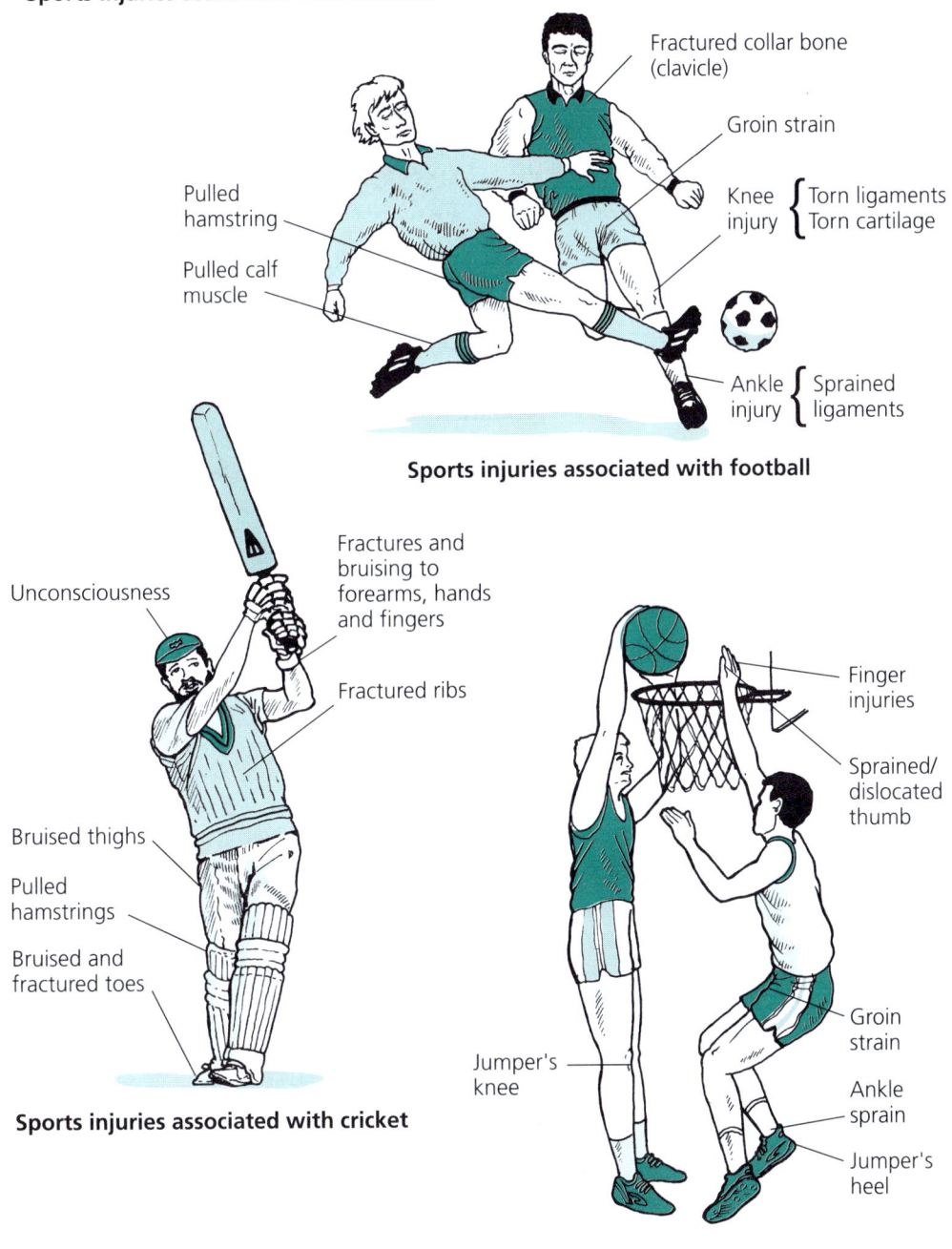

- Groin strain
- Strained knee ligaments
- Back pain and muscle strain
- Strained muscles and tendons in upper leg and hip
- Shin splints (stress fracture of tibia)
- Strained ankle ligaments

Sports injuries associated with football

- Fractured collar bone (clavicle)
- Groin strain
- Knee injury { Torn ligaments / Torn cartilage
- Pulled hamstring
- Pulled calf muscle
- Ankle injury { Sprained ligaments

Sports injuries associated with cricket

- Unconsciousness
- Fractures and bruising to forearms, hands and fingers
- Fractured ribs
- Bruised thighs
- Pulled hamstrings
- Bruised and fractured toes

Sports injuries associated with basketball

- Finger injuries
- Sprained/dislocated thumb
- Jumper's knee
- Groin strain
- Ankle sprain
- Jumper's heel

Fig. 13.6 Injuries associated with specific sports

Capabilities and limitations of the human body

PRINCIPAL TOPICS COVERED

1. The main criteria for safe practice in sporting activities are:

   correct training
   correct use of warm up and cool down
   use of protective equipment
   use of appropriate clothing
   playing the game according to the rules.

2. Knowledge of the causes and treatment of injuries does not mean that a person is capable of treating an injury.

3. Knowing what to do if an injury seems to happen during training or competition can limit the seriousness of the injury.

4. The RICE formula for treating minor injuries is: Rest, Ice, Compression and Elevation.

5. The ABC of First Aid involves checking airways, breathing and circulation. This should not be done by an untrained person.

6. Wounds in soft tissue are classified as either open or closed.

7. Hard tissue injuries are those that affect the bone.

8. Miscellaneous injuries are those which do not result in bleeding or fractures.

9. Some categories of injury are more common to specific sports.

QUESTIONS ON THIS CHAPTER

1. Explain the term 'winded'.

2. Explain the RICE formula.

3. Give two methods of treatment to help prevent blood loss from an open wound.

4. What is hypothermia, in which activity is it likely to occur and what is the recommended treatment?

5. What is a fracture?

   Examiner's tip: remember that there are four different types.

Development and organisation of sport

Chapter 14
Administration of sport

The participation in and the spectating of sporting activities touches on the lives of most of the population of this country. All boys and girls have to take part in physical education whilst at school and many pursue sports outside school hours. A large number of adults continue to be involved in sporting activities throughout their lives. Therefore it is not surprising that, with so many people involved, sport in this country has become highly organised and structured.

14.1 Structure of sport

Those who participate in sport often do so through clubs which offer either or both recreative or competitive activities. Particularly where competition is concerned sports have had to become highly structured. This provides the individual with the opportunity to advance through various levels as far as they wish, even attaining international standard. (See Fig 14.1.)

```
INDIVIDUAL
    |
CLUB COMPETITIONS
    |
REGIONAL COMPETITIONS
    |
COUNTY COMPETITIONS
    |
NATIONAL COMPETITIONS
    |
INTERNATIONAL COMPETITIONS
```

Fig. 14.1 Organisational structure of competitive sport

At the simplest level, all sports clubs have to have an organisational structure so that competitions can be arranged and games played. Administrative duties are often carried out by older club members or those who have retired from competition yet maintain an interest in it. (See Fig 14.2.)

Development and organisation of sport

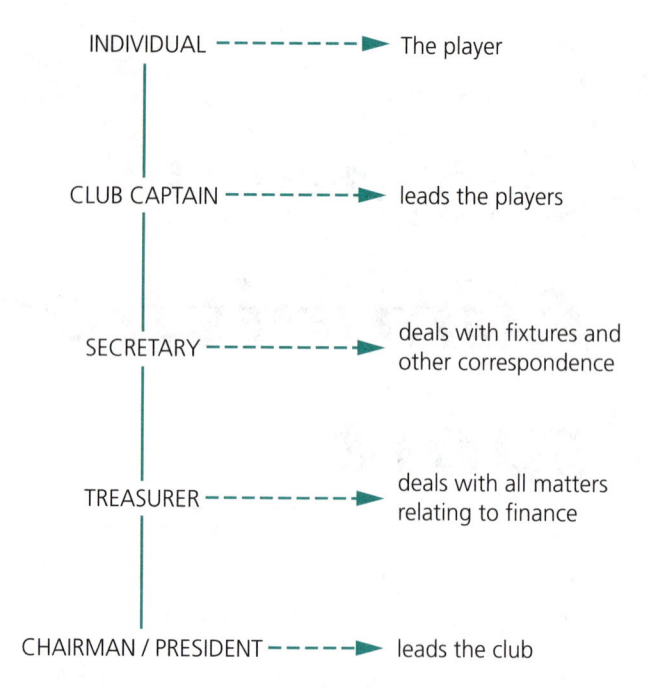

```
INDIVIDUAL  --------▶  The player
    │
    │
CLUB CAPTAIN  --------▶  leads the players
    │
    │
SECRETARY  --------▶  deals with fixtures and
                      other correspondence
    │
    │
TREASURER  --------▶  deals with all matters
                      relating to finance
    │
    │
CHAIRMAN / PRESIDENT  -----▶  leads the club
```

> **Examiner's tip**
>
> You should know the structure of sports administration at both club and national level.

Fig. 14.2 Organisational structure of a sports club

When the individual joins a club to play sport, she or he accepts a responsibility towards other players and those who organise the club, namely to play to the best of her or his ability.

By the same token the officers of the club, secretary, treasurer, president, etc., have a responsibility to the individual player to organise the club so that the individual can play the sport.

14.2 Governing bodies of sport

Each sport in the UK has its own governing body. It is the function of the governing body to:

1. establish and maintain the rules of the sport

2. organise competition in the sport

3. promote the sport

4. select international teams in the sport.

Some governing bodies have been in existence for many years whilst others have been established more recently. (See Table 14.1.)

Table 14.1 The establishment of some governing bodies in British sports

1857	The Alpine Association
1871	The Rugby Football Union
1875	The Yacht Racing Association
1884	The Amateur Boxing Association
1886	The Hockey Association
1895	The Badminton Association
1949	The Basketball Association
1967	The British Orienteering Federation

The establishment of governing bodies of sport in this country compares well with their establishment in other countries. (See Table 14.2.)

Administration of sport

Table 14.2 The foundation of national sporting associations in Great Britain, the USA and Germany

	Gt.Britain	USA	Germany
Association Football	1863	-	1900
Swimming	1869	1878	1887
Cycling	1878	1880	1884
Rowing	1879	1872	1883
Athletics	1880	1888	1898
Lawn Tennis	1886	1881	1902

Examiner's tip
You should be able to give examples of national governing bodies and be able to explain their role.

To help promote their own and other sports in this country all governing bodies of sports are represented on the **Central Council for Physical Recreation (CCPR)**.

14.3 Central Council for Physical Recreation (CCPR)

Examiner's tip
You should know what the CCPR is and how it works.

The CCPR, established in 1935, is a voluntary organisation that represents over 240 governing bodies of sport. It acts as the 'single voice' of British sport, speaking for an estimated 13 million active sports participants.

It is financed by donations from each of the governing bodies and by a donation from the **Sports Council** (see Unit 14.4), to which it acts as a consultative body. The main aims of the CCPR are:

1. to try to promote and develop sport and physical recreation
2. to give support to specialist sports bodies
3. to act as a consultative body to the Sports Council and others concerned with sport.

Overall the CCPR serves the governing bodies of sport and passes on their views to the Sports Council, central government and local authorities.

14.4 Sports Council

Examiner's tip
You should know what the UKSC is and how it works.

The original Sports Council was established by Royal Charter in 1972 and is funded by central government through the Environment Department. The aims of the Council were to:

1. ensure that all young people have the opportunity to acquire basic sports skills and physical education
2. ensure that all adults have the opportunity to take part in the sport of their choice
3. ensure that everyone has the opportunity to improve their standard in sport
4. ensure that everyone has the opportunity to reach their highest standard in sport
5. protect and develop the moral and ethical basis of sport, the human dignity of those involved in sport, and safeguard sportspeople from political, commercial and financial exploitation and from the debasing of sport through drug abuse.

In 1996 the Sports Council was replaced by the **United Kingdom Sports Council (UKSC)** and a separate Sports Council for each of the home countries: England, Wales, Scotland and Northern Ireland.

The primary function of the UKSC will be the overseeing of international sport as it relates to the United Kingdom. It will attempt to increase the influence of the UK in international sport and try to bring international sporting events to the UK.

Development and organisation of sport

The home country Sports Councils will aim to:

1. increase their programme of direct support to the National Governing Bodies (NGB)
2. help develop grass roots sport
3. provide services to support sports excellence.

Their main aim will no longer be to promote mass participation, informal recreation, leisure pursuits and health promotion. However, the NGB will receive more financial support, providing they have clear targets for the development of their specific sports from the lowest level to the highest competitive level.

The home country Sports Councils will continue to manage their own sports centres, which offer both residential and day courses to those interested (see Table 14.3 and Fig 14.3).

Table 14.3 National sports centres managed by the English Sports Council

VENUE	LOCATION	MAIN SPORTS CATERED FOR
Bisham Abbey	Buckinghamshire	tennis, soccer, hockey, squash, golf, weight training
Crystal Palace	London	athletics, swimming, judo, basketball
Lilleshall	Shropshire	soccer, table tennis, cricket, gymnastics, archery, hockey, golf
Holme Pierrepont	Nottinghamshire	water-based sports
Manchester	Lancashire	cycling

Examiner's tip

You should know the venues of the National Sports Centres and the main sports that they cater for.

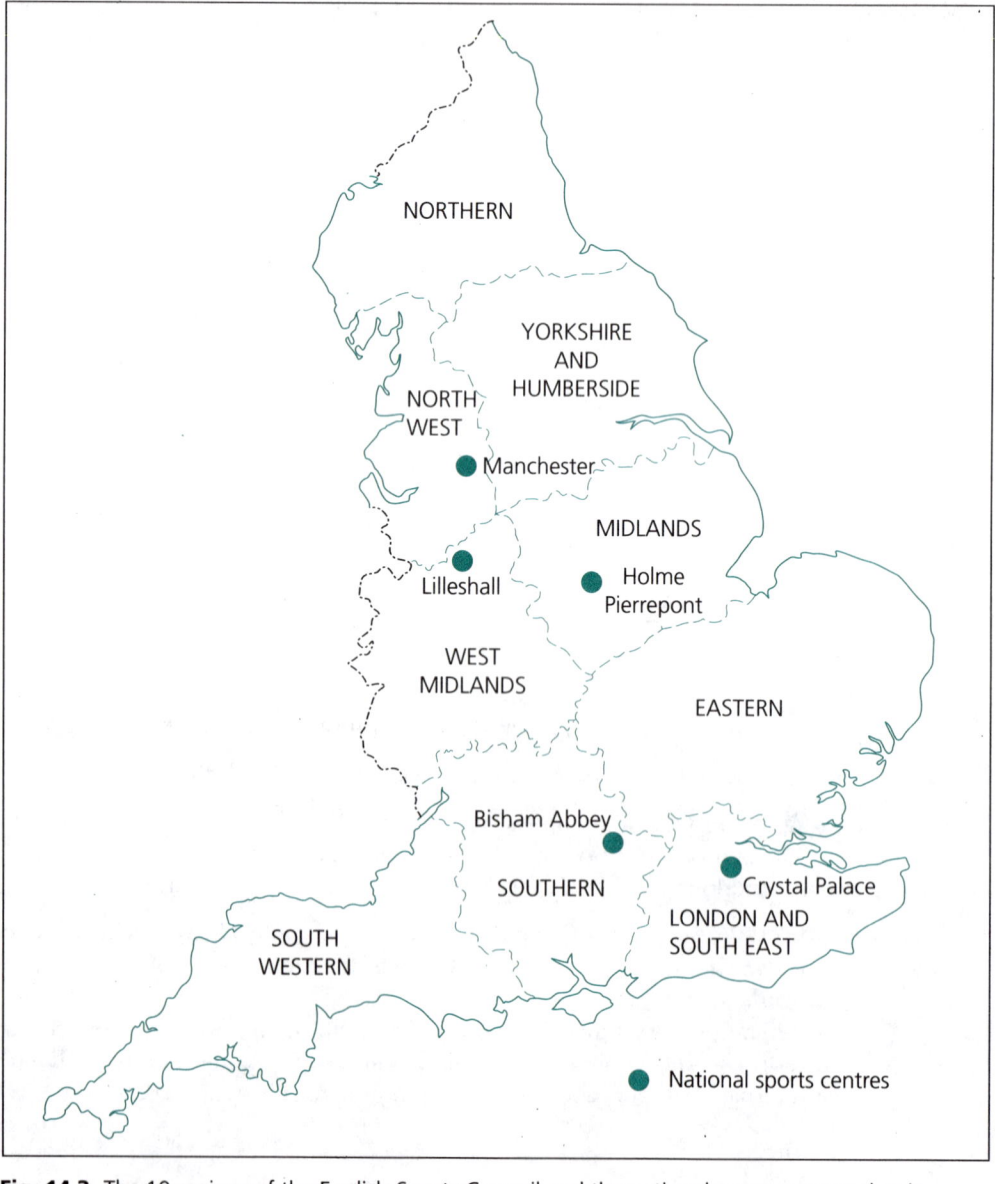

Fig. 14.3 The 10 regions of the English Sports Council and the national sports centres that it manages.

In modern day terms the UKSC is known as a **quango (Quasi-Autonomous Non-Governmental Organisation)**. This means that although it was set up by and is financed by central government it is not controlled by central government.

The home country Sports Councils will continue to allocate large sums of money, including National Lottery money, to many sports but will still not have any say in the selection of competitors for any event.

14.5 British Olympic Association (BOA)

The **BOA** is the name given to the national Olympic committee in Great Britain. This committee enters competitors in the Olympic Games. The national governing bodies of sport select their own individual teams and these are all combined together to form one British team which is controlled by the BOA.

The BOA is independent of political, religious and commercial pressures and aims to support the Olympic movement and amateur sport.

14.6 International Olympic Committee (IOC)

The **IOC** is the ultimate authority on all matters relating to the Olympic Games. Its membership is drawn from national Olympic committees and International Sports Federations.

14.7 International Sports Federations (ISF)

Each **ISF** of a sport has the ultimate responsibility for all matters relating to that sport. Each national governing body of a sport has representation on that sport's ISF. (See Fig 14.4.)

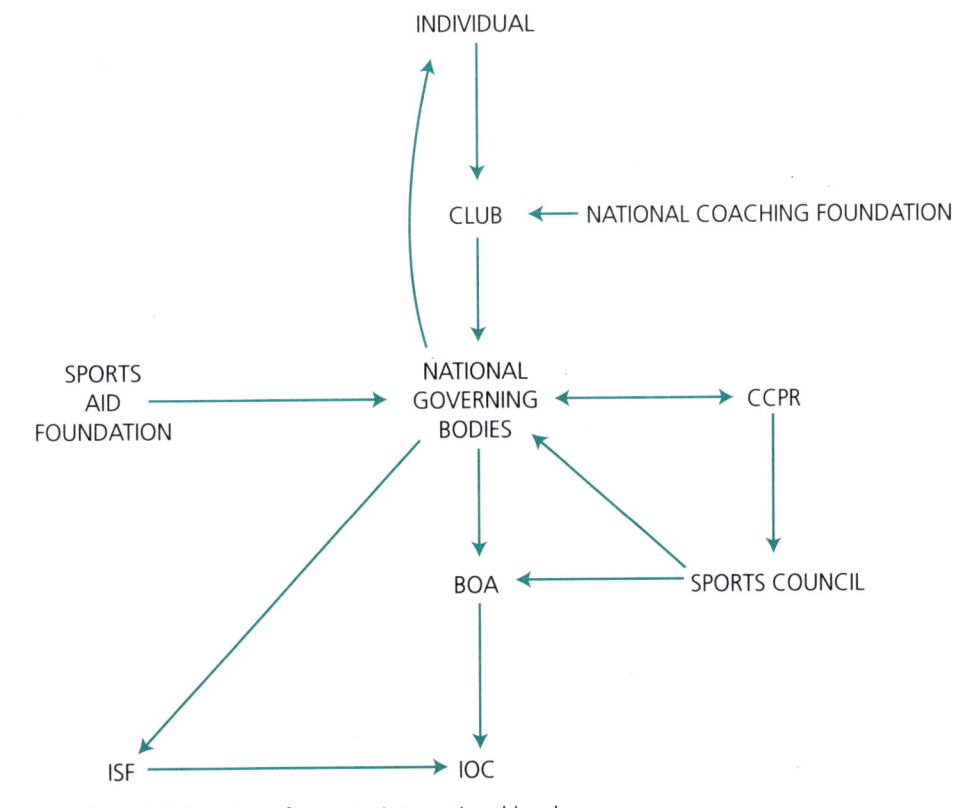

Fig. 14.4 The administration of sport to international level

Development and organisation of sport

14.8 Development of international competitions

There are two further national agencies that contribute to the development of individuals as international competitors.

❶ The Sports Aid Foundation (SAF)
This allocates grants to individuals to help them in their training and preparation for competition. It raises its money from several sources especially from industry and commerce. It allocates its funds to individuals through the governing bodies of each sport.

❷ The National Coaching Foundation
This was established to train and improve the expertise of coaches in all sports. There are 16 National Coaching Centres throughout Britain, each offering courses leading to recognised coaching qualifications at all levels. (See Fig 14.4.)

> **Examiner's tip**
> You should know the roles of the BOA, IOC, ISF, SAF, and NCF.

14.9 Recreational quangos

Those individuals who prefer to pursue sporting activities at a purely recreational level are still able to benefit from the competitive structure of sports and their respective governing bodies. There is another *quango* that has some direct influence on recreational activities.

❶ The Countryside Commission
This was established in 1968 with the objective of: *reviewing matters related to the conservation and enhancement of landscape beauty in England and Wales and to the provision and improvement of facilities of the countryside for enjoyment including the need to secure access to open air recreation.*

As with all *quangos* it receives its funds from central government. Its areas of responsibility include the National Parks, areas of outstanding natural beauty and long-distance footpaths and bridleways. It provides finance and technical assistance to local authorities and voluntary bodies in pursuit of its aims.

> **Examiner's tip**
> You should know the role of the Countryside Commission and its relationship with the National Parks.

❷ The National Parks
These are areas of countryside that the Countryside Commission has designated for recreational as well as farming use. They are areas of natural beauty, unspoilt mountain regions, heathland and some coastlines. Walkers, picnickers and climbers are welcomed in these parks. There are ten National Parks, situated mainly in the north and west of England and Wales. (See Fig 14.5.)

Administration of sport

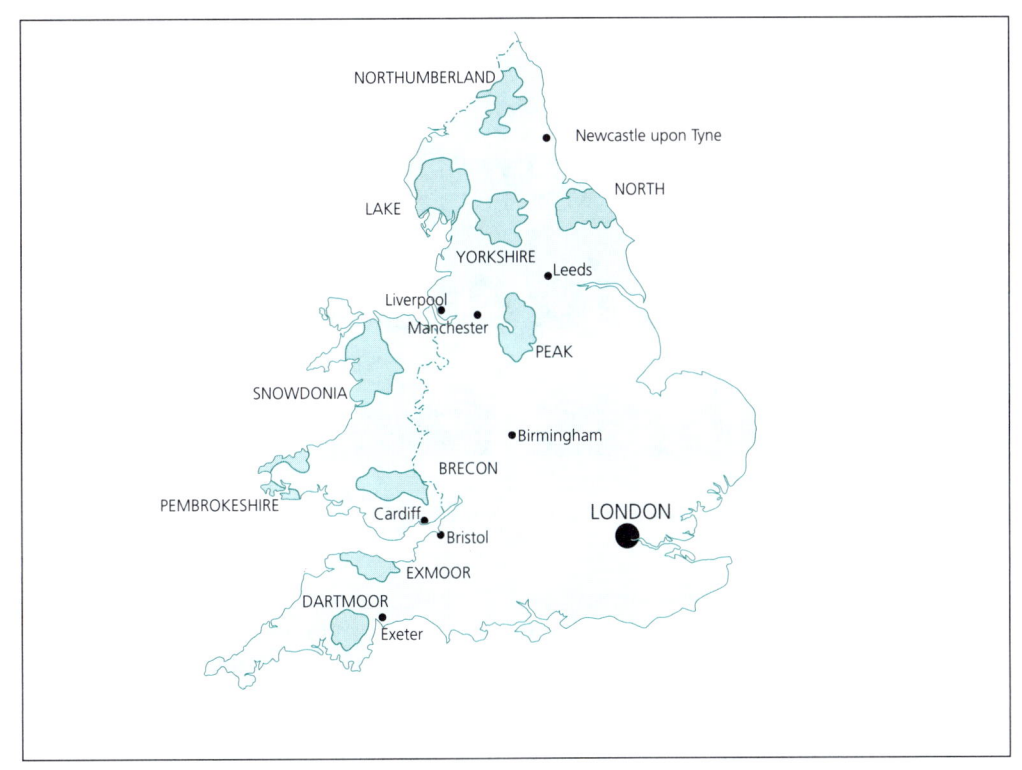

Fig. 14.5 National parks of England and Wales

PRINCIPAL TOPICS COVERED

1. The basic structure of sport is established at club level.
2. Each sport is controlled by a national governing body.
3. All national governing bodies are represented on the CCPR.
4. The CCPR serves the governing bodies of sport and acts as a consultative body to the Sports Council.
5. The Sports Council is a *quango*, runs five national sports centres and distributes funds to sports bodies.
6. The BOA is the national Olympic Committee of Great Britain and enters a British team in the Olympic Games.
7. The IOC controls all matters relating to the Olympic Games.
8. An ISF has the ultimate responsibility for its own sport.
9. The SAF and the NCF contribute to the development of British international competitors.
10. The Countryside Commission is responsible for 10 National Parks in England and Wales.

QUESTIONS ON THIS CHAPTER

1. State the name of a governing body in sport and its roles and responsibilities.

2. Give three ways in which the CCPR promotes sport.

3. What do the initials NCF represent?

4. Explain how a person might be involved in running sport at a club level.

5. Name one sport that makes use of each of the following National Sports Centres:
   (i) Holme Pierrepont   (ii) Crystal Palace

6. How could a young up-and-coming sportsperson get assistance from the SAF?

Chapter 15
Providers of sports facilities

It is often argued that Britain is a true sporting nation. Indeed, many millions of people are involved in the active participation in sports, the watching of sports or both. But although sport touches on the lives of most of the population, sport is neither organised nor provided for by central government. Central government is best described as an enabling organisation as far as sport is concerned: it makes money, technology and research information available to others so that they can provide sporting facilities.

The main providers of sports facilities in this country fall into the following broad categories:

1. **national providers**
2. **local providers**
3. **voluntary providers**
4. **commercial providers**

(See Fig 15.1.)

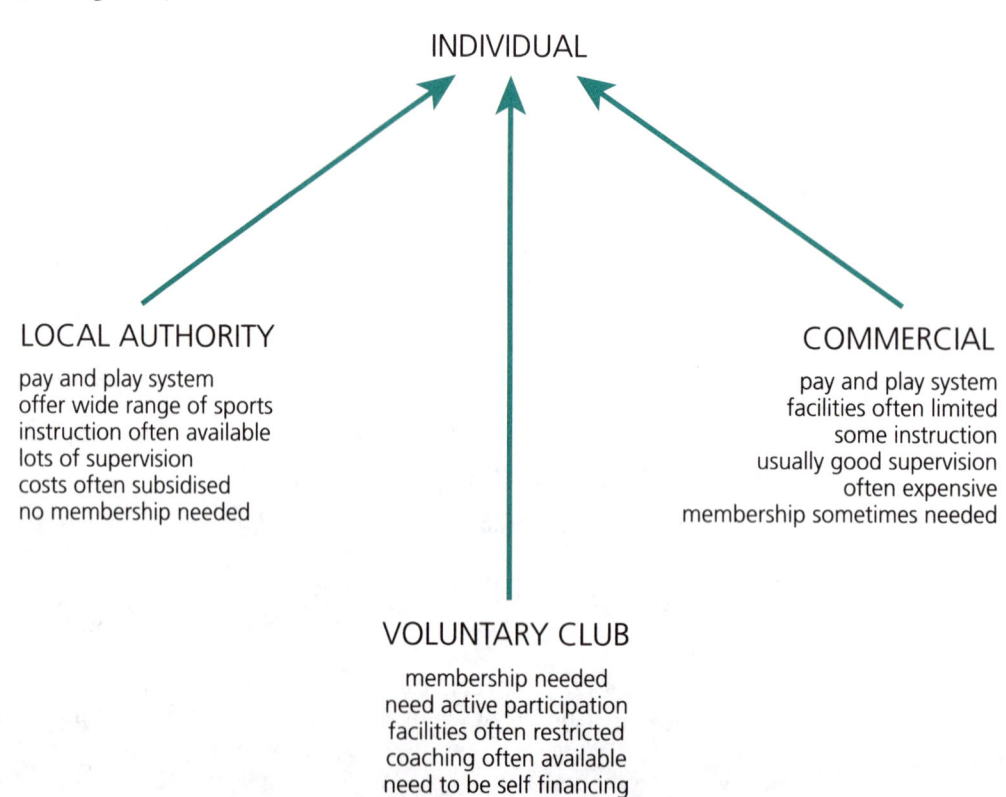

INDIVIDUAL

LOCAL AUTHORITY
pay and play system
offer wide range of sports
instruction often available
lots of supervision
costs often subsidised
no membership needed

COMMERCIAL
pay and play system
facilities often limited
some instruction
usually good supervision
often expensive
membership sometimes needed

VOLUNTARY CLUB
membership needed
need active participation
facilities often restricted
coaching often available
need to be self financing
provision is often inexpensive
run for sporting and social aspects

Fig. 15.1 Providers of sports facilities

Providers of sports facilities

15.1 National providers

The main providers of sporting facilities at a national level are the Sports Council and the governing bodies of various sports. Several of the governing bodies of sport attempt to maintain their own national sporting venues but today many base themselves at national sports centres. The Sports Councils of England and Wales operate six national sports centres at:

- Bisham Abbey
- Crystal Palace
- Holme Pierrepont
- Lilleshall
- Plas y Brenin
- Birmingham

> **Examiner's tip**
> You should be aware of the sports provision made by both the Sports Council and the Countryside Commission.

These centres often host national and international events, and also provide the setting for local events, coaching and training opportunities and public recreational use. (See Chapter 14 Unit 4.)

The Countryside Commission is a national organisation that provides local facilities such as country walks and bridleways for public use. These often extend across several local boundaries.

15.2 Local providers

By far the greater majority of sporting provision is made at a local level, and much of this by either local authorities or local clubs.

Most **local authorities** have a department which is responsible for providing sports, often together with leisure facilities. Such a **Sports Department** will not work in isolation: it will have close links with other departments such as the Engineering Department which may well maintain the machinery of a swimming pool, and the Parks Department that will be responsible for cutting the grass on football pitches. All these services are paid for either directly or indirectly by local council taxes. The most common sporting facilities provided are sports and leisure centres, swimming pools and playing fields. The National Playing Fields Association (NPFA) today does not provide playing fields and playgrounds as it originally used to do when it was set up in 1925. Now it provides expertise and advice, along with grants, to other providers of such facilities.

> **Examiner's tip**
> You should know what sporting facilities a local authority usually provides.

The changes brought about by present day legislation mean that all sport and leisure facilities that are owned by a local authority have to be run by a private company – CCT, Compulsory Competitive Tendering. However, it is the local authority which is in charge of allocating the running of such facilities to suitable operators and often dictates what provision has to be made, admission charges and staffing levels. Many local authorities go further than this by granting concessionary passes for specified groups to use council owned sports facilities. More often than not, school children and those unable to find work, together with senior citizens, are in receipt of such passes.

> **Examiner's tip**
> You should know what kind of sporting facilities your own local authority provides.

Sports centres and **leisure centres** are expensive to build and are often built in partnership with local industry and the Sports Council. They tend to provide a whole range of facilities including swimming pools, sports halls, and outdoor pitches. The main aim of such facilities is to offer sporting opportunities for the surrounding community. (See Pictures 15.1 and 15.2.)

Some local authorities also provide golf courses, outdoor pursuits centres and river facilities for specialist recreational and competitive use.

Development and organisation of sport

Pictures 15.1 Sporting and leisure facilities provided by a local authority

Providers of sports facilities

Pictures 15.2 Ample safe off-street parking for users. The indoor pool, sports halls, squash courts and outdoor fields provide for sporting activities but the centre also caters for the leisure activities of the community, halls used for concerts and social events and a permanent play area.

Development and organisation of sport

> **Examiner's tip**
> You should be able to explain what voluntary clubs are and describe the kind of facility they provide.

15.3 Voluntary providers

This title covers a large range of clubs which provide sporting opportunities because they want to. **Voluntary organisations** are those which have for their membership groups of people who freely want to join. They include local amateur football and rugby clubs, tennis clubs, athletics clubs and a whole range of other sporting organisations. Many of these hire their specialist facilities from a local authority, e.g. few athletics clubs can own their own running tracks. However, others are fortunate enough to own and run their own premises, e.g. many football, rugby and squash clubs. Very often such clubs get a regular financial grant from their local authority towards their running costs and may also get a grant from the Sports Council for the building of new facilities. The main aim of these voluntary sports clubs is not to make a profit but to provide sporting opportunities for local people at both a competitive and recreational level.

15.4 Commercial providers

Commercial providers are of two main types:

1. Those that provide facilities for their employees

Many large commercial organisations, such as banks, provide sporting facilities for their employees. Usually the employees are asked to help pay for the facilities through a voluntary levy. They may pay this a little at a time out of their wage packets. The company adds to this levy, thus ensuring that its employees enjoy subsidised sporting opportunities. Examples of this type of provision are sports fields, squash courts and fitness centres.

> **Examiner's tip**
> You should be able to differentiate between the types of commercial providers, private clubs, businesses and employee provision.

2. Those that are run on a profit-making basis

Sport today is becoming a big industry and this is reflected in the growing number of private clubs that have been established. Many of these clubs cater for only specific sports and often charge membership and entry fees, e.g. users of some private golf courses have to pay a large annual membership fee and a course fee every time they play a round. Alongside the private clubs are enterprises such as fitness centres, ten pin bowling alleys and skating rinks that are open to all members of the public. Whether they are private enterprises or private clubs, both rely on making a profit so that they can continue in business.

15.5 Finance of sport

All providers of sport have one thing in common – they all have a need to raise and spend money.

Before any facility can be built there has to be the cash available to pay for the buildings and equipment. Usually the cost of building a facility such as an ice rink, leisure centre or sports pavilion is a one-off commitment: once the facility has been built it is paid for. This is called **capital expenditure**.

> **Examiner's tip**
> You should understand the difference between capital and recurrent expenditure.

However the running and maintenance of a facility needs a continuous source of finance. The costs of wages, lighting, heating and repairs all have to be paid. These repeated types of payment are known as **recurrent expenditure**.

Sport obtains its monies for both capital and recurrent expenditure from a range of sources.

Providers of sports facilities

> **Examiner's tip**
> You should be able to explain the various sources that are available for funding sport in this country.

15.6 Obtaining money in sport

There are several ways in which money is obtained to pay for the different types of sports expenditure incurred.

1 Private sector

Private Sector finance comes in two main ways.

- Firstly by *developers* who may well decide to build a private sports facility using their own money, run the facility and take any profit that they can from the venture.
- Secondly by a *private company*, such as a brewery, who may well be prepared to make a loan to a voluntary club to help with specified costs in exchange for getting a large part of the future profits from the club's bar.

2 National taxation

National taxation is when money is obtained by central government by the raising of taxes. Every person who works has to pay income tax and VAT (Value Added Tax) in some form. The government pays out some of this income to sport: e.g. the Sports Council gets a yearly grant from central government which it spends on a range of sporting projects. The Sports Council gets its grant from the Heritage Department. Schools and youth clubs get monies from the Department for Education and Employment, some of which is spent on sport.

3 Local taxation

Local taxation is when money is obtained by a local authority through its council tax. All people living in an authority have to pay this tax. The local council spends this income on a range of services including street lighting, the police force and refuse collections. Sport and leisure departments and schools and youth clubs all get money from this source to spend on sporting activities.

4 Gambling levies

Gambling levies are often the main source of income of many voluntary sports clubs. Most small clubs have a Christmas or Summer raffle to raise funds. On a much bigger scale is the National Lottery, which has to allocate a percentage out of its income to be spent on sport. This money is allocated to sports organisations and projects on the advice of the Sports Council.

5 Sponsorship

Sponsorship also provides money for sport in a number of ways. Commerce, industry and local authorities are often prepared to invest in a sport, a sports project or even an individual sportsperson. Sponsorship is looked at in greater detail in Chapter 18 Unit 4.

6 Income

Income from the users of sports facilities is a source of money that is often overlooked. People pay to use sports facilities on a 'pay as you play' basis or in the form of club membership fees.

15.7 Spending in sport

As with all concerns, the spending of money in sport is either *capital* or *recurrent expenditure*.

Development and organisation of sport

1 Capital expenditure

Private funding is paid out by a firm that wants to build and equip its own commercial enterprise. Private squash courts and fitness centres are examples of facilities that have been paid for by their owners.

Most new sports facilities are built with monies raised for the specific project which are often assisted by grants from a range of sources. For example, a new sports pavilion could well draw monies from many of the following:

- a Sports Council grant
- a local authority grant
- a National Lottery grant
- a loan from a brewery
- money raised within the club.

The building of a new leisure centre to serve a town is often financed in a similar way. The Sports Council may well give a grant, and part of the council tax will go towards meeting some of the costs. The local authority may also obtain a loan to help meet the local cost. This loan will have to be repaid over a number of years from future council tax income.

2 Recurrent expenditure

At the moment, recurrent expenditure is not met by Sports Council or National Lottery grants: only one-off capital costs are met. However, it looks as though there may be changes in the future as far as National Lottery monies are concerned. It might be that they will be available for recurrent expenditure.

Local authorities have to pay for the upkeep of pitches and leisure centres and do this from money raised through the council tax. Very often they also make annual grants to voluntary clubs to help pay their running costs.

> **Examiner's tip**
>
> You should be able to explain how a local club might get help with its recurrent costs.

PRINCIPAL TOPICS COVERED

1. Central government does not provide sports facilities, but acts as an enabler to other providers.
2. There are four main types of provider: national, local, voluntary and commercial.
3. The Sports Council is one national provider of sports facilities.
4. Local provision is made by local authorities and voluntary clubs.
5. Local authorities mainly provide sports centres, leisure centres, swimming pools and playing fields.
6. Voluntary clubs often hire their facilities from local authorities, but many own their sports facility.
7. There are two main types of commercial provider: employers and private enterprise.
8. A private enterprise sports provider has to run at a profit in order to stay in existence.
9. Money for sport can be obtained from taxation, gambling, lotteries, the private sector and earned income.
10. Money is spent on sport for both capital and recurrent expenditure.

QUESTIONS ON THIS CHAPTER

1. In which ways might running a sports club be considered a business?
2. What is the NPFA and how has its role changed since its inception?
3. Give two sporting facilities in the commercial sector that are open to all members of the public.
4. What type of facilities for sport and physical activity might you find within a local authority?
5. How might a local cricket club fund the building of a new sports pavilion?

Chapter 16
Participation in sport

How we fill our daily lives depends on what we *have* to do, what we *want* to do and what we *can* do. How much choice we have relates to how much time we have to spend on each of these. We have no choice over what we have to do – we have to meet bodily needs, such as eating and sleeping. Most of us have to go to work or school – there is some choice in this, but not a lot. We often feel that we have a duty to perform certain jobs or tasks each day such as washing, dusting and cleaning, and sometimes we commit ourselves to certain obligations such as taking the dog for a walk. We have some degree of choice over when we will do these chores and over how much time we will spend on them.

After all these needs, duties and obligations have been met, we often have some time left when we can do just as we want – we have a freedom of choice. This freely spent time is often described as **leisure time.** (See Fig 16.1.)

THE AMOUNT OF CHOICE IN OUR DAILY LIVES

Bodily Needs	No Choice
Work	
Work Related Activities	Some Choice
Duties & Obligations	
Leisure Activities	Free Choice

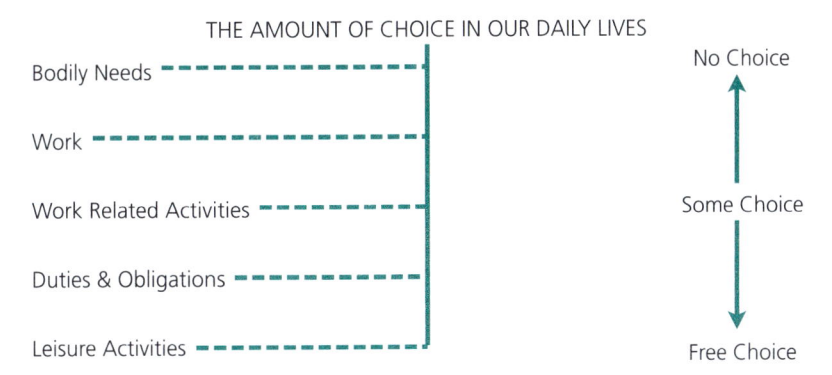

Fig. 16.1 The Leisure Time Continuum

16.1 Leisure, recreation, sport

Leisure time can best be described as:

> that time not needed to meet our social and bodily needs.

In this definition our bodily needs include eating and sleeping, and our social needs include work/school, duty and obligations.

What people do in their leisure time varies. Some spend a good deal of their leisure time following recreational activities.

Recreational activities can be defined as:

> those activities we choose to follow for their own sake.

Recreational activities tend to be planned but do not need to be *physical* activities. Stamp collecting is just as much a recreational activity as horse-riding.

Development and organisation of sport

In some instances people choose to play games as recreational activities. These can include anything from a game of billiards to a game of football. In all such cases there are clearly defined rules and very often a degree of physical involvement. On other occasions people elect to pursue a physical activity such as climbing or wind surfing in which the rules can be self-imposed. Any game or activity that includes a degree of physical involvement is often referred to as a sport.

For the purpose of this study, **sport** may be defined as:

an activity requiring physical prowess or skill together with some element of competition.

> **Examiner's tip**
> You should be able to distinguish between leisure, recreation and sport.

16.2 Leisure time

The amount of leisure time that people have has increased considerably over the last 100 years. There are many reasons for this:

> **Examiner's tip**
> You should be able to explain what has contributed to the increase in leisure time.

- **Working life**
  For most adults this is now much shorter than 100 years ago. People today do not start full time employment until they are 16, whereas in 1900 it might have been 11. Also, they are entitled to retire on a pension at the age of 60 for women and 65 for men. In addition, there are large numbers of adults whose jobs allow them to retire on a pension as much as ten years before normal retirement age.

- **Working week**
  For most people this is now much shorter than 100 years ago. It is not unusual for people to consider that a full-time job lasts for 35 hours each week, as opposed to 45 or more in the early part of the 20th century. Also, many people elect to work on a part-time basis only. The working week is now considered to be 5 days, not the 6 that was accepted in the early 1900s.

- **Unemployment**
  In addition to those retiring early, there is also a large number of the population that do not work. Some of these choose not to work, being supported by their partners; others unfortunately are unable to find employment and thus have a large amount of leisure time forced upon them.

- **Holiday time**
  This has increased over the years together with paid holiday time. Legislation forcing employers to give paid holiday time came into effect in 1938. Today people often have 3 or 4 weeks' paid holiday each year in addition to several extra paid days off for bank holidays.

- **Labour-saving devices**
  Labour-saving devices for the home have increased and have become more efficient and affordable. Most homes now have microwave cookers, washing machines and vacuum cleaners, all of which have helped to reduce the amount of time people have to spend doing their chores.

Indeed it is often argued that many people now spend far more time on leisure activities than they do working. However, not everybody spends his or her leisure time on sporting activities.

16.3 Reasons for sports participation

Most people who elect to play sport during their leisure time do so because:

1. Sport is enjoyable: it helps people to look good, feel good and very often makes them feel that they have achieved something worthwhile.

2. Sport contributes to a person's good health and aids recovery from illness. It also helps to relieve stress and tension and may well contribute to a longer life.

③ Sport is a social activity that encourages the development of friendship and social mixing. It can also stimulate acceptable competition and aesthetic awareness (the ability to appreciate physical beauty, such as the performance of physical skills).

④ Sport can satisfy that competitive element that is inherent in most people, though more strongly in some than in others.

16.4 Growth in sports participation

Just as the amount of people's leisure time has increased so has their active involvement in sport.

Surveys indicate that many more people are participating in sport, even in what were once described as minority sports, i.e. whilst sports like rugby and soccer continue to attract large numbers of players it is also true that riding, squash and volleyball have increased in popularity. There has also been an increase in interest in outdoor adventure activities such as canoeing and climbing, especially on the part of young people. There is also evidence to suggest that many people are involved in more than one sport, that they actively participate in one on a recreational level and another at a competitive level.

Over the last 30 to 40 years there has been a steady rise in the number of sporting clubs and the amount of sports provision offered to meet the ever increasing demands of the various sporting interests of the population.

16.5 User groups in sport

When considering the sporting interests of the whole population it is often advantageous to be able to divide this population into smaller, more easily identifiable groups called *user groups*. By doing this it is often possible to see which members of a community do or do not play sport, and which are or are not provided for. There are many ways in which the population can be divided or classified into groups. Perhaps the most common classification is that used by the Registrar General, a civil servant who every 10 years organises the National Census (a survey of the national population). (See Table 16.1.)

Table 16.1 Registrar General's classification of the population

CLASS	includes such people as:
A	royalty, the aristocracy, landed gentry
B	professional people such as doctor, dentists, solicitors
C1	junior managerial staff
C2	skilled workers
D	semi-skilled workers
E	unskilled workers, pensioners, unemployed

Although this system is still used today, it is hard to see how this classification can easily relate to sports participation. It would perhaps be better to divide the population by age, the amount of leisure time they have, and the size of their disposable income (that money which is left after all their bills have been paid). (See Table 16.2.)

Development and organisation of sport

Table 16.2 User groups related to age, leisure time and disposable income

AGE GROUP	AMOUNT OF LEISURE TIME	SIZE OF DISPOSABLE INCOME
young children	lots	very small
adolescents	lots	limited
young single	lots	limited but increasing
young couple	lots	large
young couple with children	little	limited
older couple	lots	fairly large
older couple with children	increasing	limited but increasing
retired	lots	rather small

This method of classification reflects not only the age of people but also illustrates the influence that family life has on both leisure time and disposable income. It also helps to show some of the factors that influence active sports participation.

16.6 Factors affecting sports participation

> **Examiner's tip**
>
> It is important to know what the main factors affecting sports participation are and how they influence participation.

Factors that affect the individual's participation in sport should not be confused with those factors that influence sport in more general ways. These are considered in Chapter 18. The following relate directly to the individual.

Age

Age is a big influence on the amount of time that people spend on sport. It is well recognised that young people up to the age of 16 spend a large amount of time on sports activities. From 18 years old there seems to be a steady decline in the participation rate but this increases again in the 30 and above age range. A second decline in the participation rate begins to show itself at approximately 50 years old.

While it is apparent that young people have the time and money to spend on sport it is evident that the first decline in participation comes at a time when the individual is most influenced by other social activities (such as going out drinking and dancing with friends) and the responsibilities of bringing up a young family. The second rise in popularity seems to coincide with that time in life when the whole family can take part in sports activities.

The second major decline in participation seems to reflect the period in life when the children have left home and people begin to look for less strenuous leisure activities. (See Fig 16.2.)

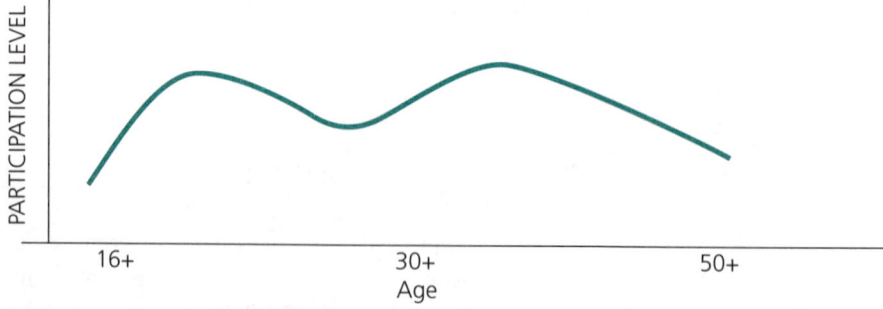

Fig. 16.2 Participation levels related to age

Attitude

The attitude of the individual is often closely related to the traditions that have developed over many years in any specific geographical area, i.e. in some parts of the country, soccer is the most dominant sport, often relegating other activities to a very minor position. Coastal areas often have a very strong tradition in water sports whilst mountainous areas have seen climbing and hill-walking flourish.

To this geographical influence must be added the development of the population's attitude towards sport in general. Although soccer was first developed in the public schools and universities during the 19th century by the so-called 'upper classes', it was for many years considered to be a game more closely associated with the 'lower classes'. The upper class game was more often considered to be rugby.

It is important to remember that the attitudes of individuals are often formed, if not strongly influenced by those closest to them. Parents who are active or interested in sport are likely to introduce their children to sport and encourage them to take part. Those adults with less active pastimes, while not discouraging an interest in sport, may not actively encourage participation.

Friends can also influence an individual's attitudes. The desire to join in and be part of a group is often a very strong driving force for both children and adults alike. What our close friends do, we may also want to do. If they are involved in a particular sport we may well want to join in with them. However, a real interest in sport may also influence the formation of friendships. Those keen on a particular sporting activity are likely to search out others with a similar interest. This in turn can lead to the making of new friends and a change in an individual's social setting.

Until some 30 or 40 years ago, an attitude most commonly adopted was that women should be allowed to take part only 'in those sports considered suitable', the 'consideration' most often seemingly being made by men! The shift in attitude relating specifically to gender is considered in greater detail in Chapter 20.

Access

Access to facilities influences the amount of time that people spend on sport. Today, sports centres, sports clubs and a whole range of sporting facilities are relatively easily accessible to all. The increased provision and development of facilities has coincided with improved road and public transport systems. An essential feature of today's sports centres and clubs is a car park, and whether they are in urban or rural areas, they are often on established bus routes making access much easier. Also the large number of public facilities are open to all potential users: there are fewer clubs with private membership.

Fashion

Fashion has influenced and has continued to influence sports participation. The running boom that started in the early 1980s was fostered by local and national fun runs and city marathons. People were encouraged to join in as much for 'the fun of it' as for the competitive element or for health reasons.

The development of a large number of aerobic clubs has seen a big rise in female participation rates. These clubs have often grown alongside the promotion of 'celebrity fitness videos' through the media, the participants being encouraged to look good as well as get fit. (See Picture 16.1.)

Picture 16.1 A step aerobics class

An often under-rated influence in the field of fashion has been the clothing industry. This industry has changed its approach to sportswear. Whereas sportswear was once purely functional, it now includes a 'fashion statement'. Today it is both common and fashionable to wear designer sports clothing both on and off the sports field. The clothes are produced in a whole range of materials, often with a spectacular use of colour to supplement design features. Today it is not necessary to look drab whilst participating in sport, even if some of the designs do reflect the clothes of past generations.

Development and organisation of sport

Finance

Finance is perhaps one of the major ruling factors in sport. In general terms, if an individual cannot pay then he or she cannot play. However, local authorities which build public sports facilities ensure that they operate at a cost that most can afford. Subsidised charges are often available for many groups within the community such as students, senior citizens and non wage-earners, and governing bodies often promote their sport at a subsidised rate. The larger costs associated with the provision of facilities are now often met from a range of sources rather than from just the user. Local authorities, the Sports Council, industry and now the National Lottery can all contribute towards the cost of sporting projects.

Schools

Schools must be recognised as an important factor relating to participation. It is most often schools, together with various types of youth clubs, that introduce sport to children. School exposes children to a whole range of sporting opportunities and by providing basic instruction enables both boys and girls to leave school with sufficient confidence to pursue a sport in later life.

16.7 Promotional campaigns

The involvement of local authorities, health authorities and the Sports Council has encouraged many people to take part in sport by using a range of promotional campaigns aimed at various groups within society. These are held at both local and national levels.

On a local level they are often run by local authorities with the support of regional sports councils in efforts to involve local people in sports participation. They often revolve around the development or provision of new facilities or specific periods of the year. Many local council sports and leisure departments run coaching and recreational courses throughout the main school holidays, often at subsidised rates. Local health authorities may well promote participation in sport alongside community health programmes.

On a national level there has been a range of campaigns designed to encourage people to take part in sport (see Fig 16.3).

> **Examiner's tip**
>
> You should be able to describe some campaigns that have been used to promote sport and state who organised them.

- WHAT'S YOUR SPORT? was a Sports Council campaign launched in 1972 to encourage all people to play sport. It was extended by a further campaign in the 1980s aimed specifically at women.

- SPORT FOR ALL – DISABLED PEOPLE was started by the Sports Council to support the United Nations International Year of Disabled People in 1981. It aimed to make people aware of the needs of the disabled as well as promoting sporting opportunities for them.

- OPENING DOORS was a joint venture between the Sports Council and the Department of the Environment in 1982. This aimed to open school, university and private facilities for community use. This dual use was seen as a way to increase the use of the facilities and help towards their financial upkeep.

- FIFTY PLUS – ALL TO PLAY FOR was started in 1983 by the Sports Council. It was aimed at older people in an attempt to stop the second decline in sports participation described in Unit 16.6.

- EVER THOUGHT OF SPORT? c.f. logo p125 was started in 1985 by the Sports Council. It was aimed at the 13 to 24 age group to try to encourage them to maintain an interest in sports participation. (See Fig 16.3.)

- PERSIL FUNFIT was a project established in 1993 aimed at increasing the participation rate of children aged 3 to 11 in fitness activities. Through schools, clubs and other organisations children's effort in following specified exercise plans are rewarded by badges and certificates. (This scheme is an example of the links that are now being made between the business community and sport.)

- SPORTSMARK SCHEME launched and run by the Sports Council in 1996 aims to give recognition to schools who are successful in competitive games and the performance of pupils. By recognising these achievements it is hoped that participation in sport at school level will be increased.
- HEC (the Health Education Council) has run and continues to run a series of topic based programmes such as *Smoking, Drugs and Alcohol* and *Healthier Eating*. Each is aimed

Fig. 16.3 An example of a Sports Council campaign logo

at improving the health of sections of the community.

The success of campaigns such as these is often difficult to assess. It is true that there are more facilities available now and more people seem to be involved in sport. How much of this is due to specific campaigns or other factors is hard to say, but they do seem to have a positive influence on many aspects of sport.

PRINCIPAL TOPICS COVERED

1. Leisure, recreation and sport are different.
2. The amount of leisure time of the individual has grown since 1900.
3. People participate in sport because it is enjoyable, it contributes to good health and provides a social and competitive environment.
4. There has been a rise in the number of people who take part in sport, together with an increase in the types of sport played.
5. People who play sport can be divided into different user groups.
6. Six of the main factors affecting sports participation are: age, attitude, access, fashion, finance, schools.
7. Sports participation has been influenced by a series of national and local campaigns run by a variety of organisations.

QUESTIONS ON THIS CHAPTER

1. Explain how the unemployed might be encouraged to make use of sporting facilities.
2. Describe one campaign organised by the Sports Council.
3. Explain the differences and similarities between a leisure activity and a sporting activity.
4. Describe two different user groups who are likely to make use of sporting facilities.
5. How can the following influence participation in sport?
   (i) attitude   (ii) fashion   (iii) age

Chapter 17

Development of international competition

The element of competition has been evident ever since people have been able to run, jump and throw. Skills such as throwing further, being more accurate and being able to run faster always seem to have gained recognition for the performer. It is not surprising, therefore, that as sports developed (often from military skills), the element of competition was maintained and fostered. As games began to be played by more and more people the development of a code of behaviour and acceptable standards of conduct evolved.

17.1 Codification of rules

> **Examiner's tip**
>
> You should be aware of the influence of the wealthy upper classes on the development of rules for horse racing, cricket and golf.

Although many sports can trace their origins back to the Middle Ages or earlier, it was during the 18th and 19th centuries that many of the games played in Britain today first established their rules.

Sports that were dominated by the upper classes were the first to establish a recognised code of rules, e.g. the Jockey Club was established to control horse racing in the 1750s and golf's first set of rules were drawn up in 1754. Cricket's first rules were generally recognised in 1788 and – unlike many sports – accepted professional players.

However, whilst golf remained exclusively an upper class sport, horse racing and cricket always involved the lower classes. Although only the wealthy could own and race horses, the poor were associated with the sport as spectators and gamblers, who enjoyed the festive occasions that race meetings became. While cricket, too, had its following of spectators and gamblers, it was played by both rich and poor together. It was not unusual to find lords playing in the same team as servants. Nevertheless, it was still controlled by the upper classes.

Despite the development of these three particular sports, it was the boys of the public schools who made perhaps the greatest impact on the codification of the rules of sports in the latter half of the 19th century. As each public school was attended only by the sons of the wealthy, these pupils could afford the time and money to play games against each other. Before any such match it was usual for the captains to meet to agree upon the rules that would be used in the forthcoming game. Eventually these boys left school and went to universities and there continued to play games, but under rules that were acceptable to all former pupils of all schools. The development of these accepted rules for sports also helped in the establishment of the governing bodies of sports, as discussed in Unit 14.2.

> **Examiner's tip**
>
> You should be able to explain the importance placed upon the amateur ethos and the ideal of fair play.

The headteachers of the public schools not only encouraged their pupils to play sport, they also encouraged them to embrace Christian ideals. This developed into the concept of 'muscular Christianity' which fostered such ideals as fair play, honesty, co-operation and playing the game for the sake of the game. This instilled in the upper classes the notion that true sportsmen could only be amateurs. That is, those who played the sport for its

Development of international competition

own sake rather than for any reward. Thus many competitions were organised for amateur sportspeople only. For example, in 1861 the West London Club made a rule that only amateurs were allowed to compete in its athletic competitions. Those it considered to be amateurs were described as:

- those who had never competed for money or cash prizes
- those who had not played sports with professionals
- those who had not earned money teaching athletic pursuits
- those who were not artisans or labourers.

Fortunately this last rule in particular was not accepted by all sports and as participation rates grew, more and more sports were played by members of all classes. The development of the road and rail systems, together with the shorter working week that evolved in the latter half of the 20th century meant that established teams from many sports could travel further to find opposition. This not only increased participation but also encouraged greater spectatorism and helped to lay the foundation for future international competitions.

17.2 International competitions

Just as the public schoolboy took his interest in games to the university, so many university graduates took their interest in games from the universities to their future professions. This was especially the case for those who entered the army and the Civil Service. As Britain had a large Empire many people were required to serve abroad for long periods of time. During this service they established sports clubs that reflected those that they had known at home. Rugby was developed in Australia, New Zealand and South Africa, and cricket in these countries and the Indian sub-continent. Again it was the wealthy upper classes who encouraged this development and controlled the games.

One of England's earliest recorded international cricket matches took place on a tour of Canada and the USA in 1859. This was followed by England's first tour to Australia in the winter of 1861–62. However, the first recorded cricket internationals did not include an English team. They are said to have taken place between Canada and the USA as early as 1844.

England's first rugby international was played against Scotland in 1871 and a national rugby team toured South Africa in 1891. England and Scotland played their first international soccer match in 1872.

As many Britons living and working overseas had assisted in the spread of games and their recognised rules, they had also fostered the ideals of fair play and amateurism. These concepts were being championed in many parts of the world and were to form a cornerstone of the first real multi-national sports competition to develop, namely the Modern Olympic Games.

Examiner's tip

You should know how the first Modern Olympic Games were founded.

17.3 Modern Olympic Games

Although the Modern Olympic Games were first staged in Athens in 1896, the concept of games played by amateur sportsmen in the spirit of fair play and friendship had been fostered in many parts of England since the 1850s. One of the most well known of such games of this period were those staged at the village of Wenlock in Shropshire. A local doctor, William Penny Brookes, established an Olympian Society in 1850 that organised a range of athletic events on an annual basis. Baron Pierre de Coubertin, a French nobleman, visited these games in 1890 and it is claimed that this visit encouraged him in his efforts to organise the first international Modern Olympic Games in 1896.

These Olympic Games can claim to be the first in which several nations came together to compete against each other at one time. Although small by today's standards, the event was one of significant importance as it set the tradition for future events. At the first modern Games 13 nations were represented by some 500 competitors in nine sports. The sports were:

Development and organisation of sport

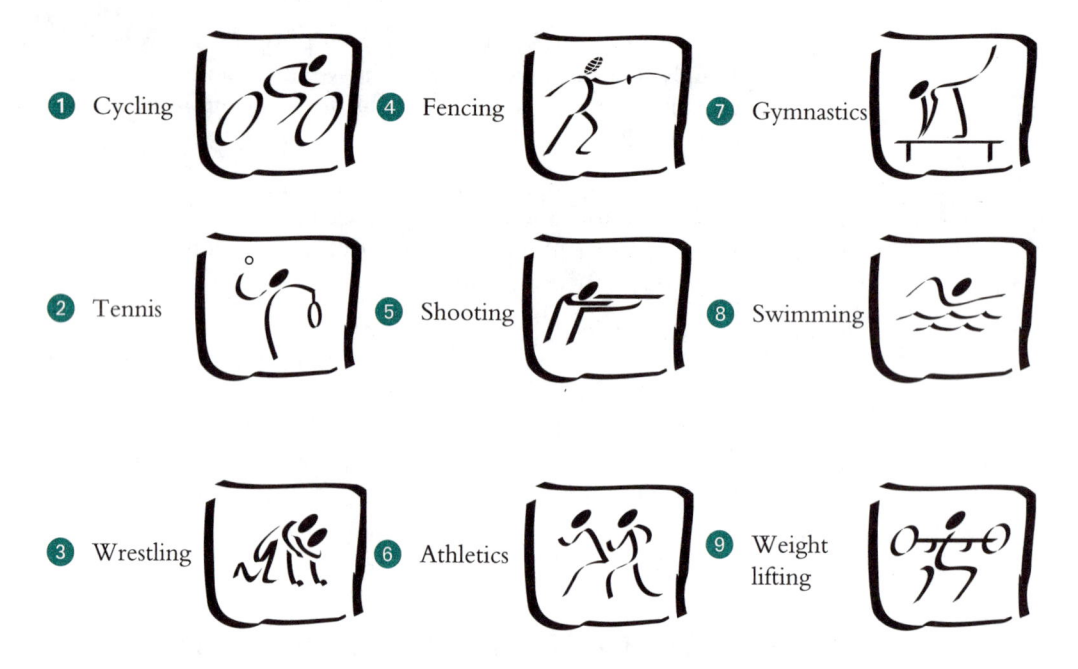

1. Cycling
2. Tennis
3. Wrestling
4. Fencing
5. Shooting
6. Athletics
7. Gymnastics
8. Swimming
9. Weight lifting

Countries did not send teams to these games. Competitors travelled to Greece at their own expense, so were drawn mainly from the upper classes. Only amateurs were allowed to take part and the events were open only to men. The accepted view at this time was that women should not take part in competitive sport.

However, at the 1900 Games in Paris women were allowed to take part despite the views of de Coubertin. He saw no place for women competitors in the games. In 1902 he is quoted as saying, "Women have but one task, that of crowning the winner with garlands." This view was in direct contrast to that of the Wenlock games which had included events for both women and girls.

Throughout this century international sporting competitions have continued to develop and many extra sports have been added to the programme of successive Modern Olympic Games. However, it can be argued that the Games have not been maintained as a truly amateur event and that the spirit of friendly competition has not been kept. Both these and other such issues are looked at more closely in Chapter 18.

PRINCIPAL TOPICS COVERED

1. The wealthy upper classes established the earliest rules for golf, cricket and horse racing.
2. The boys of the public schools contributed to the development of rules for games.
3. The graduates of the universities spread the established rules of games throughout Britain and other parts of the world.
4. The spirit of fair play and amateur status were considered important in the playing of games.
5. The first Modern Olympic Games reflected the ideals of amateur participation and the spirit of fair play and friendship.

QUESTIONS ON THIS CHAPTER

1. Describe de Coubertin's ideals for the Modern Olympic Games.

2. Explain how the rules of sports were spread throughout the world in the latter part of the 19th century.

3. Explain how the public schools and universities contributed to the codification of the rules for sports.

4. Explain why women did not take part in the first Modern Olympic Games.

Chapter 18
Major influences on sport

In the past *sport* was often regarded as the pursuit of the wealthy. Only the rich had the necessary time and money to participate in sport and it was considered acceptable as a recreational pastime. *Games* on the other hand were often regarded as activities that were played by children, the poorer classes or professional sportsmen. The approach of the latter was often more serious and the outcome was regarded as having more importance. Today however a different emphasis is put on these two terms. A definition for sport today has already been established (see Unit 16.1) and thus sport can be said to encompass all games that include physical involvement regardless of the attitude of the participants.

The emergence and acceptance of codified rules that helped in the spreading of games throughout Britain and many parts of the world has ensured that all sports can be played by rich and poor, and amateur and professional alike. The way a sport is played today depends to some extent on the amount of influence exerted on it by a range of factors.

18.1 Finance of sport

Sport receives money or financial income from a whole range of sources (see Unit 15.6). Similarly, it spends money in a range of ways. At an amateur level, sports clubs draw their income from the following sources:

1. **Membership fees**
   These form the basic income of most clubs as well as underwriting the commitment of the individual to be a member of that club.

2. **Monies raised by the membership**
   This includes a range of ways that clubs have to supplement their income. Many clubs charge team members 'match fees' whenever they play a game. Most organise raffles at specific times of the year and hold special events such as dinners and dances. These are all expected to make a profit for the club from which all the members benefit.

3. **Earned income**
   This can come from a number of sources. Money from bar and catering operations is usually made by the larger, better established clubs. To raise money from these sources clubs need to have their own club house associated with their playing facilities. Some clubs who are particularly successful and play at a sufficiently high standard may also earn money by charging admission fees to spectators. Recently, many clubs with their own grounds have found an additional income by holding car boot sales. (See Picture 18.1.)

4. **Grants**
   Grants can form a large part of the income of the amateur club. Many local authorities will provide grants to help pay for the seasonal running costs of clubs or provide facilities at reduced rates.

Development and organisation of sport

Picture 18.1 A local rugby club gains additional income from regular Sunday car boot sales. This is an example of a voluntary club putting its 'winter facilities' to good use during the off season.

The Sports Council can also provide a grant to help clubs update or extend their facilities. The Sports Council provides money for capital grants only, that is, for projects such as one-off building programmes. It will not provide money to meet the day-to-day running costs of a club.

Since 1995 a further source for grant aid has been the funds made available by the National Lottery. Money from this source has in the past been allocated along similar lines to that given by the Sports Council, namely for capital projects. However, it is anticipated that this policy may change in the near future and clubs may be able to meet some of their running costs from National Lottery funds. (See Picture 18.2.)

Picture 18.2 A voluntary club gains benefits from Lottery cash donated with the support of the Sports Council.

⑤ **Sponsorship**

This is a form of income that many amateur clubs seek but few obtain successfully. It may range from a local supplier donating a set of strips at the start of a season to a larger commercial concern paying for the costs of matches in a specific league or

Major influences on sport

competition. Firms that provide monies in this way usually want to have credit for their actions, often in the form of free advertising on shirts, in match programmes or around the ground. Successful clubs often find sponsorship easier to obtain than those who do not win competitions or trophies. (See also Unit 18.4.)

Clubs that are involved in sport on a professional basis tend to obtain income from many of the same sources as amateur clubs. However, grants from the Sports Council or National Lottery are available only under exceptional circumstances such as the running of coaching programmes for any young players.

The professional club, like an amateur club, may well charge membership fees and raise money from raffles and dances. It will also expect to make an earned income from bar and catering facilities. Most professional clubs will expect to get added income from the following sources:

- **Sponsorship and advertisement** which can be linked to both local and national commercial organisations. At the very top level of professional sport such as soccer's Premier League, clubs can expect to draw a large income from long-term sponsorship and advertising revenue. (See also Unit 18.4.)
- **Spectators**, often in large numbers, will turn out to watch professional sports clubs and individuals. Spectators will often pay a very high price to watch a feature game, such as the FA Cup Final, or a feature event such as the last day of the British Open Golf Tournament.
- **Media interest** in popular events and competitions. Whilst some amateur events, such as the annual Boat Race between Oxford and Cambridge Universities, do attract considerable media interest, many more professional events or the highlights of such events are covered by both radio and television. Broadcasting companies will often pay very high fees in order to broadcast both live coverage and highlights of events.
- **Prize monies** are available to all professional clubs and individuals. The winning of a trophy is often accompanied by a large cheque. Individuals may also be paid appearance money to ensure that they will compete in an event as well as any prize money that they may win.

> **Examiner's tip**
> You should be able to explain the different ways in which amateur and professional clubs can raise money.

18.2 Amateur v professional

There have always been people who have been prepared to perform physical skills for money, or to 'sell' their physical skills to others: e.g. in the past, a soldier could be hired to fight for one leader or another. Even the Ancient Greek Games became a professional event with money prizes being paid to event winners.

In Britain in the 18th and 19th centuries many sports developed along purely amateur lines. No amateur was expected to compete for prize money nor were they expected to instruct others for financial reward. However, the two of the more popular sports, football and rugby, did gradually evolve on a professional basis. Professional football was first legalised in 1884 with the Football League being established in 1888. Shortly after this, rugby split into two codes, the Northern Rugby Union being formed in 1895 when it separated from the Rugby Football Union. This Northern Union allowed players to be paid for missing work when they played rugby, known as 'broken time' payments. In 1922 the Northern Union changed its name to the Rugby League.

Some sports such as cricket and horse racing managed to embrace both amateur and professional participants in the same events. They also permitted gambling to be associated with the events. Other sports felt that gambling encouraged cheating and so did their utmost to keep the sport truly amateur.

Most sports would not allow amateur and professional players to play alongside each other. Cricket was one sport that did. Amateur players were always referred to as *gentlemen* and professionals as *players*. Although they played alongside each other throughout the season there was one match played each year known as the Gentlemen versus Players match. This distinction was eventually abolished in 1962.

Sports such as Rugby Union, athletics and swimming maintained strict amateur codes until very recently. Today amateur rugby players can play alongside professional players,

Development and organisation of sport

> **Examiner's tip**
> You should be able to show how professionalism is encroaching on amateur sport.

they can even move from one code to the other as the seasons change. Athletics and swimming have tried to maintain their amateur status. However the actions of both national and world controlling bodies have increasingly permitted competitors to receive indirect payments and compete for financial gain.

Today it is not unusual to see all types of sportspeople playing in Open Competitions. Open competitions are those that allow both the amateur and professional to compete against each other. Entries from foreign players are also accepted in such competitions. Amateurs can match their abilities against those of the professional, be they home based or from abroad. Open competitions serve to raise the standard of play of all the competitors.

18.3 The professional amateur

The modern Olympic Games were first established for amateur competitors. However, the 1950s and 1960s saw a change in the status of many so-called amateur competitors.

Many *Iron Curtain* countries (the communist countries of Eastern Europe controlled by the USSR) managed to achieve sporting success at all levels by drafting their best competitors into the armed forces. As soldiers they were allowed to train full time, yet still maintain their amateur status. The hypocrisy of this was shown when Russian footballers played for the army club in professional competitions yet still represented their country at the Olympic Games.

In the USA many colleges and universities began to offer sporting scholarships to able individuals. This allowed them to train full time under the control of nationally recognised coaches yet still maintain their amateur status by claiming to be students.

Today the break up of the Iron Curtain countries (the communist countries of Eastern Europe controlled by the USSR) has much reduced the number of top class sports people in the army. And whilst the sports scholarship system is still in operation in the USA all students have to follow a recognised academic course. The scholarship system has been further extended and now covers both professional and amateur sports.

Today successful competitors find that they have to train full time in order to attain the high standards needed for international competition. To enable them to do this they are allowed to compete for prize money and to get appearance money. These monies are paid into a trust fund that pays for the day-to-day living and training expenses of the athlete. In this way amateur status is maintained yet financial rewards can be gained.

18.4 Sponsorship in sport

The sponsorship of sportspersons and sporting events is as old as recorded time. Throughout history there have always been those with money who were prepared to financially support athletes or events. Very often such people were referred to not as sponsors but as *patrons*. In Victorian times when the amateur ethos was being strongly promoted, there were still members of the nobility and wealthy upper classes who would act as patrons to boxers, horse racing and even cricket teams. This form of sponsorship, or patronage, gave public recognition to the patron as well as helping promote the sport or the individual. The patron was not always seeking financial gain but more the goodwill of those watching the sport.

> **Examiner's tip**
> You should be able to describe how sports actively seek sponsorship and the benefits that they gain from this.

This is a far cry from the approach to sponsorship today. In the 1950s and 1960s many amateur governing bodies of sports found themselves short of money to both promote their sport and run show-piece events. To help overcome this problem many sought the help of big business. In exchange for a cash contribution a company could tie its name to a specific sporting project or event. One of the earliest of such ventures was the introduction of the Athletics 5 Star Award Scheme. The costs of this scheme were originally met by the Walls Ice Cream company. Their name appeared on every certificate given to every child who gained an award. Whilst Walls were supporting a worthy cause, they were also getting good advertising exposure at the same time.

Many governing bodies entered into such agreements with companies and the money paid by them was distributed by the governing bodies throughout the sport.

Major influences on sport

Today many companies bypass the governing bodies and sponsor individual sportspersons directly. The individuals in turn agree to wear the sponsor's logo on clothing and equipment and the more successful the individual the more sponsorship he or she can obtain.

Many firms are prepared to sponsor specific sporting events. If an event is particularly successful then the sponsor may be prepared to advertise the event as well as put money into it. Examples of this type of sponsorship of amateur events are that of BUPA's sponsorship of the Great North Fun Run, Flora's sponsorship of the London Marathon and Beefeater Gin's sponsorship of the Boat Race. (See Picture 18.3.)

Picture 18.3 BUPA sponsor the Great North Fun Run

Perhaps the most expensive sponsorship deals ever arranged in amateur sport were those organised by the controllers of the 1996 Olympics Games in Atlanta. These were sometimes called the Pepsi Cola Games after their main sponsor, although many other firms also paid vast sums to sponsor parts of the Games.

For professional sports and sports clubs sponsorship is treated in a slightly different way. It is true that sports still want cash contributions from companies. However a sport is more likely to sell itself to the highest bidder for a set period of time. The 1996 FA Cup Competition was called the Littlewoods Cup, and first class cricket has several sponsors. (See Table 18.1). Legislation proposed in 1997 is expected to stop all advertising at and sponsorship of sporting events by tobacco-related products.

Table 18.1 Sponsors of first class cricket competitions for the 1996 season

County League matches	Britannic Assurance
Sunday League matches	AXA Equity and Law
Knock-out Cup competitions	NatWest Bank
	Benson and Hedges
Test matches	Texaco
	Cornhill

Whilst sports can use the money earned from such sponsorship deals to further the game itself, the companies concerned get plenty of national advertising exposure. In effect today the meaning of the word sponsorship has changed from that of Victorian times. In the past a sponsor helped to promote an individual, a sport or an event. Today the successful individual, sport or event acts as an exclusive form of advertising for the company prepared to pay the highest price.

From this it would now seem that the more successful a sport is, the more it can charge for sponsorship. Unfortunately this is not always correct. Some sports readily get sponsorship. Nearly all professional soccer clubs have their own sponsor and play in sponsored leagues. Amateur athletics matches and Rugby Union games have had little problem finding sponsors. But some sports such as hockey, canoeing and judo have difficulty getting high-value sponsorship deals, no matter how successful they are at international level. This often reflects the difficulty that the sport has in attracting large numbers of spectators. Few spectators often means little media interest and this in turn means that sponsors will get little advertising return for their money.

18.5 The media in sport

The media can be divided into two main areas, namely:

1. **the written word** – which includes newspapers, magazines, books
2. **broadcasting** – which includes radio commentary and discussion, television and films.

Each of these influence sport to some extent.

The written word

There has always been a large amount of written coverage of sports events. Many of the newspapers and journals of the late 19th century included reports on a variety of sporting activities. As is the custom today, these often featured on the back pages of publications. Many books were also printed relating to a range of sporting activities and were usually descriptive, or of a slightly educational nature. Most of the newspapers and books confined themselves to those sports that were of interest to the middle and upper classes as these were the buyers of the publications.

Today sport is written about extensively. All newspapers carry a substantial coverage of sporting features – although still on the back pages. However, not only are sports reported on, but they are also discussed, with opinions aired and comments made. The reporting tends not to be as objective as in the past. Local and regional papers often report matches with a local bias. They often 'excuse' the local side for losing rather than accepting that the non-local side 'won' the fixture. There is occasionally evidence of this at the national level too. The range of sports events covered also varies from paper to paper. Some tend to cover only soccer and racing in the winter and cricket and racing in the summer. Others will include a broader range of sports, often giving coverage to less popular sports. A common feature of all newspaper coverage appears to be the desire to sensationalise a story. Factual reports seem to be of less importance than a story of an incident that can be made to look sensational.

There are also many more books published relating to sport than hitherto. These cover a wide spectrum of topics. There are those of an educational nature which tell you how to play the sport, those that describe the successes of individuals or teams, and those that are purely descriptive in nature. Most common of all are the autobiographies that most well-known sportspersons now produce.

Broadcasting

- The development of *radio* brought a wider, different audience to sport. Those who would not or could not read about sport were often prepared to listen to it. Radio could report on events taking place all over the world almost as they happened. Also, more important events were reported 'live'. Surprisingly, the development of radio coverage of sport did not seem to detract from newspaper coverage or reduce the number of people prepared to watch sport live.
- The advent of *television*, especially when more than one channel became available, had a much bigger impact on sport. Spectatorism began to fall away as more sports began to get coverage. The independent television stations had to find sports that were not 'tied' exclusively to the BBC. For a long time they could provide only limited coverage of cricket, football and tennis. To counteract this they promoted a different range of sporting events. Horse racing and Rugby League were strongly featured and wrestling became a national favourite in the 1960s and 1970s.

> **E**xaminer's tip
>
> You should be able to show how sponsorship and advertising are closely linked in sport.

The controlling bodies of sports and sports events soon realised that the media, especially television, was capable of making a big impact on a sport's popularity. Events were being shown live from all round the world and the level of spectatorism was falling off badly. To help offset the loss of income from falling spectatorism, sports began to sell themselves to the many television companies. This ensured the particular sport an income as well as maintaining popularity.

The increased popularity that a sport could gain from extensive television coverage also provided two further spin-offs. Firstly, sports with a strong television following could attract better advertising and increased levels of sponsorship. In many cases, sponsorship really became advertising. Soccer players and racing drivers have now become moving advertising space. They advertise the name of the sponsor who is prepared to pay the highest price. Secondly, the extensive television coverage, supported by glossy magazine coverage, has helped to promote some sports men and women into stars. Some have become as well known as pop or film stars and can command large fees just for appearing at an event as well as for success in their chosen sport.

Sports have not always benefited from increased media interest. Very often it is the television companies that decide which sports will be given coverage. They want to broadcast only those sports which have 'spectator appeal', those that will draw a large audience. To help maintain this status, some sports have changed their rules to make them more attractive to watch. Rugby League introduced the six tackle rule so that the game would flow better, soccer changed the off-side law so that more goals could be scored and cricket developed limited over and one-day matches which proved more exciting than three-day games. Many sports were prepared to reschedule their playing times to fit in with broadcasting times. The television companies can now dictate to soccer's Premier League which games will be played on Saturdays, which on Sundays, and which through the week.

Whilst many sports, individual sportspersons and sporting events have flourished through increased media interest there are many that have not. Those without the previously mentioned 'spectator appeal' get very little television attention and find it hard to attract money into the sport from both sponsors and spectators. This can lead indirectly to a lowering of standards within a sport. A sport without good television coverage will find it hard to maintain a strong international fixture list and will have difficulty paying for good 'grass roots' coaching programmes.

Many people involved in sport at all levels often wonder who benefits most from media interest in sport. Certainly interest can bring about an increase in popularity and revenue to a sport. However this is not the main aim of the media.

Sports reporting, be it visual, oral or written, is used first and foremost to promote that section of the media. Reports on soccer matches and the printing of racing results help to sell newspapers. Television and radio coverage of events help to maintain an audience that can bring advertising and other revenue to the broadcaster. Books written by sports personalities are designed to earn them money from royalties.

Whether sports gain more from media coverage than the media gain from sport is open to question.

18.6 Politics and sport

Examiner's tip

It is important to be able to give examples to show how some governments have tried to use international sporting events to further their own political ideals.

Sports, like some wars, can bind a nation together. Just as a population might pull together to fight a common enemy, so it is possible that a population will unite in supporting a national sporting team. Success at international level can create a national feeling of goodwill. This may be one of the reasons why many governments in the past have put large amounts of money into national sportsmen and sportswomen.

At the same time, many governments have been prepared to use sport to further their own political ideals or influence. This has been seen many times at international level, even at the Olympic Games. Despite the fact that the Olympic Games were founded to promote international goodwill and friendship they have been used many times by various governments to try to prove a political point.

Development and organisation of sport

1936   The Berlin Games were manipulated by the Nazi government of Germany to promote that country's political ideals. Many German dissidents were imprisoned so that they could not disrupt the games, competitors were not allowed to travel freely within the country and only Germans of so-called Aryan descent were allowed to compete for Germany. Owing to Hitler's extreme racial prejudices, he refused to acknowledge the success of Jesse Owens, the black American athlete who won four gold medals.

1956   The Melbourne Games saw Spain and Holland withdraw in protest against the Russian invasion of Hungary. Communist China also withdrew rather than compete against the nationalist Chinese from Taiwan.

1964   At the Tokyo Games, the invitation to South Africa was withdrawn because of that country's policy of apartheid.

1968   At the Mexico City Games, the invitation to South Africa was again withdrawn because many of the black African states held anti-apartheid views. Also, many black American athletes chose to demonstrate against racial problems in their own country by giving the black power salute on the winner's rostrum.

1972   The Munich Games were perhaps those that have been most influenced by politics. Rhodesia, now Zimbabwe, had followed IOC guidance and selected a multi-racial team. However, many black African countries refused to accept this and on the eve of the Games threatened to walk out. To stop this, the Rhodesian team was sent home, despite the IOC President, Avery Brundage, claiming openly that this was caused by political blackmail. The Games were further disrupted when Arab nationalists, attempting to promote their own political ideals, invaded the Olympic village and killed several Israeli competitors.

1976   The Montreal Games were boycotted by several Arab and black African nations who refused to compete against New Zealand. This country had previously played against South Africa – by then expelled from the Olympic movement – at rugby, a non-Olympic sport.

1980   The Moscow Games were criticised by many countries because of Russia's poor record in the matter of human rights. Also, just before the start of the games, Russia invaded Afghanistan, and the USA led a boycott by many western nations in protest.

1984   The Los Angeles Games were used by the Russians and many Eastern Bloc countries in a tit-for-tat boycott against the Americans following the American boycott of the previous Games.

Although the Olympic Games are seen as the most important international sporting competition staged, many athletes from Britain and the Commonwealth countries see the Commonwealth Games as an event of almost equal importance. These Games have also been used to promote political ideals.

The development of the apartheid system in South Africa not only impinged on the Olympic Games but also on the Commonwealth Games. South Africa was expelled from the Olympic movement in 1970 but for several years before this many countries had tried to isolate that country from all sporting events. In 1977 at a meeting of the political Commonwealth leaders a declaration on apartheid in sport was made. The declaration, known as the Gleneagles Agreement, not only condemned apartheid in sport but went on to say that individual governments were to:

> '...take every possible practical step to discourage sporting competition with South Africa...'

This declaration was supposed to be binding on the sporting authorities of each of the Commonwealth countries. However, in Britain and New Zealand the authorities that control sport are independent of national government control. Some sports chose to ignore their governments' advice and continued to arrange fixtures with South Africa. This was because some people thought that sport should not be mixed with politics; that sportspeople who had trained long and hard for international competition shouldn't have to forefeit the opportunity for the sake of proving a political point. They also didn't want the black population of South Africa to be denied the chance to enjoy international fixtures or experience top level sport. (Several years later, other sporting authorities were to adopt a similar approach towards participation in the 1980 Moscow Olympics.) Rugby and cricket were to maintain links with South Africa for several years. By the late 1970s the sporting authorities of the Commonwealth nations managed to help break even these links. It was only when apartheid was eventually dismantled that full sporting links with South Africa were re-established.

PRINCIPAL TOPICS COVERED IN THIS CHAPTER

1. The major influences that affect sport are considered to be:
   finance
   the division between amateurs and professionals
   the emergence of the professional amateur
   sponsorship
   the media
   politics.

2. Sports can gain their income from a range of sources:
   membership fees
   earned income
   grants
   prize money
   sponsorship
   advertising revenue.

3. Amateur and professional players have been competing in sporting events in Britain since the middle of the 19th century.

4. The raising of the status of many athletes has brought about a change in the rules relating to amateurism.

5. Sponsorship has helped many sports to increase in popularity and now influences the staging of many sporting events.

6. Media interest in sport has grown throughout the 20th century and has helped change the nature of many sports.

7. Governments have tried to use sporting events to further their own political ideals.

QUESTIONS ON THIS CHAPTER

1 Explain how television might affect the development of a sport.

2 What are the advantages of 'Open' competitions to the amateur sportsperson?

3 Explain how political problems affected the Olympic Games staged in 1976.

4 Explain how an amateur club raises its annual income.

5 Explain why the partnership between sport and sponsorship is important.

Chapter 19
Changing attitudes in sport

Sport today includes many more activities than it did in the past and the attitudes that people held towards participation in the past have changed over the years.

It is accepted that many modern day sports were first fully established and developed in the late 19th century. Along with the defined and accepted sets of rules, players were expected to behave themselves with an acceptable attitude of fair play. Indeed this was considered so important in soccer that it was written into the laws of the game that players could be, and still can be, punished for 'ungentlemanly conduct'. Sport was considered to be a gentlemanly pursuit.

Sport today is played by many people from a whole range of differing backgrounds, which has helped to bring about a change in attitude towards it.

19.1 Attitude towards winning

To many people today the playing of sport is a serious matter. The element of competition is very strong and only winners seem to get any recognition for their efforts. Although this attitude has been fostered to some extent by media coverage and sponsorship it is also evident in the way that some parents encourage their children to take part.

Most parents claim that they want their children to enjoy sport, e.g. that they should learn to swim for pleasure and safety, or that they should be playing team games for fun. They often also claim that they, the parents, only watch and only encourage their children to participate because they are interested in their children's activities.

Too often, the truth is far from this. Some parents seem not only to encourage their offspring to play to the best of their abilities, but also to condone or encourage behaviour that is not in the spirit of the game. Words of encouragement either before or during the event will sometimes include suggestions that opponents should be dealt with in a less than sporting manner. The aim is often to stop skilful opponents from playing the game by any means possible and thus ensure success. The attitude of 'win at all costs' is not only promoted in young players by parents but also by the actions of professional sportsmen and clubs. Youngsters will often copy the actions of their sporting idols and adopt what is often incorrectly called a 'professional attitude' towards games that are supposed to be fun. Such actions may not be regarded as cheating: they may well fall within the rules of the game, but can sometimes best be described as the 'bending' of the rules: e.g. in a game of soccer, is it acceptable to water the sides of the pitch because you know that your opponents have fast wingers who like hard, dry ground? In a game of cricket, when does 'polishing' the ball become tampering with it and thus cheating? What is seen at senior club level and international level is often reflected in games played by the young.

> **Examiner's tip**
>
> You should be able to explain how people's attitude towards winning has changed.

Changing attitudes in sport

19.2 Abuse of drugs

> **Examiner's tip**
>
> You should be able to describe the rise of drug abuse in sport and the methods adopted to combat this.

Today the rewards that go with success at national and international level encourage many athletes to strive to be successful at any cost. This is apparent from the way that drugs seem to have become more evident in top class sports.

There is a long history of drug abuse in international sport: e.g. it is claimed that in the changing rooms used by competitors at the 1952 Winter Olympics held in Oslo, many used ampoules and syringes were found scattered about the floor. At the 1960 Games held in Rome, Jensen, the Danish cyclist, died as a result of drug abuse. Tommy Simpson, the British cyclist, died in the 1967 Tour de France after taking an overdose of stimulants.

Whilst sports tried to legislate against the use of some drugs in competition, other drugs were thought to be being used in training. It is claimed that prior to the 1964 Tokyo Olympics many athletes were using anabolic steroids. These drugs, taken at five to ten times their recommended medical dose could increase an athlete's body weight by up to 70 pounds a year, advantageous for throwers and lifters. Unfortunately it was not possible at this time to detect the use of these drugs, especially if the athlete stopped using them a couple of weeks before competition.

The 1988 Games held in Seoul, South Korea, underlined the extent to which drugs were being used in sport. Ben Johnson, the Canadian sprinter, was seen by millions to win the 100 metres final. Shortly after, he was stripped of his gold medal, following the discovery that he had used forbidden drugs. A further penalty was later imposed by his home country: that he should be excluded from athletics for two years. At these same Games it was surmised that many competitors had used performance enhancing drugs to help them reach the standard necessary for this type of competition.

Whilst most people condemn the use of drugs in sport, there are many coaches, trainers and members of the medical profession who are prepared to supply drugs to athletes. Not only this, but they are also prepared to develop 'new' drug preparations that they hope cannot be detected. Although the taking of such drugs might enhance performance in the short term, it is accepted that they might cause long term damage to the athlete or even premature death.

Today all sports have random testing programmes of athletes both in competitions and during their training.

19.3 Spectatorism

Spectators have an important part to play in sport. They not only provide income for the clubs or teams that they watch but they contribute to the game by showing their appreciation of skilful play and the efforts of the players.

Before television made its full impact on society, spectators flocked to many sporting events in huge numbers – football matches in particular. During the late 1940s and early 1950s football games enjoyed a huge following of fans prepared to support their favourite teams both at home and away matches. However, by the mid 1960s, these numbers had fallen away considerably. There were three main reasons for this:

1. Television began to broadcast many more events live, and regularly showed edited highlights of further matches. As more households became able to purchase television sets, so more people were prepared to stay at home to watch their sport in comfort.

2. The sports themselves, especially football, had done little to cater for the needs of the watching public. The huge crowds that had in earlier times gone to watch football matches were provided with very poor facilities. Most spectators were expected to stand on sloping terraces open to the wind and rain at all times. Toilet facilities were few in number and of a very poor standard, and there were few catering or refreshment outlets. People were crowded together with little thought being given to their comfort or to their ability to see the game.

3. There developed in the mid 1960s a huge rise in hooliganism associated especially with soccer matches. This drove many people away from watching the games on the

Development and organisation of sport

terraces. Parents were afraid to take young children to watch matches and began to stay at home to watch other sports on television in safety and comfort. This, of course, began to deprive the soccer clubs of a large amount of income.

19.4 Crowd violence

> **Examiner's tip**
>
> You should be able to explain the underlying causes of crowd violence associated with sport and the measures that are being taken to combat this.

The problems associated with crowd control at football matches and the vandalism created by travelling spectators became so serious that football clubs began to suffer a heavy loss of income. In an effort to reverse this trend, research was conducted into crowd behaviour which identified three main causes of the anti-social behaviour seen.

① Alcohol abuse

Alcohol abuse appeared to be the major contributory cause of much of the crowd violence.

Violence associated with alcohol was not confined to the match itself. Visiting fans would often cause damage to pubs before games and up to several hours after the game was over. Gangs of so-called supporters were often seen fighting in the streets once the game was over.

At soccer grounds today, alcoholic drinks are not served and fans are not allowed to take such drinks into matches. Although some may try to consume alcohol before a match, entry is restricted to those who are sober and restrictions are placed on the number of outlets that can serve alcoholic drinks before a game.

② Tradition

Tradition was also seen as a contributory factor to crowd violence. Many spectators had grown up knowing nothing but violence on the terraces and accepted this as part of watching a soccer match. This was also found to be closely linked to the poor economic situation of many fans. Those from the more socially deprived areas seemed to take out their frustrations with life in general at the soccer match.

③ Loyalty

Loyalty of a very intense nature towards club or country was also seen as a contributory factor. Opposing supporters saw each other as the enemy. The noise and excitement of the game could inflame the crowds and lead to aggressive behaviour towards visiting fans. Visitors would be subjected to verbal abuse and often physical abuse.

Even today, crowd violence can be caused by intense loyalty to one's own country. At the 1996 under-15 World Challenge cricket final, some 200 Pakistan supporters invaded the Lords pitch and stole the wickets, forcing the game to stop. This was intended to prevent the Indian team from scoring the last six runs needed to win the match. Police had to restore order before the Indian team could go on and win the match by four wickets.

Whatever the reasons for crowd violence, it has an undesirable effect on sport and those who promote it. Many groups of fans of both club and national teams have gained poor reputations and are therefore unwelcome when they travel to away matches. Sometimes they are even excluded from certain events. English soccer clubs were banned from playing in Europe for several years during the 1980s because of the actions of groups of spectators.

In an endeavour to combat crowd violence and encourage an increase in spectatorism some policies have been implemented by soccer clubs. The development of all-seater stadia and the segregation of opposing fans has helped to reduce violence at many soccer matches. Restrictions on the sale of alcohol in or near grounds and the speedy removal of visiting fans from town centres by police chaperone has further reduced hooliganism. Many clubs have developed special facilities for family viewing so that young children can watch games with their parents in comparative safety. The improved supervision of grounds including the use of closed circuit television links with local police control points helps to defuse potential flash points of violence and keep known trouble makers away from matches.

Surprisingly, cricket has been slow to follow the lead of soccer clubs. It is true that there has never been as much pre- or post-match violence associated with this game but crowd violence at the game is becoming more and more evident. Spectators have been known to invade pitches – though not often in this country. However, many players often suffer strong verbal abuse from spectators while a match is in progress. Spectators are not above throwing debris at players or of barracking umpires who make unpopular decisions. Constant singing and chanting throughout play seem to follow the fortunes of some teams. Unlike at soccer matches, cricket spectators have direct access to alcoholic drinks throughout the day. Perhaps this could be the root cause of the rise in anti-social behaviour at cricket matches.

PRINCIPAL TOPICS COVERED

1. A 'win at all costs' attitude is evident today in sport at most levels.
2. This attitude is supported by the common bending of the rules to achieve a win.
3. Drug abuse has been evident in international sport since the early 1950s.
4. There is a concerted effort in international sport to ban the use of illegal drugs.
5. Some new drug preparations are hard to detect.
6. The steady fall in spectatorism in the mid-60s was mainly owing to the rise in popularity of television, the poor facilities provided for spectators and the increase in hooliganism among spectators.
7. The main underlying causes of crowd violence at soccer matches are seen as alcohol abuse, tradition, and intense loyalty to club or country.
8. Methods used to combat crowd violence include the provision of all-seater stadia, segregation of fans, restrictions on the sale of alcohol and improved ground control.

QUESTIONS ON THIS CHAPTER

1. Outline the reasons against taking drugs in sport.

2. Explain how the behaviour of professional performers might influence the behaviour of young performers in the playing of their sport.

3. Give two reasons why spectatorism of sporting events sporting events declined in the early 1960s.

4. Identify the factors which have contributed to crowd violence amongst football supporters.

5. State which groups of athletes might take anabolic steroids and why.

Chapter 20
Social concepts in sport

As sport in this country has grown and developed over the last 100 years, the number of games played has increased, as has the range of opportunities to play them. However, this increase in opportunities to participate has had to be adjusted in recent years. This adjustment was necessary to meet the needs of those groups of people who have found themselves disadvantaged as far as sporting opportunities are concerned. Those who often find themselves at such a disadvantage are usually those who suffer from some kind of discrimination, e.g. because they are female, or have some form of disability.

20.1 Discrimination in sport

The population of Great Britain originally developed from four major racial groups: English, Irish, Scottish and Welsh. Over the last 50 years two other major ethnic groups have been added, namely those of Afro-Caribbean origin and those of Asian origin. These six major racial identities are each in turn influenced by a range of religious beliefs, including the Roman Catholic, Muslim and Protestant faiths. The sporting attitudes of these mixed racial/religious communities are also influenced by gender, age, regional location and tradition.

In effect, the main causes of discrimination in Britain can often be traced to one or more of the following:

- **race**
- **religion**
- **gender**
- **age**
- **tradition**

> **Examiner's tip**
>
> You can remember the main causes of discrimination in British sport by the mnemonic "G. Re. A. T. R." (greater) = Gender, Religion, Age, Tradition, Race.

Race

Sporting fixtures have traditionally been held between the four home countries (England, Scotland, Wales, Northern Ireland) for many years and these serve to emphasise local nationalistic pride. Many sports originally discriminated against people because of their country of birth. If you were born in England, you played for England – or you played for no one else. However, this attitude has now changed and many sports allow a person to 'choose' his or her nationality. The sportsperson can choose their own birthplace, that of one of their parents or one of their four grandparents. Some sports, such as professional cricket, now allow each home county to play up to two registered overseas players in their teams. Yorkshire cricket club, who for many years allowed only those born in Yorkshire to represent the county, now accepts overseas players in the team.

Professional soccer has recently had to change its attitude towards overseas players. In the past, clubs could field only a restricted number of foreign players, but as many players as they wanted from the home countries. In 1995 Bosnan, a Belgian footballer, was refused permission by his club to play for any other club. He took his case to the European court who ruled that no club could restrict a player's right to work as a professional player for any club within the European Community. Following the 'Bosnan' case, the European Community ruled that it was illegal to discriminate against the employment of football players because of their place of birth. Today, clubs can employ any players, born in any country.

Although there have been many changes of attitude by those running sport, it often seems that some racial groups continue to be overlooked. Overall, the number of black sportsmen and sportswomen who have achieved success in sports in this country has increased. However, the increase still does not reflect the total percentage of such groups within the country. Whether such sportspersons have been denied sporting opportunities because of their colour is open to question.

Religion

At first sight it would seem that sports have not suffered discrimination on religious grounds for many years. It is true that several of the top soccer clubs in Britain were originally founded as church boys' clubs. These were either Protestant or Roman Catholic clubs and would not accept players from the other faith. Examples of these are Everton and Liverpool, and Glasgow Rangers and Celtic. Today such discrimination has largely disappeared. Even the Irish Olympic boxing team is drawn from clubs from both Northern Ireland and Eire and includes boxers from all faiths.

However, women who follow the Muslim faith are still restricted in the sports in which they can participate. Their religion dictates their dress code, which in turn restricts participation in many sports, especially those that take place when men are present.

Gender

Traditionally, women have never had equality of opportunity with men in sport and to some extent this is evident today. In the past, decisions relating to women's sports were made mainly by men who thought that they were acting for the good of women. This encouraged the development of separate governing bodies of sport for women and thus an increase in sporting opportunities followed. This topic is looked at more fully in Unit 20.2.

Age

With the development of the modern welfare state it might be assumed that all age groups would be fully catered for. However, there is evidence to suggest that this is not so in Britain. Schools and youth clubs have always supplied sporting opportunities for the young but very often clubs are not available for post-school youth sport. This post-school 'gap' in sports participation was identified in the early 1960s but not enough was done immediately to fill it. The Sports Council felt the need to run the campaign *Ever Thought of Sport?* in 1985, aimed especially at the 13 to 24 age group to try to bridge the post-school sporting gap. This followed the successful 1983 campaign *Fifty Plus – all to play for* aimed at the older generation. (See Fig 20.1.) Both these campaigns and other initiatives have helped to bring about greater sports provision for all age groups in the community. Yet still some groups are poorly catered for. Older people and young mothers are often offered only off-peak opportunities whilst others can choose when they wish to play.

Fig. 20.1 The logo for the *Fifty Plus* campaign

Development and organisation of sport

Tradition

This has played a large part in the development of most sports in this country. Many sports were developed by more wealthy sportsmen and became the sports of the wealthy. Others developed into so-called 'working class' sports. Soccer, along with Rugby League, became identified with the working man. Rugby Union became associated with the upper classes and public schools. Cricket seems to have always drawn from all social groups whilst horse racing, known as 'the sport of kings', can only be participated in by the wealthy but has always been extremely popular with the working man as a spectator sport. Rowing, sailing, skiing, tennis and golf were all originally seen to be upper class sports. One reason for this may be that such sports require a fairly large financial outlay before they can be played. This barrier though is now being steadily broken down. The provision of facilities by local authorities and clubs and the steady rise in the standard of living of many people have brought many such sports within the reach of many more individuals.

20.2 Women in sport

To say that women have always been excluded from sport is not altogether correct. What is correct is that women have throughout time been given little opportunity to take part in sport and have rarely been able to compete alongside men on equal terms.

There is evidence to suggest that women took part in female-only games in ancient Greece at the same time as the original Olympic Games were being staged. These women-only games were held to celebrate the goddess Hera. Later, women-only games were held at Olympia, the home of the Olympic Games, and in Sparta around 500 BC. By 100 AD similar games were being held in many Greek towns and cities.

In the Middle Ages in Britain, upper class women were active in riding, hunting, tennis and archery. However, poor women were unfortunately tied to the home or were needed to work.

Traditionally there are four major reasons why sport for women did not develop as fast as that for men. These are:

- clothing
- class
- motherhood
- men

> **Examiner's tip**
> "CM CM" = Clothing and Motherhood, Class and Men (the major reasons why sports for women have developed slowly).

Clothing

Although there are many records of women taking part in a range of sports throughout the 19th century (see Table 20.1) many found it difficult to play because of the clothing they wore. Sportswear for women was very similar to everyday clothing. It was long and all-covering for the sake of respectability as well as fashion. (See Fig 20.2.)

Fig. 20.2 Ladies' hockey match 1893

The first real piece of women's clothing designed for a modern sport was the culotte style trousers pioneered by the American, Fanny Bloomer. These trousers, which became known as 'bloomers' were designed for cycling, a sport that was very popular with women from 1880 onwards.

The development of less restrictive and more suitable clothing continued into the 20th century. Skirts became progressively shorter, clothes much looser, and women were no longer expected to wear their whalebone corsets when they played sport. During World War I between 1914 and 1918, many women were needed to take on jobs previously done by men, so it became acceptable for them to wear trousers. Competitors at Wimbledon were the first to wear 'short' trousers in 1931, and at the same time many gave up the wearing of stockings in favour of the new style 'bobby sox'.

The changes in style of women's sports clothing continue to this day. These changes reflect not only the suitability of the clothes to the sports concerned, but also the fashion of the day. The 1980s saw a massive change in the design of leotards, tights and leggings. New fabrics and a whole range of colours were incorporated into their design and these clothes became popular as much for fashion as for their suitability for sport.

Today, women's sportswear is both fashionable and relevant to the event. Women enjoy being seen in the clothing, yet still find it suitable for their sport.

Class

The status of women in society has had considerable influence on the amount of sport that they have played. In the Middle Ages only the wealthy upper class woman had the time to play recreative sports. Middle class women were busy in the house and poorer women had to work in the fields alongside their men folk: they had little time for sport.

Later, in Queen Victoria's time, the fashion was for upper class girls to follow the royal lead and marry, having large families. Education for girls wasn't considered necessary until the end of the Victorian era, when the first girls' schools were founded, offering the daughters of the upper classes sports such as swimming, gymnastics, dancing and tennis. But sport still remained unavailable for most women, not only because it was considered 'improper' but also because they had little time and money. Poor women worked long hours in the mills and mines. Even the servants of the wealthy were expected to work long hours for very low wages.

The two World Wars brought about a radical change to the lives of many woman, both rich and poor alike. Many women worked in jobs previously done by men and proved that they could do them just as well. Later the improvement in post-war standards of living began to erode the huge gap between the lower and upper classes and more women found themselves able to participate in a whole range of sporting activities.

The development of a broader, more enlightened education system first introduced in 1944 meant that more and more women and girls from all groups in society were introduced to a range of sports. Today, sport is not the province of the wealthy. It is available at moderate rates to all. Now it is only at the highest levels of sporting competition that women tend to find themselves held back through lack of money. Prize money for women's events is still much lower than that of similar events for men, and sponsorship is not as easy to obtain for women as it is for men.

Motherhood

It has traditionally been the role of women to act as the homemaker and carer of the family. Women have always been expected to stay at home to look after children, aged parents and to act as the 'housewife'. For instance, even though the wealthy Victorian woman could afford to employ a housekeeper and servants, she spent most of her time supervising them. Women from poorer backgrounds had to combine having children with cooking, cleaning and often also working outside the home.

This traditional perceived role of women has persisted throughout a large part of the 20th century. It is only recently that it has been accepted that women can combine the role of motherhood with that of sports performer. Fanny Blankers-Koen won the 100m hurdles at the 1948 Olympics when she was the mother of two children and Mary Rand won gold in the long jump at the Tokyo Olympics shortly after giving birth to her daughter. There are now many women who successfully take part in top-flight sport while acting as both mother and wife. (See Pic 20.1.)

Picture 20.1 Women today play a wide range of sports, few can now be regarded as only 'men's sports'.

Men

There is no denying the fact that men have contributed most to the slow development of women's sport. It was as much men as women who promoted the idea that clothes worn by Victorian women should be 'respectable' rather than suitable for sport. Women have been poorly catered for in the Olympic Games mainly because men felt that most events were 'too strenuous for women'. Women were considered to be the weaker sex. In the 1928 Games held in Amsterdam, several women collapsed at the end of the 800m. Men thus decided that the event was too hard for women and should be withdrawn. It did not reappear on the Olympic programme until 1960. Women were not allowed to compete in the 400m until 1964, and the 1500m until 1972. The first women's marathon was not held until the Los Angeles Games of 1984.

Most governing bodies of team sports tended to exclude women. The Hockey Association, all male, refused to acknowledge the Ladies' Hockey Association when it was founded in 1895 and the Football Association refused to recognise the Women's Football Association (established in 1969) until 1993. Even today, boys and girls above the age of 11 are not allowed to play football together. Sports where men and women do compete on equal terms are the equestrian sports, show jumping and three day eventing. In these sports women have repeatedly proved that they are not only equal to but often better than their male counterparts.

Women in sport today

Despite the Sports Council's campaigns *Sport for All* started in 1972 and *Come Alive* in 1977, women do not seem to have obtained equal opportunity in sport. It's true that there are more opportunities than previously and still more are being promoted. The Sex Discrimination Act of 1975 allows women to go to court if they feel their rights are being abused in sport as well as in the workplace. However, this Act also makes the concession that:

"When the physical strength or stamina of the average woman puts her at a disadvantage to the average man – as a competitor – then discrimination can take place."

Unfortunately many sporting bodies use this clause to encourage the separate development of men's and women's sport. This separate development helps to promote the view that men's sport is better and worth more than women's sport. Male Wimbledon champions win far more in prize money than female champions. It also seems to promote far more opportunities for men than women to play professional sport.

It is perhaps somewhat ironic that men who are supposedly better at sport than women, have been instrumental in the development of sex tests for women competitors only. Women have to undergo a test to prove that they are women before they can compete in the Olympic Games, yet men do not have to prove that they are men!

Table 20.1 Early recorded dates of female sports participation

1591	painting of Queen Elizabeth I shooting with a cross bow
1714	Queen Anne involved in horse racing and introduced betting
1835	first recorded all-female cricket match
1874	first lady's bicycle produced with a side saddle
1885	first college founded to train women as PE teachers (first men's college did not open until 1933)
1886	the 'Original Ladies' Cricketers' formed: two professional ladies' teams that toured Britain giving exhibition matches
1887	first lady's bicycle built with lowered crossbar
1895	Ladies' 'South' football team established
1895	Ladies Hockey Association founded
1900	women allowed to compete in the Modern Olympic Games

20.3 The disabled and sport

Examiner's tip

Disabled people can play sport – be aware of changes that have been made to meet the needs of these athletes.

One of the underlying philosophies of all sporting activities today is that they should be available to all. This should include all those people with some form of disability. As a sub-group within society, disabled men and women can be classed as a minority group and have often in past years been identified as a low participation group. Disabled people often find it difficult to participate in sporting activities for a variety of reasons. Many are unemployed or work in low income jobs and thus have little disposable income to spend on sport. Many need the services of carer or friend to provide assistance in getting to and from activities or to assist them while they are playing their chosen sport. Many others lack the confidence to enter a sporting arena dominated by large numbers of able-bodied participants. Many venues for sports weren't initially equipped suitably for disabled access.

In an effort to counteract some of the problems faced by disabled people, the United Nations nominated 1981 as the International Year for Disabled People. The aim of this was to encourage the provision of extra facilities for disabled people in general and to make all people aware of the abilities of disabled people. It also hoped to promote an understanding of some of the problems regularly faced by disabled people. In this country the Sports Council added its own campaign to that of the United Nations. This campaign, *Sport for All – Disabled People*, had as its main aims:

- to make people aware of the needs of the disabled sportsperson
- to encourage the disabled to take part in sport
- to encourage the able-bodied to take part in sport with the disabled
- to ensure that disabled people enjoyed sport for its own sake.

Although the success of campaigns is often difficult to assess, one achievement noted was that more and more centres have, over the years, provided more specialist facilities for the disabled. Today, no centre should be without access ramps, lifts to all floors and suitable toilet and changing facilities. Many are also thoughtful enough to put notice boards at a conveniently lower level for wheelchair users.

The aims of this Sports Council campaign further developed the work done much earlier in Britain. In 1948 Sir Ludwig Guttman had founded the Stoke Mandeville Games for the paralysed. These Games took place on the day that the Olympic Games started in London and helped to show that sport was not just for the able-bodied. These Games have continued to develop over the years and are now held every four years in the same city as the Olympic Games. Usually these Games take place after those for the able-bodied, though in Barcelona in 1992 some events were included in the main programme of the Games themselves. At the recent Atlanta Games Britain's disabled competitors won many more medals than their able-bodied colleagues. However despite this success, it was the able-bodied competitors who got the bulk of the media coverage.

Development and organisation of sport

The British Disabled Sports Foundation places disabled competitors into two main groups for competition purposes. **S1** denotes those who are physically mobile, while **W1** denotes those who are confined to a wheelchair. Within these two main groups there are many sub-divisions so that differing degrees of mobility can be identified and activities can be more fairly competed in. Activities are categorised into three main groups for the disabled:

1. those in which competition is held on equal terms with the able-bodied — e.g. archery, bowls
2. those where the sport has been modified to suit a specific handicap — e.g. wheelchair basketball
3. those sports that have been specifically designed for disabled people — e.g. goal ball for the visually handicapped

Many disabled competitors still need some assistance during competition. Visually impaired athletes run attached by a short cord to a sighted runner and blind swimmers are allowed to use the lane markers to help them swim in a straight line. Assistants also use a stick to touch the blind swimmer as they approach the end of the pool so that they know when to turn and where the finish is.

Those who have watched disabled people playing sport either for recreation or for competition cannot deny that such participants enjoy the sport and play with a fine competitive edge. Indeed, the efforts seen in such events often seem greater than those seen in able-bodied competition. It is therefore surprising that little real recognition is given to the achievements of disabled sportspersons. Few people will remember the name of Neroli Fairhall from New Zealand. Neroli was confined to a wheelchair following a motor cycle accident in 1969. In 1982 she took part in the Commonwealth Games, against able-bodied competitors, and won the gold medal for archery. Although she shot from her wheelchair she had to conform to the same rules as all other entrants.

Today, many sports and leisure centres offer recreative classes designed for specific groups of disabled people. These are usually very well supported, not only by individuals but also by clubs. PHAB (Physically Handicapped and Able Bodied) clubs are run in many localities and aim to provide recreative activities that the disabled and able-bodied can play together. Many major events such as the London Marathon and the Great North Run integrate disabled with able-bodied competitors.

PRINCIPAL TOPICS COVERED

1. The main causes of discrimination in sport are: race, religion, gender, age and tradition.
2. The main reasons why sporting opportunities for women have not developed as fast as those for men are: clothing, class, motherhood and men.
3. The Sports Council has attempted to obtain equal opportunities in sport for women by running several national campaigns.
4. Many disabled people have been denied access to sporting opportunities.
5. Today, sporting facilities include special facilities to encourage disabled people to take part.

QUESTIONS ON THIS CHAPTER

1. Give two reasons why women are now taking part in physical activity.

2. What disadvantages do women have to overcome in order to take part in sport?

3. What was Sir Ludwig Guttman's contribution to sport for the disabled?

4. List three examples of discrimination in sport and suggest ways in which they might be countered.

5. Describe three ways in which sports centres have been adapted to make them more suitable for disabled visitors.

Chapter 21
Analytical investigation (for NEAB candidates only)

As part of the internally assessed coursework for the full Physical Education course, one board, the NEAB, requires candidates to submit an analytical investigation based on one or more of the activities contained in the scheme.

This piece of work is expected to be between 1500 and 3000 words in length, and candidates are not expected to exceed the upper limit. Although the length of the piece of work is defined by words, the Board encourages the inclusion of diagrams, photographs, graphs, audio recordings and video recordings. (If, however, a visual or audio recording is submitted it must be accompanied by a written commentary.)

The assessment of this investigation is based on four themes:

1. planning
2. implementation
3. analysis
4. evaluation

- The planning and implementation themes together can be awarded up to 20 marks.
- The analysis and evaluation themes can be awarded up to 20 marks each.
- These marks are added together and, when scaled, can contribute up to 20% towards the final grade awarded.

It is recommended that candidates make preparations for completing the analytical investigation part of their entry as soon as possible. As all coursework marks have to be submitted to the Board by the end of April in the year the examination is to be taken, it is essential that the analytical analysis is completed well before this time. If the investigation is completed early then it will allow more time for examination preparation and revision.

It is recommended that the topic to be studied in the investigation is chosen in consultation with your teacher so that he or she can watch over your progress and help you to avoid time-wasting mistakes.

A list of topics suitable for analytical investigation is published in the NEAB syllabus, but these are only samples. You can choose any topic that relates to the activities contained in the syllabus. Some further suggestions are made at the end of this chapter.

Remember:

your analytical investigation must be based on one or more of the physical activities listed in the syllabus.

Coursework (for NEAB candidates only)

General advice

① Choose the topic to be studied in conjunction with your teacher.

② Prepare an 'action plan' for yourself. Include in it all the things you are expecting to do, the order in which you intend to do them and a proposed time schedule.

③ Although your action plan will help you to complete the work, it can and should be altered to meet any unforeseen circumstances.

The following two topics, Investigation A and Investigation B, have been chosen as examples to show how the investigation might be tackled and presented.

21.1 Sample analytical investigations

Investigation A

To improve the chip shot in golf of three players.

Action Plan

TASKS	TO BE COMPLETED BY END OF WEEK
1. Find three golfers who are prepared to help you with your investigation.	1
2. Find a suitable course where you can conduct any testing and training.	1
3. Research into the shot to fully acquaint yourself with the skill of chipping in golf.	2
4. Design some tests that will relate to the chip shot.	3
5. Carry out the tests and analyse the chip shots of the three golfers.	3
6. Design a training programme that will improve the chipping ability of the golfers.	4
7. Complete the training programme.	7
8. Re-test the golfers.	8
9. Analyse the results obtained.	10
10. Write up your findings for submission.	10

Throughout the time that you are following your plan you should:

① keep a record or diary of all that you do

② keep a register of attendance for the three golfers whom you are training

③ keep a careful note of any test results

④ note any changes that you have had to make to your plan

⑤ take photographs throughout your testing and training. *Do not leave this job until last.* Also try to take two or three shots of each topic, to try to ensure that you obtain at least one good photograph.

As can be seen from the action plan, this investigation is scheduled to take 10 weeks. You could be 'rained off' for two or three sessions or your golfers might not be available every session. If this were to happen, then you would have to adjust your programme by either extending it or by condensing it.

Analytical investigation (for NEAB candidates only)

Investigation B

To improve the shotput of four athletes of different ages by using a weight training programme.

Action Plan

TASKS	TO BE COMPLETED BY END OF WEEK
1. Find four shotputters who are prepared to help you in your work by following weight training programmes devised by you.	1
2. Make sure that you can have the use of the necessary equipment so that your weight training programmes can be followed.	1
3. Research into weight training, taking advice from any source that can give help. You should consult weight training books, any shotput coaches you know and your teacher.	2
4. Test your shotputters and record the results.	3
5. Devise suitable training programmes for your shoputters and get them approved by your teacher.	4
6. Conduct the training programmes with your four shotputters.	4
7. Complete the training programmes and re-test your four shotputters.	8
8. Analyse the results you have obtained.	10
9. Write up your findings for submission.	10
NOTE: With this particular type of investigation: • you should make sure that you are using shot of the correct weight for your tests • you will probably see different rates of improvement that might well relate to the age of your shotputters.	

Throughout the time that you are following your plan you should:

① keep a record or diary of all that you do

② keep a register of attendance for the four shotputters whom you are training

③ keep a careful note of any test results

④ note any changes that you have had to make to your plan

⑤ take photographs throughout your testing and training. *Do not leave this job until last.* Also try to take two or three shots of each topic, to try to ensure that you obtain at least one good photograph.

As can be seen from the action plan, this investigation is scheduled to take 10 weeks. You could find that you cannot use your weights on a particular night or your shotputters might not be available every session. If this sort of situation were to arise you would have to either extend or condense your programme.

If investigations of the above type are followed it is best to try to start them at the beginning of a school term. Then, if you do find that you fall behind your schedule, you can use some of your holiday time to complete the writing up of your submission.

Coursework (for NEAB candidates only)

21.2 Presentation

The way you present your investigation is most important. You should aim to show all your hard work in a good light. When writing up your final submission you should include the following:

1. State the aim of your investigation and the broad outline of what you intended to do.

2. Report your research findings and explain the tests that you used.

3. Describe in detail your training programme. Do not forget to include suitable warm up activities as well as any skill practices. Record the length and location of each training session.

4. Describe your first testing session and record your results. Include any observations on your subjects that you think are important, such as their style or skill level.

5. Describe your training sessions in the order that you did them. It is a good idea to present each session one at a time, with the aim of each session clearly stated. Record any observations you have made about the progress, success or failure of the subjects at the end of each session.

6. Describe your second testing session and record your results.

7. Analyse and evaluate the results you have obtained. Explain why you think your subjects have improved or not as the case might be. If possible, include graphs to illustrate your results. Always try to relate your findings to your original aim and the observations you made during the first testing session. A good way to help illustrate your analysis is to prepare a 'player profile' for each of your subjects. Include a photograph of each along with their age, experience, test results and your observations.

8. The final section should include a short observation of how you feel the investigation has gone, identify any problems you discovered and how you overcame them.

9. Your last page should include a list of all the sources of information used, all the books and magazines you consulted and any other help you had to complete your work.

21.3 Suitable topics for investigation

The following broad areas of study are offered in addition to those specific topics suggested by the Board in its syllabus. These lists are neither prescriptive nor exhaustive. They are offered to help you choose a topic that you will find interesting and be able to follow with a degree of confidence.

Any form of fitness test related to a specific activity

With this type of topic you can choose a sport that you enjoy playing or have an interest in. You might also be able to use one or more of the tests that are listed in Chapter 12 of this book.

- You should test a number of players, fellow students, who play your sport on a given day.
- You should then get them to follow a selected training programme.
- You should then test them on completion of the training programme.
- You can then analyse the results of your tests.

Analytical investigation (for NEAB candidates only)

Any form of training programme related to a specific activity

With this type of topic you can choose a sport that you enjoy playing or have an interest in. You may have to find a skills test that relates to your sport or you can devise your own skills test.

- You should test a number of players, or fellow students who play your sport, on a given day, using your skills test.
- You should then get them to follow a selected training programme that relates to the skills you are trying to improve.
- You should then test them on completion of the training programme using the same test as before.
- You can then analyse the results of your tests.

Analysis of a game

This task demands that you choose a sport you know well. In this type of topic you would aim to find out if the skills of the players matched the requirements of the game (e.g. discovering if the fastest runners are playing in the positions that require the most speed).

- You would first have to analyse a game to see which positions require the fastest runners. These might be the wingers in rugby, the attacks in basketball or the strikers in football or hockey. They could be players in other positions. Your analysis would establish this.
- Your analysis would establish the distance over which a player is expected to be fastest: 10m, 20m, 50m etc.
- You would then test your school/college/club team to see who is fastest and what positions they normally play in.
- You can then analyse the results of your tests.

Coaching or teaching of the basic skills to relative newcomers to a sport

For this type of study you need not only a good knowledge of your chosen sport but also a supply of willing younger students.

- You would select the skills you wished to teach, work out a programme of lessons and make sure that your sports hall, gymnasium or playing field is available.
- You should then teach the programme of lessons which you have developed.
- Your final session should include some sort of assessment of your students. Your final analysis could be a pupil profile of each of your students, identifying their strengths, weaknesses and any improvement observed. Remember that your register of attendance for your teaching sessions could indicate why your students have or have not performed well.

Some of the difficulties with this type of study are:
- your students might prove unreliable in attendance
- you might not always be able to get the use of the gymnasium or playing fields when you want
- you should always have a member of staff present at all sessions: you might be taking the session, but technically they have to be 'in charge'.

Remember that although the way you present your Analytical Investigation will not necessarily gain you any extra marks, it should be done in such a way that it will not lose you any marks. If your handwriting is difficult for others to read, it might be better to produce your report on a word processor. This may take a little more time but it can be to your advantage. Your teacher and the external moderator will be able to read your submission easily and may well be impressed with your standard of presentation. A spell check is an added advantage.

Note: up to 3 extra marks can be awarded for good spelling, punctuation and grammar.

Whatever topic you choose to study, consult at regular intervals with your teacher or lecturer. Keep them informed of your progress and let them know if you are having any difficulties. They may well be able to help you to sort them out.

Chapter 22
Performance improvement programme (for NEAB candidates only)

As part of the internally assessed coursework for Physical Education (short course), one board, the NEAB, requires candidates to submit a report on a completed Performance Improvement Programme based on one activity. It is expected that the chosen activity will be one of those offered for assessment in the practical performance part of the examination.

This piece of work must be submitted on the Board's own printed form and is expected to show a candidate's ability to analyse and improve their own and others' performance.

The programme is internally assessed and 20 marks are awarded for each of the following sections:

1. analysis
2. planning and implementation
3. evaluation

The final mark is scaled and contributes up to 10% of the final grade awarded.

A list of topics suitable for your performance improvement programme are published in the NEAB syllabus, but these are only examples. You can choose any topic that relates to the activity you have chosen to be assessed in.

The following three activities, Activity A, Activity B and Activity C, have been chosen as examples to show how a topic might be tackled and presented.

22.1 Sample performance improvement programmes

ACTIVITY A: Shooting in hockey

Objective: To improve shooting accuracy over a distance of 14 metres.

Performance improvement programme (for NEAB candidates only)

SECTION ONE: Analysis of current performance

To carry out the analysis of the existing shooting accuracy I have set up the following test situation.

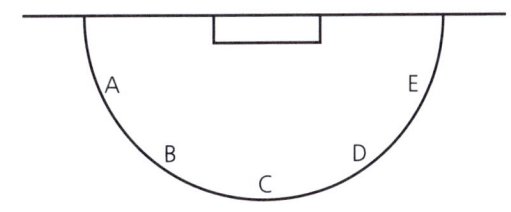

- 5 cones are placed evenly round the shooting circle and 1m inside the circle.
- From about 2m outside the circle Mary was asked to dribble approximately 3m and take a shot from one of the cones.
- She repeated this five times for each cone.
- I observed all her attempts.
- I recorded her accuracy.
- I made a note of any problem that she had.

Results:

CONE	SCORE
A	2
B	3
C	4
D	2
E	0

Observations:

- Mary had most difficulty scoring from the right side.
- Mary had some difficulty in controlling the ball as she dribbled into the shooting circle.
- Mary looked to see where the cone was before she took her shot.
- Mary did not look up to see where the goal was before she took her shot.
- Mary tried to shoot when the ball was too far away from her feet.

SECTION TWO: Performance Improvement Programme Implementation

The dribble — The ball should be fairly close to the feet and just in front and to the side of the feet.

The shot — The shot should be taken from fairly close to the feet on the right side.
Mary should look to see where the goal is every time before she shoots.

Programme:

1. I explained to Mary what I thought her problems were in shooting and dribbling.
2. Practice was given in dribbling technique. Emphasis was placed on close ball control and on telling Mary to keep looking up to see where she was going.
3. Mary was told to look at the goal every time before shooting.
4. Extra practice was given to the dribbling and shooting from the right hand side of the circle.
5. At the end of the training session I reminded Mary of the main points of the session.

The training session lasted for 30 minutes.

SECTION THREE: Analysis of performance after following programme

I used the same shooting set-up as before and recorded the results.

Coursework (for NEAB candidates only)

Results:

CONE	SCORE
A	2
B	4
C	5
D	4
E	2

Observations:

- Mary has improved her shooting overall.
- Mary has improved her shooting most of all from the right side of the circle.
- Mary has more control of the ball when she is dribbling.
- Mary looks to see where the goal is before she shoots.

SECTION FOUR: Evaluation of programme

- I think that the time spent telling Mary where she was making mistakes helped her to improve.
- I think that the time spent on the practice dribbling and shooting was effective.
- Mary's overall success rate went up from 11/25 to 17/25.
- If Mary were to practise this programme every week in training, her shooting would improve even more.

ACTIVITY B: Shooting in netball

Objective: To improve the shooting accuracy from the edge of the circle.

SECTION ONE: Analysis of current performance

To carry out the analysis of the existing accuracy I have set up following test.
Three cones are set just inside the shooting circle, one directly in front of the goal and one each at an angle of 45° from the goal.

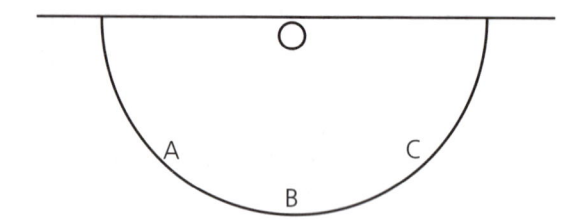

- Carol was asked to take 10 shots from each of the cones.
- I watched all of her attempts.
- I recorded her success rate.
- I made a note of any problem she had in shooting.

Results:

CONE	SCORE
A	3
B	3
C	2

Observations:

- Carol tended to shoot the ball from below her chin and from the side of her body.
- On most of the occasions that she did not score, I noticed that the ball did not reach the goal.
- On most occasions that she did not score, the ball was not thrown high enough to go in the goal.
- Carol tended to rush her shots.

156

Performance improvement programme (for NEAB candidates only)

SECTION TWO: Performance Improvement Programme Implementation

- When shooting, it would be better if Carol could shoot the ball from above shoulder height and from in front of her face.
- It would be better if Carol could practise shooting from closer to the goal until she is more accurate, and then move further out from the goal.
- It would be better if Carol were to look carefully at the goal before every shot.

Programme:

1. I explained to Carol where I felt she should shoot the ball from in relation to her shoulders and head.

2. I explained to her that I wanted her to practise shooting from very close to the goal, two paces from it, in line with the cone.

3. When she could get 3 out of 4 shots into the goal, she was to move a further step from the goal and practise again.

4. Carol should continue with this practice, moving back towards each cone in turn.

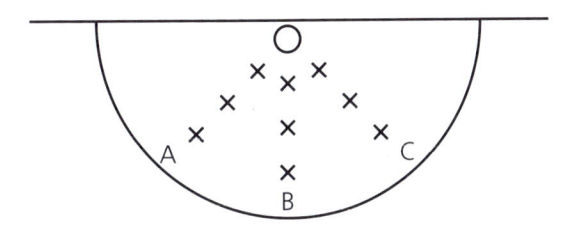

5. Carol was to think of looking carefully at the goal before each shot was taken.

6. At the end of the session I reminded Carol of the best way to hold the ball for shooting and to have a short pause before every shot.

Carol completed 3 training sessions, each lasting for 20 minutes.

SECTION THREE: Analysis of performance after following programme

I used the same shooting test as before and recorded Carol's scores.

Results:

CONE	SCORE
A	6
B	7
C	5

Observations:

- Carol has improved her accuracy at shooting from the edge of the circle.
- Carol has improved her style of shooting.
- Carol now looks carefully at the goal every time before she shoots.
- Carol is now able to reach the goal every time she shoots.

SECTION FOUR: Evaluation of programme

- I think that the time spent telling Carol how to shoot more effectively helped her to improve.
- Starting the shooting practice close to the goal gave Carol confidence.
- Carol's overall success rate went up from 8/30 to 19/30.
- Carol needs to spend a lot more time on this practice: a good shooter at netball should be able to get a success rate of 9/10 from anywhere in the circle.

Coursework (for NEAB candidates only)

ACTIVITY C Sprint starts

Objective: To use starting blocks correctly to improve speed over first 20m of a sprint race.

SECTION ONE: Analysis of current performance

- I observed Jack as he ran the first 20 metres of a sprint.
- I timed him over this distance 5 times with a suitable rest between races.
- I noted the position of his feet in the starting blocks before he started to sprint.
- I noted his body position when he was in the blocks before the race started.

Results:

Race 1	5.1 secs
Race 2	4.9 secs
Race 3	5.3 secs
Race 4	5.1 secs
Race 5	4.8 secs

Observations:

- Jack's average time for the 5 races was 5.04 secs
- Jack was looking down at the track between his hands when he was in the 'set' position.
- Jack seemed to be about to overbalance when he was in the 'set' position.
- Jack's feet were very close together when they were in the starting blocks.
- Jack's feet were very close to the start line when he was in the starting blocks.
- Jack said he felt squashed up when he was in the 'set' position in the starting blocks.

SECTION TWO: Performance Improvement Programme Implementation

The start

- The starting blocks needed to be further back from the start line.
- More space was needed between the front and rear starting blocks.
- Jack needed to lift up his head in the 'set' position and look down the track towards the finishing line.

Programme

1. I had a discussion with Jack to point out why he felt squashed up at the start of the race.
2. I explained to Jack that I would adjust the position of the starting blocks behind the start line and also the space between each block until he felt comfortable.
3. I adjusted the blocks during a 30 minute session, during which Jack tried the different settings until he found one in which he felt comfortable.
4. In a 10 minute session, Jack tried his sprint starts, practising looking down the track.
5. In a re-cap session, I reminded Jack of the position his head should be in during the 'set' part of the start.

SECTION THREE: Analysis of performance after following programme

- I retested Jack 5 times over a 20m sprint.

Performance improvement programme (for NEAB candidates only)

Results:

Race 1	4.7 secs
Race 2	4.4 secs
Race 3	4.6 secs
Race 4	4.6 secs
Race 5	4.2 secs

Observations:

- Jack's average speed for the 5 races was 4.5 secs.
- Jack did not seem as squashed up as before in the 'set' position.
- Jack was looking down the track in the 'set' position.
- Jack was not overbalancing in the 'set' position.
- All Jack's times have improved.

SECTION FOUR: Evaluation of programme

- I think that Jack has got faster because he is more comfortable in the starting blocks now and because he is more stable in the 'set' position.
- His average time for the 20m sprint has improved by 0.5 secs.
- I think that with more practice of his sprint starts, Jack should improve further.
- Although he is looking down the track better in the 'set' position, I think that Jack's overall body position needs to be studied in greater detail.

22.2 General advice

1. You should try to avoid having any spelling mistakes in your work: get someone to check this for you.

2. When deciding what kind of performance you want to improve, it is best if you can choose a skill that is easy to test on its own. Those skills that have to be tested in a game situation are harder to analyse.

3. Try to give yourself plenty of time to do the work. It is best if you can complete this part of your assessment a long time before you start your revision programme.

4. Check regularly with your teacher before you start and while you are doing the programme.

Chapter 23
Test yourself: questions

There now follows a series of questions, some of which are taken from past GCSE examination papers and others which have been prepared in a similar style.

The questions are divided into three groups to reflect the style of questions most commonly set. These are of three types:

- TYPE A: single, short-answer questions that require only a one- or two-word answer or the labelling of a diagram
- TYPE B: longer structured questions with an incline of difficulty. These often start with a simple short-answer question but go on to ask questions where longer, more detailed answers are required.
- TYPE C: open-ended questions that require an answer in the form of an essay.

It is useful to note that at the end of all examination questions asked a mark value is given. This is an indication of the number of facts or pieces of information required for that answer.

Examination papers often come in booklet form: space has to be given for the answer. This is provided by a number of lines on which you are expected to write your answer. The amount of space or number of lines is an indication of how much the examiners are expecting you to write. If you find that you are 'running out of space', especially for a type A or B question, then you might be trying to give too complicated an answer.

Type A and B questions require factual answers. Those that have an incline of difficulty might expect you to give several facts related to each other.

Try to be concise: you should be able to answer these types of questions in an uncomplicated way.

With the Type C questions it is often best to note all the points that spring to mind as soon as they occur to you after reading the question. This will help you to organise your thoughts before you start trying to write the essay type of answer. As you write your essay answer you can tick off or cross out the points as you include them.

The Type C questions are designed to test not only your factual knowledge, but also to allow you to show your skills of description, analysis, interpretation and evaluation. These are harder questions and consequently are worth the greater number of marks.

If you are not sure how much information to supply for this type of question, then give more rather than less.

Remember: If you give no answer, then you will gain no marks.

Questions Type A

		Board	Mark
1	Give another name for the kneecap.	NEAB 96	(1)
2	Name ONE bone in the chest.	NEAB 95	(1)
3	State ONE function of the skeleton.	NICCEA 96	(1)
4	Where in the body do you find the heart?	MEG 94	(1)
5	Where in the body would you find the scapula?		(1)
6	What carries blood away from the heart?		(1)
7	What do the initials CCPR stand for?		(1)
8	Name a sport that can be played by one or more players in teams.	MEG 94	(1)
9	What is an amateur sportsperson?	NEAB 95	(1)
10	Name a city that has hosted one of the last four Olympic Games.		(1)
11	Give TWO symptoms of shock.	NEAB 95	(2)
12	Name TWO organs protected by the chest.		(2)
13	Name TWO types of muscle found in the body.		(2)
14	The respiratory system deals with the exchange of TWO gases. Name them.	NEAB 95	(2)
15	What types of movement do the following sets of muscles bring about? Give ONE example for each. a) Flexors b) Extensors c) Adductors d) Abductors	SEG 93	 (2) (2) (2) (2)
16	Name in full the following organisations: a) IOC b) BOA	NEAB 96	(2)
17	Give TWO functions of the management committee of a sports club.	NEAB 95	(2)
18	Name TWO campaigns the National Sports Council has promoted.		(2)
19	State TWO of the main aims of the Sports Council.		(2)
20	Name TWO nutrients which fuel most of our energy needs.	SEG 92	(2)

Test yourself

Questions Type B

21

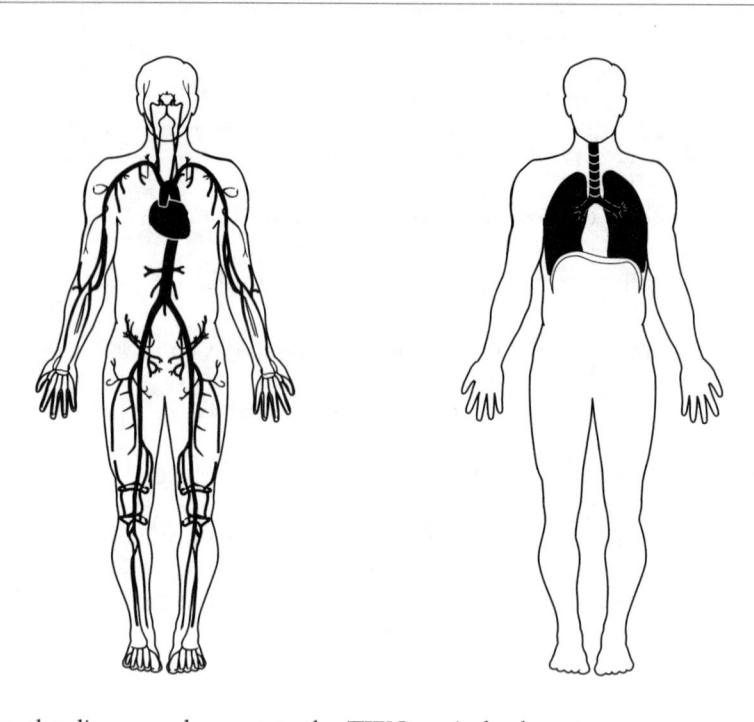

a) From the diagrams above, state the TWO main body systems. (2)
b) For the body systems, state the following:
   i)   THREE of the main organs and vessels of EACH system (6)
   ii) TWO disorders that can affect EACH of the body systems (2)
   iii) FIVE means by which the effectiveness of these body systems can be improved (5)
c) State the following:
   i) THREE reasons why it is necessary to maintain personal hygiene (3)
   ii) THREE ways in which hygiene can be maintained   *SEG 94* (3)

22 a) Name ONE of the regions of the vertebral column. (1)
b) Briefly describe a freely movable (synovial) joint. (1)
c) Write down the numbers 1 to 4 on your answer paper and name the muscles indicated by these numbers on the following diagram. (4)

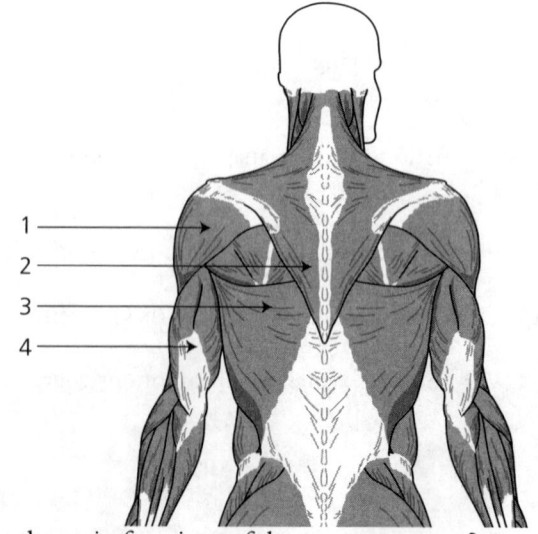

d) What are the main functions of the nervous system? (5)
e) How does the heart operate in order to move blood around the body?   *MEG 94* (8)

23

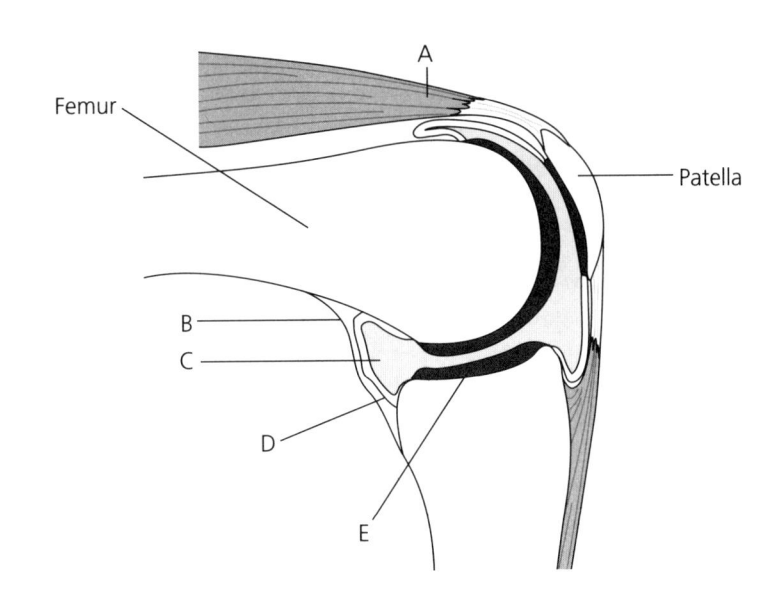

[Diagram of the knee joint showing Femur, Patella, and labels A, B, C, D, E]

a) The diagram above shows the knee joint. Name the parts labelled A – E from the diagram. *(5)*
b) Excluding the knee joint, name THREE other types of joint and give ONE example of each. *SEG 92* *(6)*

24 a) What is meant by the word 'stamina'? *(1)*
b) What external factors occurring during physical activities could cause injury? *(2)*
c) Write down FOUR effects that hard exercise has on muscles. *(4)*
d) i) What does 'principal of overload' mean? *(1)*
   ii) Relate your answer to activities of your choice. *(4)*
e) The Harvard Step Test is a well known measurement of fitness. Explain fully:
   i) the organisation of the test *(2)*
   ii) the theory behind the test *(3)*
   iii) the interpretation of data collected from the results of carrying out the test *MEG 94* *(3)*

25 a) Flexibility is important for performers.
   i) State THREE reasons why it is important, giving ONE example for EACH from a sporting situation. *(6)* *(4)*
   ii) Describe a test designed to test flexibility in the lower limbs. *(2)*
b) State the relationship between flexibility and:
   i) age *(2)*
   ii) strength *(2)*
c) Define what is meant by strength. *(3)*
d) How can strength be improved through:
   i) overload *(2)*
   ii) progression? *SEG 94* *(2)*

26 a) What component of fitness would you be testing if you used a hand-grip dynamometer? *(1)*
b) Give TWO ways of monitoring the condition of the heart. *(2)*
c) Give THREE exercises which show muscular stamina in the upper body. *(3)*
d) What factors would you take into consideration when deciding upon a method of training? *(4)*
e) How can weight training be used to improve physical fitness? Give examples to illustrate your answer. *NEAB 94* *(5)*

27 a) Give another name for cardiovascular fitness. *(1)*
b) Give TWO reasons why swimming is a good way to keep fit. *(2)*
c) State THREE important principles of training. *(3)*
d) What are the factors that can affect physical fitness? *(4)*

Test yourself

  e) Choose a competitive physical activity and describe how a training programme could change throughout the year.   NEAB 93   (5)

28 a) Name ONE type of skill that is common to both netball and basketball. (1)
  b) What is meant by the word 'skill'? (2)
  c) Consider any ball game. What problems can a player, who lacks skill, experience during a full game? (4)
  d) Give FIVE factors that can limit the level of skill a person can reach in sport. (5)
  e) Copy this information processing diagram on to your answer paper, fill in the boxes and describe the skill learning process.   MEG 94   (8)

[Diagram: INPUT → [ ] → [ ], with feedback loop from a box below back to INPUT]

29 a) What was the purpose of the campaign *50+ All to Play For*? (1)
  b) Give TWO reasons why some physical activities tend to be associated with older people. (2)
  c) Give THREE social reasons why fewer teenage girls take part in sport than teenage boys. (3)
  d) What has been done to help increase participation in sport for people with disabilities? (4)
  e) Spectators are an important part of sport. How might crowd behaviour affect the performer?   NEAB 95   (5)

30 a) What do the initials NCF stand for? (1)
  b) Give TWO examples of how the police can help in the organisation of a sports event. (2)
  c) Briefly describe the representative honours a promising 400m runner might achieve on the way to becoming an international athlete. (4)
  d) What advantages are there for sport in this country as a result of the Olympic bids? (5)
  e) i) What is sponsorship? (1)
    ii) Explain how sponsorship can help both an individual sports person AND a National Governing Body of Sport.   MEG 94   (7)

31 a) Give ONE advantage of radio coverage of sport. (1)
  b) State TWO main purposes of the CCPR. (2)
  c) Name FOUR different facilities that are available for physical activities in your area. (4)
  d) Describe the possible impact of satellite TV on sport in this country. (5)
  e) Name TWO Sports Council campaigns that have promoted participation in sport and give reasons why they were introduced.   MEG 94   (8)

32 a) Name a physical activity played by females. (1)
  b) Give TWO Sports Council campaigns which aimed at increasing sports participation in physical activities. (2)
  c) State THREE reasons why fewer women than men take part in physical activities. (3)
  d) What benefits can people gain from playing team activities? (4)
  e) Why do some sports performers become famous sports 'stars'?   NEAB 93   (5)

33 a) State ONE national venue, naming the sport played there. (2)
   b) Facilities are vitally important for the provision of sport.
   Answer the following:
   i) Where should they be located? (2)
   ii) Who could have ownership or control? (2)
   iii) State TWO developments which could be made and the benefits they would bring about. *SEG 94* (4)

Questions Type C

34 State the advice you should give to the people who are overweight on how to lose fat. *NICCEA 96* (8)

35 As someone who is in charge of a *Fit for Life* campaign, state the arguments you should use to convince people of the benefits of exercise. *NICCEA 96* (10)

36 a) What are the main benefits of training? (5)
   b) Name ONE physical activity and state what method of training would be most beneficial. Give examples of the intended outcomes and progression which would be built into the training programme. (10)
   c) What do you understand by the term 'match fit'? In your answer, refer to BOTH general and specific fitness. *SEG 94* (10)

37 Look at the illustrations below.
   The Sports Council was launched in 1972 to replace the Central Council for Physical Recreation as a focus for sports issues. Outline the structure and functions of the Sports Council. Pay particular attention to the part played by 'campaigns'. *NEAB 94* (15)

SPORTS COUNCIL

TARGET
320,00 more Teenagers & under-24s by 1987

TARGET
Refurbish 200 pools by 1987

Sportify the Over 45s!

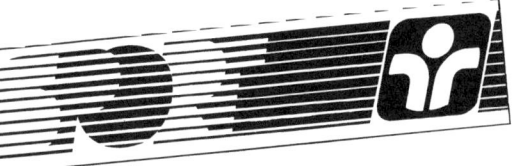

Test yourself

38 Look at the illustration below.
Select ONE of the following areas of physical activity: athletics; dance; games; gymnastics; outdoor pursuits; swimming.

Be a sport!

	Boys	Girls
Athletics	37.1	33.3
Basketball	12.7	4.5
Dancing	4.9	31.5
Football	72.0	14.5
Gymnastics	5.0	16.3
Hockey	6.5	3.5
Judo	16.0	6.7
Netball	3.3	35.0
Riding a bicycle	71.7	60.5
Roller-skating	7.3	26.0
Rugby	11.8	2.5
Swimming	53.1	55.0
Play no sports	3.8	5.8

Which sport do you play outside lesson time, and how often?

Percentage of 10 to 11 year-olds answering "once a week" or "more than once a week".

Outline the physical and social attractions and benefits for young people. NEAB 95 (15)

39 The relationship between the media and sponsorship of sport is a close one. Is there now a very thin line between assistance and interference in televised sport? Give examples to illustrate your answers. SEG 94 (15)

Chapter 24
Test yourself: answers

Please note that the answers which follow are the author's only and that the various examining groups accept no responsibility for the methods or accuracy of working in the answers given.

Answers Type A

1 patella

2 Choice of:
- sternum (breast bone)
- ribs
- clavicle (collar bone)

3 Choice of:
- support
- protection
- blood production
- movement

4 Choice of:
- between the lungs
- behind the sternum

   Note: 'in the chest' is not sufficiently specific

5 upper back between shoulder and spine (known as shoulder blade)

6 arteries

7 Central Council for Physical Recreation

8 Choice of:
- badminton
- tennis
- table tennis
- golf

9 Choice of:
- someone who does not get paid for playing
- someone who plays the game as a hobby
- someone who does not play for a living

Test yourself

10 Choice of:
- Atlanta
- Barcelona
- Seoul
- Los Angeles

11 Choice of TWO from:
- vomiting
- rapid, weak pulse rate
- shallow breathing
- cold with clammy skin
- thirsty
- dilated pupils
- confusion

12 heart and lungs

13 Choice of two from:
- smooth or involuntary
- skeletal or voluntary or striated or striped
- cardiac

14 oxygen and carbon dioxide

15 a) closing of joint - e.g. bending arm

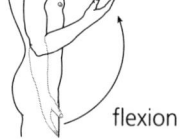

flexion

b) opening of joint - e.g. straightening of of elbow

extension

c) movement towards body - e.g. lowering of arm

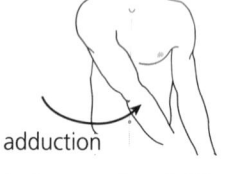

adduction

d) movement away from the body - e.g. raising of arm

abduction

16 a) International Olympic Committee
b) British Olympic Association

17 Choice of any TWO which explain how they run the club:
- represent members
- take decisions
- select teams
- raise money
- organise events
- arrange fixtures

18 Choice of TWO from:
- *Ever Thought of Sport?*
- *What's Your Sport?*
- *50+ All to Play For*
- *Sport for All – Disabled Sport*
- *Sportify the Over 45s!*

19 Choice of TWO from:
- ensure that all young people have the opportunity to acquire basic sports skills and physical education
- ensure that all adults have the opportunity to take part in the sport of their choice
- ensure that everyone has the opportunity to improve their standard in sport

- ensure that everyone has the opportunity to reach their highest standard in sport
- protect and develop the moral and ethical basis of sport, the human dignity of those involved in sport, and safeguard sports men and women from political, commercial and financial exploitation and from the debasing of sport through drug abuse

20 Carbohydrate and fat

Answers Type B

21 (a) circulatory system and respiratory system
   (b) i) - heart, arteries, veins
         - THREE from: lungs, diaphragm, trachea, bronchioles, alveoli, intercostal muscles
       ii) Four from:
         - increased cholesterol levels
         - heart attacks
         - thrombosis
         - cancers
         - pneumonia
         - tuberculosis
         - smoking related disorders
       iii) FIVE from:
         - increased stamina/endurance work
         - correct balanced diet
         - strengthening of abdominal and intercostal muscles
         - avoid smoking and pollutants
         - regular exercise
         - healthy lifestyle
         - avoid obesity
         - low cholesterol levels
   c) i) THREE from:
         - to keep clean
         - to keep healthy
         - to keep clear of disease
         - to avoid unpleasant body odours
      ii) THREE from:
         - skin care by regular washing/showering
         - regular cleaning of hair and teeth to avoid disease and decay
         - particular care of feet; nail cutting
         - regular change of clothing to clean clothing
         - regular washing of arm pits and genital area

SEG 94

22 a) ONE from:
      cervical, thoracic, lumbar sacrum, coccyx
   b) TWO from:
      - they all have a layer of tough, smooth cartilage covering the ends of bones
      - there is synovial fluid within a membrane that helps to give friction-free movement
      - the bones are held together by ligaments
   c) Muscles are: 1) deltoid   2) trapezius   3) latissimus dorsi   4) triceps
   d) Any FIVE from:
      - receive sensations from within the body
      - receive sensations from outside the body
      - act upon stimuli - automatically
      - act upon stimuli - after thought
      - store information for later use
      - pass messages to different parts of the body

Test yourself

- control the normal functions of the body
e) Blood pumped from left ventricle of heart through aorta
through the systemic system (around the body)
to the major organs of the body (brain, stomach, etc.)
through the capillaries into the veins to right atrium of heart
from right ventricle around pulmonary system (lungs)

Note: a suitable diagram would be as follows:

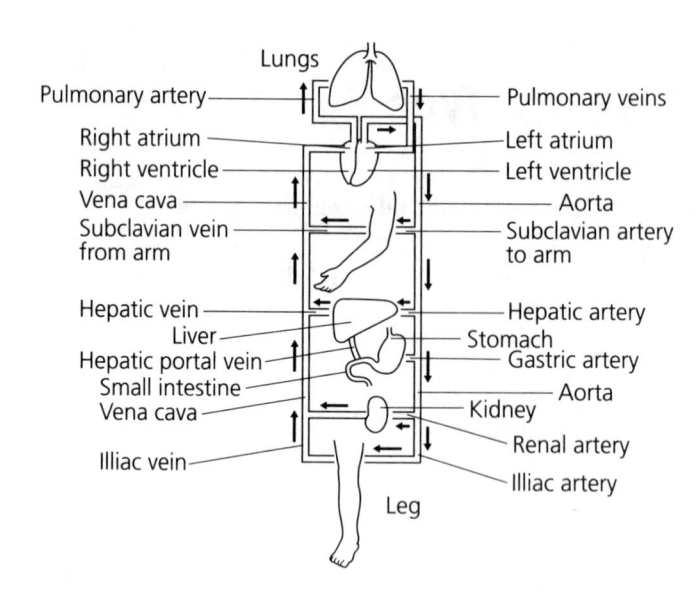

[Diagram of circulatory system with labels: Lungs, Pulmonary artery, Pulmonary veins, Right atrium, Left atrium, Right ventricle, Left ventricle, Vena cava, Aorta, Subclavian vein from arm, Subclavian artery to arm, Hepatic vein, Hepatic artery, Liver, Stomach, Hepatic portal vein, Gastric artery, Small intestine, Aorta, Vena cava, Kidney, Illiac vein, Renal artery, Illiac artery, Leg]

MEG 94

23 a) A = tendon from quadriceps muscle
B = ligament
C = synovial fluid
D = synovial membrane
E = articular cartilage
b) Any three from:

- ball and socket	hip joint
- saddle	base of thumb
- condyloid	wrist
- pivot	neck
- slightly movable	spine (vertebrae)
- immovable	skull (cranium)

SEG 92

24 a) the ability to exercise the whole body for long periods of time
OR
the ability to play a sport for a long period of time
b) Any TWO from:
- weather
- playing surface
- unsuitable clothing
- sub-standard equipment
- contact with another player
c) Any FOUR from:
- makes muscles stronger
- muscles become warm and ache
- produce more waste products such as lactic acid, HO_2, CO
- need more oxygen
- blood capillaries are enlarged
- muscle tone is improved
d) i) improving the body systems by making them work harder
ii) any FOUR from:
- means we need to work harder
- this extra demand is known as stress

Test yourself: answers

- aerobic ability, muscular strength and endurance can be improved by placing them under increased stress
- flexibility can be increased in the same way
- the intensity of the exercises can be increased
- the frequency of the exercises can be increased
- any increase in the stress situation is working in the overload principle
- hard training sessions should be interspersed with light training sessions to help tissue recovery

e) i)
- subject stands facing block 40/45 cm high, steps on and off it for 5 mins at rate of 30 steps per min.
- at end of exercise subject sits down and has pulse taken after 1 min, 2 min, 3 min rest

ii)
- is a test of cardiovascular fitness
- based on theory that a fit person will show a smaller increase in heart rate during exercise
- and that a fit person's heart rate will return to normal faster than that of an unfit person

iii)
- approximate scores of 90+ = really fit; 65+ = average fitness; 50 or less = poor fitness
- individual score is calculated by:
multiply length of exercise in seconds by 100
then divide by 2 times the sum of pulse counts
- the score obtained can be compared with established published norms

MEG 94

25 a) i) Any THREE from:
- flexibility exercises in warm up loosens muscles e.g. prevents muscle tears
- flexibility exercises increase range of movement e.g. stride length of sprinter
- greater flexibility means less likely to overstretch e.g. lunging in fencing
- flexibility exercises train muscles to work together in groups to help create skilful movements e.g. gymnastic activities

ii) sit and reach test
Subject sits with legs straight in front and feet flat (against marker). Subject then reaches as far forward as possible along calibrated slide. Legs are kept straight at all times.

b) i) Flexibility decreases with age. Also as muscle size increases at age 14/16 flexibility decreases unless exercises maintained.
ii) Strength training increases muscle bulk which decreases flexibility.

c) The ability of a <u>muscle</u> to <u>apply force</u> and <u>overcome resistance</u>. *Each underlined part is worth 1 point.*

d) i) Muscles become stronger if they are worked harder than they are used to working. This can be achieved by increasing the intensity or duration of an exercise.
ii) Overload must be increased progressively to allow the muscles to adapt gradually to the extra stresses being applied.

SEG 94

26 a) strength
b) Any TWO from:
- heart monitor machine
- blood test
- Harvard Step Test
- taking ECG
- taking pulse rate
- taking X rays

Test yourself

          – taking blood pressure
- c) *Note: Exercises are asked for, not activities.*
  Any THREE from:
  - dips
  - pull-ups
  - exercises with weights (not weight lifting)
  - sit-ups
  - chins
- d) Any FOUR from:
  - suitability for purpose relating to activity
  - suitability relating to needs of performer
  - must satisfy principles of training
  - availability
  - cost
  - time
  - equipment
  - safety
  - supervision necessary
  - age
  - sex
  - body type
  - state of health
- e) Weight training can improve fitness in terms of:
  muscle strength, muscle power, muscular endurance, some cardio-vascular endurance.
  Programme to show varying load in relation to number of repetitions and sets.
      e.g. for strength: high load, low reps, long recovery
          for stamina: low load, high reps, shorter recovery
  Note: Examples should show appropriate loads to activities.

NEAB 94

27 a) stamina or endurance or aerobic
    b) Any TWO from:
- good for mobility
- good for strength
- good for power
- good for local and general stamina
- good for all-round body conditioning
- good for recovery from injury
- relaxing exercise

    c) Any THREE from:
- overload
- intensity
- duration
- frequency
- progression
- specificity
- reversibility

    d) Any FOUR from:
- age
- sex
- metabolism
- body type
- injury
- diet
- environment
- altitude
- lifestyle
- smoking
- drinking

Test yourself: answers

   e) Must choose a competitive activity.
   - Programme must reflect time of year: close season, pre-season, season, peak
   - Training should: vary from light to intense, from gaining fitness to keeping fitness, switch from fitness to technique to tuning

NEAB 93

28 a) Choose from:
passing and catching, intercepting a catch, shooting into a ring, marking and dodging
   b) A skill is a learned response that brings about a predetermined result with maximum certainty, often with minimum outlay of time and energy.
   c) Any FOUR from:
   - *unskilful players* keep the ball to themselves
   - *unskilful players* are often self-conscious
   - *unskilful players* are not always in the right place at the right time
   - need to work harder than a skilful player
   - are more prone to injury
   - waste energy and tire sooner
   - are more likely to upset other players
   - are more likely to slow down a move
   d) Any FIVE from:
   - physique
   - age
   - sex
   - ability
   - mental approach
   - social development
   - time available for practice
   - facilities available
   - quality of teaching
   - motivation
   - disability
   - correct equipment available
   - fitness
   e) 1 mark for each of the following in the correct box:
   decision making ⟶ output
   ⟵ feedback ⟵
   and, 5 further marks for any FIVE of the following:
   - input is receiving information from hearing, seeing, feeling
   - this results in the decision making process taking place
   - the performer decides what to do
   - this results in the output which is the performance of a skill
   - the decision reached is based upon all the information received
   - feedback provides further information on the results of the action taken which is fed back into the process

MEG 94

29 a) to increase the number of older people taking part in physical activities
   b) Any TWO from:
   - more leisure time available
   - gentler sport
   - less chance of injury
   - less aggressive
   - less physical
   - slower pace
   - more sociable
   c) Any THREE from:

Test yourself

          – religion
          – culture
          – tradition
          – it is what girls don't do
          – fewer activities available
          – fewer activities to suit girls
          – pregnancy
          – girls have other outside interests

    d) – 1981 was nominated International Year for Disabled People
        – the Sports Council ran a *Sport for All – Disabled People* campaign
        – in 1948 Sir Ludwig Guttman founded the Stoke Mandeville Games for the paralysed
        – the British Disabled Sports Foundation encourages disabled sports competitions
        – many sports and leisure centres run recreative classes for specific groups of disabled people
        – PHAB clubs are run in many localities
        – major events such as the London Marathon integrate disabled with able-bodied competitors

    e) Noise, quietness and gestures affect players in different ways:
- encourage; motivate; inspire; help concentration; help players relax; support; give sense of well-being
- distract; pressurise; scare; isolate; force mistakes; frighten; break concentration

NEAB 95

30 a) National Coaching Foundation
    b) Any TWO from:
        – segregate supporters
        – ensure safety in ground or centre
        – control crowds queuing or outside
        – control crowds in ground
        – traffic control
        – liaise with officials
        – provide escort duties

    c) Any FOUR from:
        – progression through school teams:
        – school team
        – district team
        – county team
        – regional representation
        – National Championships
        – Junior International Squads
        – progression through club teams:
        – junior club representation
        – higher club team representation
        – county representation

    d) Any FIVE from:
        – increased financial support from central government
        – increased financial support from industry
        – improved facilities
        – new facilities built
        – greater awareness generated among performers and spectators
        – increased participation rated
        – inner city regeneration based on sport
        – improved transport system
        – range of sports associations join together to present a united front
        – standards in sports raised

    e) i) Financial or other support given by a company, person or business to an individual, team or sport in order to gain publicity

       ii)
- Individual benefits: kit supplied, accommodation and entrance fees paid, direct payment, coaching fees paid, travel costs met, better facilities and equipment paid for, can concentrate on training alone.
- Governing body benefits: operate coaching schemes, pay for advertising, can

Test yourself: answers

give monies to local clubs, can provide better facilities, can pay for top class coaches, can organise better competitions with better 'prizes' to attract better opposition

MEG 94

31 a) ONE from:
cheap, live, can be listened to anywhere, can sound exciting, broadcast from all round the world, hosted by stars, ideal for blind

b) TWO from:
- encourage people to take part in sport
- improve and develop sport in this country
- act as centre of debate for governing bodies
- pass on views of NGB to Sports Councils

c) Any FOUR from:
- local parks
- leisure centres
- waterways
- National Parks
- health centres
- swimming pools
- amateur sports teams
- private sports clubs

d) FIVE comments from:
- increase in live coverage of sports from all round the world
- make people more aware of different sports
- may lead to increased participation
- may discourage live spectatorism
- may lead to loss of income to sports clubs
- may improve sponsorship deals
- may change rules of sports
- only major clubs in demand so gulf between rich and poor enlarged
- increase awareness of women in sports

e) TWO from:

Campaign	Target group
Sport for All	All potential users
Women in Action/Milk in Action for Women	Women
50+ All to Play For	Men and women 50+
What's Your Sport?	Young, unemployed, women, disabled
Ever Thought of Sport?	13/24 year olds
Sport for All - Disabled People	Disabled people

Sport for All was the first ever campaign launched. Main objectives were:
- to influence opinion about the value of sport in society
- to increase participation in sport
- to promote sport

Sport for All was not specifically aimed at improving fitness.

Other campaigns aimed at:
- improving and extending existing facilities
- making better use of facilities
- encouraging spectators to become players
- encouraging those who have left school to take part
- specific groups who were not taking part in sport

Note: You will need to describe the group your chosen campaign was aimed at and be able to describe why this was necessary.

MEG 94

32 a) ONE from:
netball, synchronised swimming, rhythmic gymnastics, aerobics

b) Any TWO from:

Test yourself

       - *What's Your Sport?*
       - *Women in Sport*
       - *What's on for Women/She's got It*
       - *Sport for All*
       - *Ever Thought of Sport?*
       - *1991 Year of Sport*

  c) Any THREE along the lines of:
      - they have not been encouraged - no history
      - stigma of not being feminine to play sport
      - traditional role of woman as housewife and mother
      - not allowed to play certain sports e.g. snooker
      - no sessions or events organised for women
      - most of top administrators are men

  d) Any FOUR from:
      - any benefits of fitness
      - development of character qualities such as loyalty, co-operation, reliability, interdependence
      - socialising factors such as making friends, meeting friends, talking, having fun, team work
      - performance factors such as playing at a higher standard, improving own quality of play

  e) Any FIVE from:
      - remembered for good and bad reasons
      - outstanding quality, success, entertaining
      - style of personality - good looking for media
      - 'off field' exploits - records, sponsored walks
      - novelty of background come from
      - being in the 'fashion'
      - belonging to high profile club
      - levels of sportsmanship
      - commitment and dedication
      - using position to support 'good causes'

NEAB 93

Answers Type C

33 a) *1 mark for the venue and 1 mark for the correct sport*
     e.g. Twickenham - Rugby Union
           Wembley   - soccer
           Lords   - cricket

  b) i) Any TWO from:
        - close to centre of population
        - where there is easy access
        - good public transport system
        - good parking

     ii) both Private Sector (sports clubs and organisations) and Public Sector (local authorities) must be mentioned

     iii) Any TWO suitable developments including the benefits they bring
        e.g. indoor tennis courts for all year round play
            covered training areas for all year round practice
            indoor jumping pits for all weather practice

SEG 94

34 *Note: To gain full marks you must show that you have a good understanding of the principles which apply when aiming to achieve a safe weight reduction.*
A person should:
- seek advice from a dietician
- go on a calorie controlled diet
- not go on a low calorie controlled diet i.e. one of less than 1000 calories
- look at their present diet with a view to cutting back on fatty foods

Test yourself: answers

- avoid frying foods; whenever possible, poach or boil
- limit the amount of sugar in the diet
- limit the amount of alcohol in the diet
- eat complex carbohydrates where possible
- eat foods high in fibre
- increase their daily exercise; include where possible aerobic endurance exercise

NICCEA 96

35 *Note: To gain full marks you should show that you have a good understanding of the benefits of exercise. You should include in your answer as much of the following as possible.*
Through exercise:
- you will be able to continue with hard physical exercise for a long period of time
- you will get stronger and find things easier to do
- you will become more flexible
- you will be able to control your weight better
- you will be able to delay the ageing process
- you will be able to look good and feel good
- you will find that you can sleep better
- you will find that you are less likely to succumb to illnesses
- you will find that you will recover more quickly from injury
- you will find that you can combat the bad habits of smoking, drinking and taking drugs
- you will enjoy yourself

NICCEA 96

36 a) Training improves the following:
strength, stamina/endurance, suppleness/flexibility, co-ordination, cardio-vascular fitness, cardio-respiratory fitness, power, performance, motivation, technique, appearance, social factors, tactics and set plays
Note: Up to five marks are awarded for this section. Your answer could be in the form of a list. You would be expected to include at least 5 of the above.

b) A physical activity and method of training must be stated. Acceptable methods include: continuous, fartleck, repetition, interval, sprint in conjunction with interval sprinting and shuttle runs, circuit, weight
Up to 4 marks are awarded for a named activity together with a suitable training method.
Up to 2 marks are awarded if you state the intended outcome of your chosen method.
Up to 4 marks are awarded if you show that progression is built into your programme.

c) This is a general term relating to the ability to participate fully in a game or a chosen physical activity to a high standard. Usually this is achieved through regular match play or participation.
Up to 2 marks are awarded for a suitable definition of 'match fit'.
Up to 4 marks if you relate your definition to general fitness.
Up to 4 marks if you relate your definition to specific fitness.

SEG 94

37 This question is best answered in three separate parts.

Part 1 Structure:
- it is an advisory body on sport
- it advises both central government and the NGB of sport
- it is run by a committee of invited members and professional officers
- this committee is based in London
- there are 10 regional Sports Councils in England
- there are 5 national Sports Councils, one for each of the home countries and one for the whole of GB

Part 2 Functions (five main aims)
- ensure all young people have the opportunity to acquire basic sports skills and receive physical education
- ensure the adult population has the opportunity to take part in the sport of their choice
- ensure that everybody has the opportunity to improve their personal standard in sport
- ensure that everybody has the opportunity to reach their highest standard of sporting excellence

Test yourself

- protect and develop the moral and ethical basis of sport by safeguarding sportsmen and women from political, commercial and financial exploitation, and from the debasing of sport by drug abuse and at a national level:
- run their respective national sports centres
- liaise with the governing bodies of sports
- raise additional finance for sport

Part 3 Campaigns:
The aims of the Sports Council have been promoted through the many campaigns that it has run. For each campaign that you list, you must be able to include the target group in order to get a mark. If you can, include the date of the campaign.

72	*Sport for All*	all ages
75/6	*Sport for all the Family*	all ages
79	*Sport for All - Come Alive*	all ages
82	*Sport for All - Disabled*	disabled
83/4	*50+ All to Play For*	over 50s
85/6	*Ever Thought of Sport*	13/24 yr olds
87/8	*What's Your Sport?*	all ages and women
89	*Milk in Action for Women*	women
89	*She's got It - Get It*	women

NEAB 94

38 *To gain full marks when answering this question both the physical and social aspects must be covered.*

All the activity groups will reflect many of the following attractions and benefits. An activity may:
- suit different character traits, e.g. play alone or with a partner, contact or non-contact, aesthetic or dangerous
- allow for the acquisition of skill, knowledge and physical fitness
- provide enjoyment, thrills
- suit the abilities of the participants
- provide for a sense of fulfilment, success
- allow individuals to meet new people and make new friends
- fit in with the amount of time a person has available
- provide opportunities for travel
- be cheap to do
- have facilities easily available
- be easy to learn
- require only the minimum of equipment
- help to build character
- keep people off the streets and out of trouble

NEAB 95

39 *It is important to refer to both assistance and interference when this question is answered.*

Your answer should include as many as possible of the following examples:
- promotion of existing sport, increased prize money and participation
- more exposure and promotion of minority sports, thereby raising their profits
- the timing of events may be dictated by the sponsors
- rules may be changed to accommodate easier TV scheduling, e.g. half time periods extended so that TV can give an up-date on another sport
- some events or sports will get saturation coverage
- some sports/teams will encourage a 'win at all costs' approach so that they can retain media interest
- media may wish to decide what is acceptable sponsorship, e.g. refuse to cover events with high profile tobacco or drinks sponsorship
- participants are put under greater pressure to perform 'to order', e.g. when TV coverage is live
- standards may be being raised by increased interest and support

SEG 94

Note: All examination boards give extra marks for correct spelling, punctuation and grammar. These marks are awarded over and above those given for factual information. All answers to Type B and Type C questions contribute towards these extra marks.

Chapter 25
Answers to chapter questions

The following answers relate to those questions posed at the end of preceding chapters.

2.1 (i) at joints
(ii) breast bone found where the ribs meet
(iii) the hip and shoulder joints

2.2 (i) tibia
(ii) clavicle
(iii) vertebral column

2.3

joint	how strong	position in body	range of movement
ball and socket	very strong	hip/shoulder	full
hinge	fairly strong	elbow	limited
saddle	fairly weak	base of thumb	limited
condyloid	weak	wrist	2 ways only
pivot	fairly strong	neck	rotation only
slightly movable	weak	spine	depends on position

any 5 of the above

2.4 ligaments

2.5
- blood leaks from the damaged blood vessels and forms a clot round the damaged bone
- after a few days the damaged ends of the bone become soft and a connective tissue develops round more soft bone called a callus, and holds the bone in place
- osteoblasts begin to strengthen the bone deposit collagen and other salts to aid in the repair
- after a few weeks, new soft bone starts to bridge the gap of the broken bone. The callus also hardens and the material surrounding the broken bone is reabsorbed into the body.

Test yourself

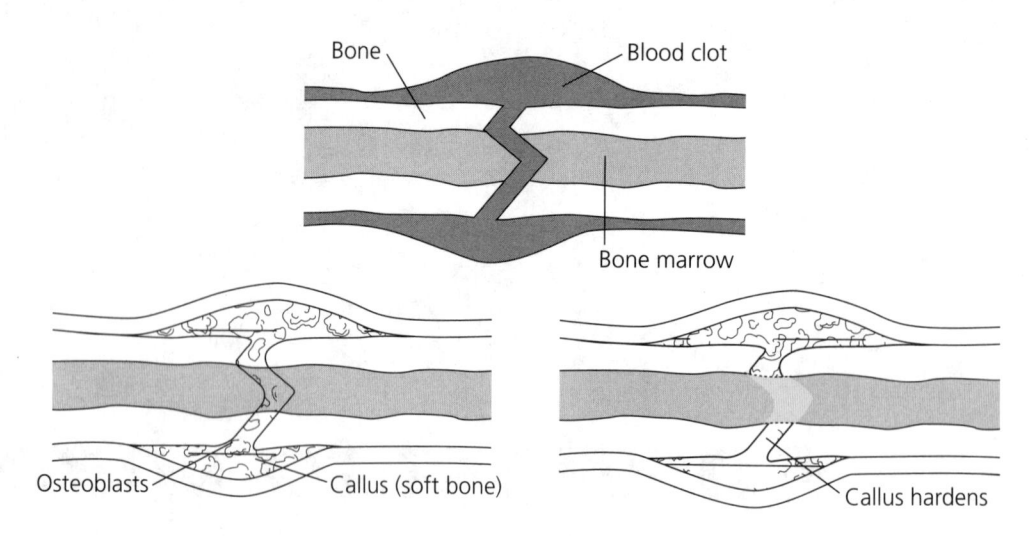

[Diagram showing bone healing stages: Bone with blood clot and bone marrow; osteoblasts forming callus (soft bone); callus hardens]

3.1 (i) front of upper arm
(ii) back of thigh
(iii) across back and top of shoulder, from base of neck to shoulder

3.2 As one muscle contracts an opposite one relaxes. When the elbow bends, the biceps at the front of the upper arm contract and at the same time the triceps at the back of the upper arm relax.

3.3 Voluntary or skeletal muscles are made up of many individual fibres that are controlled by the nervous system. We can tell voluntary muscles when to contract and when to relax.

Involuntary or smooth muscles are made up of layers or sheets of fibres. They contract and relax automatically as the needs of the body dictate. We have no control over these muscles.

3.4 The muscle fibres get shorter
The muscle fibres get fatter
More fibres are prepared for work
The blood supply to the muscles is improved
The muscle reacts more quickly to stimuli

3.5 ATP provides energy for contraction: this produces ADP
ADP combines with glycogen to produce ATP: this produces a by-product called pyruvic acid

If energy production continues the pyruvic acid is turned into lactic acid; the build up of lactic acid makes muscular contraction difficult; the continued build up of lactic acid will bring about a feeling of fatigue and eventually muscular contraction will cease.

4.1 Reaction time is the speed at which a decision is made. This includes the time taken to: detect the stimuli, decide what action to take, start to carry out the response decided upon

4.2 A motor unit includes a single motor nerve and all the muscle fibres it controls.

4.3 They are taken low down the Central Nervous System.

5.1 Heart:
makes a small increase in size
develops a slower resting rate
stroke volume is increased
returns to resting rate faster after activity
improves the prevention of coronary disease

Answers to chapter questions

Blood:
- the number of red cells is increased
- its ability to transport oxygen is improved
- supply to muscle fibres is improved
- return of deoxygenated blood to heart is improved

5.2 When muscles work they create heat. As the blood moves round the body it transports this heat to the cooler parts so that an even temperature can be maintained. This is often near the surface of the skin and when we get hot we tend to go red.

5.3 All arteries carry blood away from the heart. This includes the pulmonary artery which is the only artery to carry deoxygenated blood.
All veins carry blood to the heart. This includes the pulmonary vein which is the only vein to carry oxygenated blood.

5.4 The upper chambers are the left and right atria; the lower chambers are called the left and right ventricles.

5.5 At the site of an open wound, the blood will begin to clot. The platelets combine together to form a temporary plug. Then enzymes in the platelets react with the air and cause the fibrinogen from the plasma to change into fibrin. The fibres of fibrin form a mesh which seals the wound.

6.1 the size of the chest increases
chest expansion increases
resting breathing rate is lowered
exchange of gas is improved
inspiratory and expiratory reserve volumes increase
tidal volume increases during exercise

6.2 The main organs are: nasal passages, trachea or windpipe, lungs

6.3 Vital capacity is the combined total of the Tidal Volume, plus Inspiratory Reserve Volume, plus Expiratory Reserve Volume.

6.4 Oxygen uptake is the amount of oxygen that is absorbed into the blood during each breath.

As the rate of exercise increases, the rate of uptake increases.

Examiner's Tip: Oxygen uptake must not be confused with oxygen intake. We breathe in far more oxygen in each breath than is taken up or absorbed into the blood.

7.1 A balanced diet should include: proteins, carbohydrates, fats, vitamins and minerals.

7.2 Carbohydrates are energy providers.

7.3 During hard physical exercise blood is diverted from the digestive system to the muscles. Any food in the alimentary canal cannot be absorbed. This can cause discomfort and contribute to under-performance.

7.4 Proteins are obtained from: meats, cheese, fish, eggs, soya, nuts.

7.5 This is the wave-like motion of the walls of the oesophagus. It is caused by the contraction of the smooth muscles that make up the walls as they force a bolus of food towards the stomach.

8.1 Strength – the ability to use the muscles to apply force to overcome a resistance.
Stamina – the ability to perform strenuous activity over a long period of time.
Speed – the shortest time taken to move the body or a body part over a specific distance.
Suppleness – the range of movement possible at a joint or joints.

Test yourself

8.2

	AT REST	DURING ACTIVITY
Pulse rate	75 bts/min	190+ bts/min
Stroke volume	100 ml/bt	200 ml/bt
Cardiac output	7 lt/min	35+ lt/min

During physical activity they all rise. Pulse rate more than doubles, stroke volume doubles and cardiac output increases up to five-fold.

8.3 Explosive strength is used in both the shot put and high jump events. During the use of explosive strength the body moves fast over a short distance, the state of the muscles changes quickly and all this happens in a short space of time.

8.4 The arm action in butterfly swimming has to be recovered above the water and stretch as far forward as possible. This requires an extensive range of movement.

The leg action of the swimmer must be compensated by the movement of the hips and lower back. The greater the range of movement in these areas, the more effective the leg kick can be.

8.5 For an individual to perform at his best he or she must have the right attitude. He must want to win and be prepared in his mind for competition.

9.1 Any two of the following methods can be selected:

Interval training: alternative sessions of high intensity work and rest periods

Continuous training: working for long periods at a steady stress level below maximum effort

Fartlek training: sharp bursts of very intensive activity interspersed by period of low level activity and medium stress activity

Circuit training: the completion of a series of exercises in a set order with little or no rest between. Each exercise should concentrate on a different part of the body.

Weight training: the using of weights to put stress on different parts of the body. Stress can be increased by increasing the number of reps performed and by making the weights heavier.

9.2 Progression is the steady increase in the amount of stress that is included in a training session. A long distance runner will steadily increase his weekly work rate over a period of time. He must not try to increase the rate too quickly or he could cause injury, nor must the increase be too slow as the body will not be kept under stress.

9.3 (i) Strength - the ability to use the muscles to apply force to overcome a resistance. Weight training.

(ii) Suppleness - the range of movement possible at a joint or joints. Stretching exercises for the hamstrings

9.4 During isometric contraction the muscle fibres are put under stress but remain the same length throughout the exercise. Pushing against a wall is an isometric exercise.

9.5 Warm ups are needed in order to:
- prepare the body and mind for work
- so that the muscles can be stretched without the risk of causing injury
- increase the blood supply to the muscles
- prepare the joints to work over a greater range

9.6 A training session must have three main parts: a warm up session; the main training session and a cool down session.

Answers to chapter questions

Activity	Rugby
warm up	light exercises for the whole body: jogging; flexibility exercises, progressive strength exercises, ball handling exercises
training session	to include skills work, strength and speed work: further ball practice exercises un-opposed and opposed, strength work on scrummage machines, against tackle bags, pushing and lifting exercises, sprint work over short distances, shuttle runs, agility runs.
cool down	to include gradual run down to walking pace, light un-opposed flexibility exercises

10.1 Skill is a learned ability to bring about pre-determined results with maximum certainty, often with the minimum outlay of time or energy, or both.

10.2 Open skill - performing a tackle during a game of hockey
Closed skill - performing a hand stand

10.3 Extrinsic motivation is when a person works hard to gain an external reward such as a trophy or prize money.

10.4

INPUT → DECISION MAKING → OUTPUT
FEEDBACK

10.5 Arousal can be described as how prepared the individual is to take part in an event.
Too much arousal can lead to anxiety and inhibit performance.
Too little arousal will not affect performance.

These points are illustrated by the graph that looks like a U upside down.

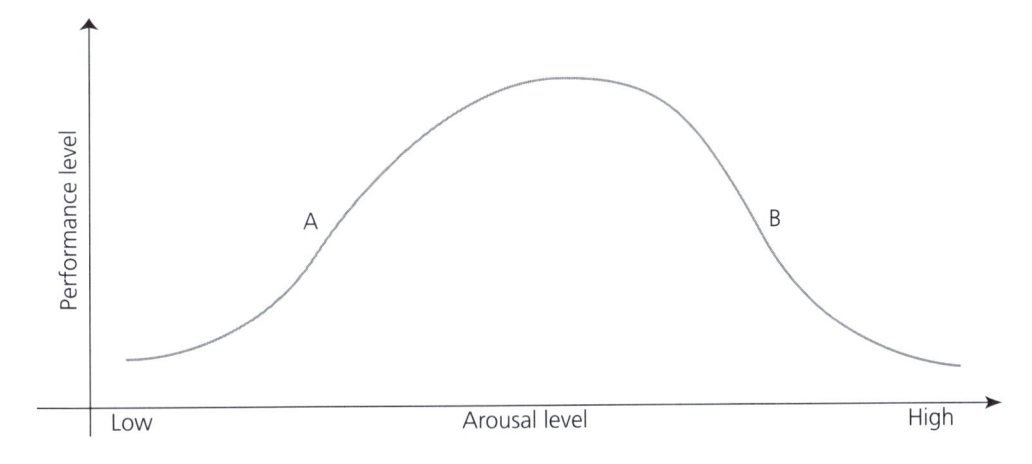

(Graph: Performance level vs Arousal level, inverted U curve with points A and B marked)

11.1 Tobacco smoke includes two main products: nicotine and tar.
 - Nicotine when inhaled increases heart rate and can cause high blood pressure.
 - Tar when inhaled can accumulate on the inner surface of the lungs and prevent the efficient exchange of gases between the lungs and the blood capillaries. This reduces the individual's capacity to transport oxygen round the body.

11.2 Injuries can be avoided by:
 - following the correct type of training for the activity
 - the adequate use of warm up activities before any form of physical work is undertaken
 - the use of the correct protective equipment for the sport concerned
 - the wearing of the correct clothing for the sport concerned
 - playing to the rules of the sport and not cheating

Test yourself

11.3 A weight lifter will be a mesomorph. He or she will have broad shoulders and be very muscular.

11.4 Training should acclimatise the individual for known competitive conditions
The main factors to be considered are:
- weather: what temperature the event will take place in
- state of the track or field: how long or short the grass will be, what type of playing surface is to be used
- venue: is it at altitude or sea level; is there high or low humidity?

11.5 Ectomorphs are extremely tall, thin people: they are more likely to be suited to the high jump event.

Mesomorphs are muscular, broad shouldered people who are more likely to be suited to a gymnastic event.

Endomorphs carry a large amount of body fat and are more likely to be suited to cross channel swimming.

11.6 Anabolic steroids:
- are used to develop muscle strength and bulk
- can aid recovery from injury
- can produce aggressive behaviour
- can cause damage to the liver and other internal organs

12.1 (i) 12 min run test
(ii) sit and reach

12.2 Testing can identify those physical deficiencies that need to be improved in order to gain fitness.

Re-testing can indicate the levels of improvement reached during a training programme.

12.3 After the age of 11 or 12, most people tend to lose a degree of suppleness. This is especially noticeable in boys as they develop large muscle mass during adolescence and this restrict suppleness. It is accepted that the older a person is the less flexible they become.

12.4 The principal external factor that might affect the score gained for the 12 min run test is the weather. Heat, cold, humidity, rain and wind can all affect performance.

12.5 Testing the individual before he or she starts a training programme can identify those physical deficiencies that need to be most concentrated on in order to attain fitness.

13.1 Caused by a blow to the solar plexus which can make the diaphragm go into spasm.

13.2 The recommended first aid treatment when a fracture is not suspected is to follow the RICE formula.

REST	- stop using the injured part as soon as possible
ICE	- apply ice to the injured area to help reduce the swelling and any muscle spasm
COMPRESSION	- use elastic bandages or compression pads to help reduce swelling
ELEVATION	- if movement does not cause pain, the injured area should be raised above the level of the heart to reduce blood flow to that area and to help drain away any waste fluids.

13.4 Hypothermia is the lowering of the body temperature below 35 degrees centigrade.

It is likely to occur whilst sailing or canoeing in very cold conditions, and whilst climbing or walking in cold weather.

The recommended treatment is to bring the patient's body temperature back to normal (36/37 degrees centigrade) in a steady, sustained manner.

13.5 A fracture is the breaking of a bone in the body. The broken bone may or may not break the surface of the skin.

Examiner's tip: you should be able to explain the difference between the different types of fracture.

14.1 Examples are: FA - Football Association
AAA - Amateur Athletics Association

The main roles of a governing body are to:
- establish and maintain the rules of their sport
- organise competition in the sport
- promote the sport
- select international teams in the sport

14.2 The CCPR promotes sport by:
- giving support to specialist sports bodies
- acting as a consultative body to the Sports Council and others concerned with sport
- acting as a forum for the governing bodies of sport

14.3 National Coaching Foundation

14.4 To help run a sport at club level a person could:
- act as an official at the club, e.g. Captain, Secretary, Treasurer
- act as the club's representative to regional or other sports committees
- act as trainer, coach, first aider
- promote social or fund-raising events for the club

14.5 (i) Holme Pierrepont - rowing, canoeing
(ii) Crystal Palace - athletics, swimming, judo, basketball

14.6 They would have to apply to the Sports Aid Foundation through the Governing Body of their sport. A grant could then be awarded and passed to the individual via the Governing Body.

15.1 A sports club that is run as a business is one that runs at a profit for its owners. It is privately owned but can run as a private club or be open to members of the public.

15.2 The National Playing Fields Association was originally set up in 1925 to provide playing fields and playgrounds. Now it provides expertise along with grants to other providers of such facilities.

15.3 skating rinks and ten pin bowling alleys

15.4 sports/leisure centres, swimming baths, golf courses, outdoor pursuits centres, bridleways, cycle tracks

15.5 It could obtain money from:
- a Sports Council grant
- a National Lottery grant
- a local authority grant
- a loan from a commercial source such as a brewery or bank
- sponsorship
- its own members through affiliation fees and fund raising activities

16.1 - by providing reduced cost entry

Test yourself

- by providing daytime use of facilities
- by advertising facilities available
- by offering courses leading to coaching qualifications and thus improved job opportunities

16.2 Examples:

CAMPAIGN	TARGET GROUP
Ever Thought of Sport	13/24 year olds
50+ All to Play For	the over 50s
What's Your Sport?	all groups of people
Sport For All – Disabled	disabled groups

Examiner's tip: Make sure you know the campaigns and the groups they were aimed at.

16.3 A leisure activity takes place during a person's leisure time, that is, that time not needed to meet a person's social or bodily needs. Such activities may range from stamp collecting to horse riding.

A sporting activity also takes place in a person's leisure time but includes only those activities that require physical prowess or skill together with some element of competition.

16.4 People who use sporting facilities can be divided into recognisable groups. This division can be based on factors including age, sex, income, family commitments.

One such group can be described as 'Young Single Persons'. These have a large amount of leisure time and high disposable income.

Another group could be described as 'Retired Persons'. These also have a large amount of leisure time but only a limited amount of disposable income.

Examiner's tip: You should be able to split the whole community into user groups, using a range of criteria.

16.5 The attitude that a person adopts towards sport participation can be based on:
- tradition of the area in which they live
- tradition of family activity
- the 'class' to which a person considers him- or herself to belong
- attitudes of friends towards sports

Fashion can influence participation:
- some sports are 'in fashion' at a particular time and so many people want to join in
- some sportswear is fashionable to wear and so it encourages participation

The age of a person can affect sports participation:
- the very young have plenty of time to play sport but no money to pay for it
- older people have both the time and money to spend on sport
- people in their late teens and early twenties are the most likely group to be involved in contact sports
- some older people have family commitments such as young children or aged parents to look after and so restrict the amount of time available to spend on sport.

17.1 De Coubertin wanted the Modern Olympic Games to be a sporting stage for amateur sportsmen to compete, one nation against another in the spirit of fair play and sportsmanship. He did not feel that women should be included in the competition.

17.2 The rules of many sports were spread throughout the world by civil servants, traders and soldiers. Britain had a huge Empire that spread all over the world. The Empire had strong trading links with GB. To help administer and control this Empire, British soldiers, traders and civil servants had to be stationed abroad for many years at a time. Whilst living abroad, they established the games that they had learned during their time at schools and universities in Britain.

17.3 At the start of the 19th century many of the public schools played similar sports, but all had their own sets of rules. On leaving school, many of these pupils went on to university. At university they met pupils from many schools and in order to continue playing games they had to produce a set of rules for all to play by. These formed the basis of national rules that were established later in the century.

17.4 De Coubertin did not approve of women taking part in sport. He felt that sports should be only for men who could play in the true spirit of fair play and sportsmanship. De Coubertin felt that the only part for women in the Modern Olympic Games was to crown the winners with garlands.

18.1 Television can affect sport by:
- bringing a sport to the attention of many people and making it more popular
- showing negative aspects of a sport and making it less popular
- making it wealthy by paying large sums for broadcasting rights
- making the players into stars or super sportspersons
- making it so popular that it will attract sponsorship from commercial organisations

18.2 Open competitions allow amateur and professional players to compete against each other, and players from other countries to compete in the event. This can serve to raise the standard of both the amateur player and the home professional player. Amateur players get the opportunity to learn from the professional players and can judge whether they are capable of joining the professional ranks. Interest in the competition will also be raised if players from abroad are allowed to compete.

18.3 The 1976 Olympic Games were held in Montreal in Canada. Just before the Games were due to start, many African and Arab nations called on the organising committee to expel New Zealand as its rugby players had recently toured South Africa. This tour was seen to be an act of support for South Africa's policy of apartheid. However, the IOC ruled that as rugby was not an Olympic sport it had no control over who played whom and refused to expel New Zealand. Thus many African and Arab countries decided to boycott the games and returned home.

18.4 Amateur clubs might raise their annual income from:
- membership fees
- fund raising projects such as raffles and social events
- earned income from bar sales and admission fees
- local authority grants
- sponsorship

18.5 Sponsorship provides sport with a large financial income.
It can make sports more popular by promoting events.
It can provide the income to promote coaching and development in a sport.
It can under-write the cost of sporting events.
It can help to bring world class overseas players to the game.
It can help in the finance of amateur national teams.
Many sports could not operate at the level that they do without the money obtained through sponsorship deals.

19.1 Taking drugs in sport:
- is a form of cheating
- can cause liver damage
- can cause impotence and hair loss in males
- can lead to heart disorders
- can cause physical and psychological damage
- can become addictive
- can cause death

19.2 Professional performers can:
- be role models for young players and fans
- have their actions on and off the field of play imitated by younger players

Test yourself

- set correct standards for a game, in the way it is played, administered and coached
- encourage young players to play the game in a spirit of fair play and honesty
- encourage young players to abide by the rules of the sport and its officials

19.3 The availability of TV sets for large numbers of the population meant that people could stay at home and watch sport in comfort
The TV introduced a large number of people to 'new' sports that they found interesting.
Many grounds provided very poor accommodation for spectators.
Many sports were associated with hooligan behaviour which was widely reported.
Many families felt unsafe in large crowds at sporting events.

19.4 The major contributing factors to crowd violence at football matches are:
- alcohol abuse, inside and outside the ground
- tradition of past spectators: some sports are recognised as being supported by hooligan elements
- loyalty to either club or country and the perceiving of the opposition supporters as the 'enemy'

19.5 Anabolic steroids are likely to be taken by:
- those athletes recovering from injury, to aid recovery but under strict medical supervision
- those athletes who are involved in power events when muscle bulk and body size are important. The steroids, if taken during training, will increase muscle bulk very quickly. Sprinters and weight lifters are likely to be included in this group.
- those athletes who feel the need to increase their aggressive nature for competitive purposes. The steroids can increase this trait. Boxers and rugby players are likely to be in this group.

20.1 Any two from:
- more opportunities available
- more acceptance of women playing sport
- more 'mother and toddler' groups available
- women now have a greater disposable income of their own
- some sports are fashionable for women
- campaigns are run to encourage women to take part in sport
- there is more suitable fashionable clothing for women to wear while taking part in sport
- there are now more 'women only' sports clubs

20.2 Women have:
- fewer opportunities to take part in sport
- opportunities are often restricted to off-peak times of the day
- insufficient creche facilities to give women the time to play sport
- women are still expected to 'look after the home and children' even if they also have a job outside the home
- women often have to make do with sub-standard facilities for their sport
- in some sports women are not taken seriously
- some sports refuse to allow women to play sport with men

20.3 All age groups but especially 13/24 and 45/49 mixed age groups, plus all other women's age groups

20.4 Any three from:
- methods of counteraction

- race   by providing more opportunities for minority groups
             by education
             by using the law to counter racial discrimination
             by banning racial abusers from sporting events

Answers to chapter questions

- religion   by not staging events on sensitive religious occasions
            by accepting a suitable venue for religious minorities

- gender   by providing equality of opportunity
           by providing equality in prizes
           by providing equality in resources
           by providing suitable creche facilities
           by education

- age   by providing equality of opportunity
       by providing sports to match age groups
       by providing adequate supervision where necessary
       by use of campaigns

- tradition   by use of education and campaigns
             by providing suitable resources for all
             by providing opportunities for all

20.5 Any three from:
- provision of ramps for easy access
- placing of notice boards at convenient height
- removal of 'turnstiles' at entry points
- fitting of automatically opening doors
- provision of suitable toilet, changing and showering facilities
- provision of hoists in swimming pools
- fitting of 'hard of hearing' units at reception counters
- provision of lifts to all floors with control buttons at convenient heights
- fitting of wider doors for wheelchairs

Index

ABC of First Aid 98, 104
abdominals 90, 169
abduction 27, 28, 29, 161, 168
access 123, 125
    disabled 148
actin 31, 32
adduction 27, 28, 29, 161, 168
advertising 131, 133, 134, 135, 137, 174
adenosine diphosphate (ADP) 33, 34, 36, 180
adenosine triphosphate (ATP) 33, 34, 36, 180
administration of sport 105-111
aerobic 172
    activity 65
    capacity 66, 72, 171
    system 34, 36
aerobics 63, 102, 103, 123, 175
age 28, 43, 67, 82, 88, 95, 122, 125, 142, 143, 148, 163, 171, 172, 184
agility 63, 64, 72
agonist 33
agonistic muscle action 33
air 49, 50, 51, 52
    pressure 50
alcohol 85, 140, 114, 188
alimentary canal 54, 55, 57, 59
altitude 84, 172
alveolus 21, 48, 49, 50, 53, 169
amateur 116, 126, 127, 128, 129, 130, 131, 132, 133, 136, 137, 161, 175, 187
anabolic steroids 84, 85, 139, 141, 184, 188
anaerobic
    activities 66
    capacity 72
    system 34, 36
analgesics 84
ankle 18, 24, 69, 103
anorexia nervosa 84
antagonist 33
antibodies 46
antitoxins 46
anti-depressants 84
anus 21, 54, 55
apartheid 136, 137
archery 62, 63, 75, 85, 108, 147, 148
arm curls 68
arousal 77, 79, 183
artery 42, 43, 44, 46, 47, 167, 169, 181

aorta 42, 43, 170
    pulmonary 42, 43, 44, 49
asthma 84
athletics 108, 116, 128, 131, 131, 133, 166
atrophy 66, 125
attitude 63, 64, 122, 123, 138, 141, 186
atrium 42, 170, 181

bacteria 46
badminton 86, 102, 167
balance 63, 64, 85
basketball 81, 82, 103, 108, 164, 166
    wheelchair 147
bench press 67, 68, 69
beta-blockers 85
biceps 19, 31, 33, 36
billiards 120
Bisham Abbey 108, 113
bladder 31
Blankers-Koen, Fanny 145
blisters 99
blood 20, 21, 22, 25, 35, 41, 43, 44, 45, 46, 47, 50, 60, 72, 73, 85, 99, 102, 162, 170, 181
    cells 28, 45, 52, 53, 65, 84
    circulation 42, 43, 47, 98, 104
    clotting 45, 46, 180, 181
    deoxygenated 41, 42, 44, 47, 181
    oxygenated 41, 42, 44, 181
    plasma 45, 46, 181
    platelets 45, 46, 181
    pooling 73
    pressure 41, 44, 45, 46, 47, 85, 172
    vessels 20, 24, 25, 31, 41, 43, 44, 47, 100
Bloomer, Fanny 144
Boat Race, the 131, 133
body type (see also somatotype) 81, 82, 85, 172
bolus 55
bone 18, 19, 22, 24, 25, 26, 27, 28, 29, 30, 31, 35, 82, 100, 161, 169
    broken (see also fracture) 25, 81, 97, 100, 179
    callus 25, 179
    compact 24, 29
    flat 24, 29
    irregular 24, 29

    long (tubular) 22, 24, 27, 29
    marrow 22, 24, 28, 180
    short 24, 29
    spongy 24, 29
books 134, 135
Bosnan Case, the 142, 143
bowel 55
bowls 147
boxing 132
brain 19, 20, 22, 28, 37, 38, 39, 40, 64
    stem 19, 37, 38, 39
breathing 21, 34, 48, 49, 50, 51, 52, 53, 60, 98, 104
British Disabled Sports Foundation 147, 174
British Olympic Association (BOA) 109, 111, 161, 168
bronchiole 21, 48, 49, 53, 169
bronchus 21, 48, 49, 53
Brookes, William Penny 127
bruises 81, 99, 100, 103

calcium 24, 28
cannabis 84
canoeing 74, 101, 121, 134
capillary 43, 45, 46, 49, 50, 170
carbohydrate 56, 57, 58, 59, 79, 169, 177, 181
    loading 57, 58, 59
carbon dioxide 20, 34, 44, 45, 50, 168, 170
cardiac output (Q) 60, 64, 182
cardiovascular 62, 93, 94, 95, 163, 171
carpals 22, 23, 26
cartilage 24, 27, 28, 29, 99, 103, 169
    articular 24, 29, 170
    menisci 29, 100
Central Council for Physical Recreation (CCPR) 107, 109, 111, 161, 164, 165, 167, 185
central government 112, 117, 118, 174
central nervous system (CNS) 37, 38, 39, 40, 75, 76, 180
chafing 99
cheating 138, 141, 183
circulatory system 20, 41, 43, 169
class 127, 129, 135, 143, 144, 145, 148
    lower 123, 126
    upper 123, 126, 128

Index

clavicle (collar bone) 18, 23, 30, 103, 167, 179
climbing 120, 121, 122
clothing (see also sportswear) 144, 148
clubs 105, 106, 109, 111, 116, 123, 127, 129, 130, 138, 143, 185
   private 116, 123, 175
coccyx 22, 23, 169
Commonwealth 136, 137
competition 57, 59, 73, 78, 79, 83, 85, 96, 104, 105, 110, 121, 126, 136, 138
   open 132, 137, 187
contraction 31, 33, 35, 36, 46, 51, 69, 102
   isometric 69, 73, 182
   isotonic 69, 73
cool down 72, 73, 96, 182, 183
co-ordination 39, 63, 64, 85, 101
Coubertin, Baron Pierre de 127, 128, 186, 187
Countryside Commission 110, 111, 113
coronary heart disease 46, 47, 180
coursework 1, 11, 16, 149-159
CP (creatine phosphate) system 34
cramp 62, 101, 102
cranium (skull) 18, 22, 23, 27
cricket 84, 103, 108, 118, 126, 127, 128, 131, 132, 133, 134, 135, 137, 138, 140, 141, 143, 176
Crystal Palace 108, 111, 113, 185
cuts 81, 99
cycling 68, 101, 128, 166

dancers/dancing 63, 145, 166
decision-making 76, 77, 78, 79, 173, 183
dehydration 101
deltoid 19, 31, 169
diaphragm 21, 48, 50, 51, 57, 101, 169, 184
diastolic pressure 46
diet 56, 57, 59, 85, 102, 172
diffusion 50
digestion 54, 55, 57
digestive system 21, 54, 57, 181
dips 91, 92, 172
disabled people 124, 147, 148, 164, 174, 188
discrimination 142, 143, 148, 188
dislocation 103
diuretics 84, 85
drugs 84, 85, 139, 141, 177, 187

ears 22, 38
ectomorph 81, 82, 85, 184
endomorph 81, 82, 85, 184
endomysium 33

endurance (see also stamina) 66, 69, 94, 95, 169, 171, 172
   tests of 93, 94
energy 34, 35, 56, 57, 58, 59, 62, 161, 181
   systems 33, 34, 35
English Sports Council 108
environment 83, 172
enzyme 45, 46, 181
epimysium 31, 31, 33
epiphysis 24
Ever Thought Of Sport? 124, 143, 168, 175, 176
expenditure
   capital 116, 117, 118
   recurrent 116, 117, 118
expiration 51, 53
expiratory reserve volume (ERV) 52, 181
extension 27, 28, 29, 33, 168
extensor 33, 35, 161
external chest compression 98
exteroceptor 38, 75
eyes 22, 38

Fairhall, Neroli 148
fashion 123, 125, 144, 186
fat 56, 57, 59, 79, 82, 165, 169, 181
   deposits in arteries 46
fatigue 64, 79, 84, 180
feedback 75, 76, 78, 173, 183
femur 22, 23, 26, 27, 29
fencing 62, 128
fibrinogen 45, 46, 181
fibula 23
Fifty Plus - All To Play For 124, 143, 164, 168, 175
finance 116, 117, 124, 125, 129, 137, 174
First Aid 96, 97, 98
fitness 60, 65, 67, 72, 73, 74
   cardiovascular 62, 72, 93, 94, 95, 163, 171
   centre 116, 118
   motor 60, 63, 64
   physical 60, 61, 64
5 Star Award Scheme 132
flexibility (see also suppleness) 62, 63, 65, 72, 80, 82, 163, 171
flexion 27, 28, 29, 33, 168
flexor 33, 35, 161
food 20, 21, 34, 54, 56, 57, 58, 59, 85
football (see soccer)
fracture 81, 97, 100, 104, 185
   closed 100
   compound 100
   open 100
   stress 100, 101, 103
front squat 69, 70

games 120, 126, 127, 129, 138, 166
gamblers/gambling 117, 118, 126, 131
gas 20, 21, 48, 50, 53, 57, 85, 161, 181
gastrocnemius 19, 31
gender (see also sex) 123, 142, 143, 148
gluteus maximus 19, 31
glycogen 34, 57, 73, 180
goal setting 78
golf 108, 113, 116, 128, 130, 131, 143, 167
grant 116, 118, 129, 137, 185, 187
Guttman, Sir Ludwig 147, 148, 174
gymnastics 62, 63, 81, 82, 108, 128, 145, 166
   rhythmic 175

haemoglobin 45, 50
handgrip dynamometer 91, 92, 163
hallucinogens 84
hamstrings 19, 31, 36, 88, 103
hard tissue injuries 100, 102, 104
hayfever 84
health authority 124
Health Education Council 125
heart 20, 22, 31, 41, 42, 43, 44, 45, 47, 60, 97, 161, 162, 168, 169, 180
   attack 46, 169
heel lift 69, 72
high jump 62
hill-walking 101, 110, 122
hockey 35, 74, 75, 84, 108, 134, 166
   ice 80
holiday time 120
Holme Pierrepont 108, 111, 113, 185
horse
   racing 126, 128, 131, 132, 134
   riding 119, 121
hooliganism 139, 140, 141, 188
humerus 22, 23, 26, 33
hurdling 63
hyperthermia 101
hypothermia 101, 104, 185

illness 42, 79, 80, 84, 85, 120
impulse, nervous 38, 39, 40
information processing 75, 76, 77, 78, 79, 164
injury 63, 66, 72, 80, 81, 84, 85, 96, 97, 100, 102, 163, 183
input 75, 76, 77, 78, 173, 183
insertion, point of 33, 35
inspiration 50, 51, 53
inspiratory reserve volume (IRV) 51, 181

Index

International Olympic
    Committee (IOC) 84, 109, 111,
    136, 161, 168, 187
International Sports Federations
    (ISF) 109, 111
International Year for Disabled
    People 147
intestine 31, 43, 57
    small 20, 21, 54, 45, 55
    large 21, 54, 55
inverted U theory 77
Iron Curtain 132, 136

jaw 22, 23, 24
Jockey Club, the 126
jogging 34, 68, 73
joints 18, 22, 25, 28, 29, 33, 35, 62,
    63, 72, 88, 100, 163, 168, 170,
    179
    ball and socket 25, 26, 29, 30,
        170
    condyloid 25, 26, 29, 179
    hinge 25, 26, 29, 170
    immovable 25, 27, 29, 170
    movable 30
    pivot 25, 26, 29, 170
    saddle 25, 26, 29, 170
    slightly movable 25, 26, 29, 170
    synovial 25, 26, 27, 29
Johnson, Ben 139
judo 108, 134, 166

karate 62
keep fit 102
kidneys 20, 43, 45
Knapp, Barbara 74
knee 27, 29
    bend (deep) 69, 71

labour-saving devices 120
lactic acid 34, 35, 36, 62, 170, 180
    system 34, 35
larynx (voice box) 21
latissimus dorsi 19, 31, 169
laxatives 84
leg press 67
leisure
    centre 113, 116, 117, 118, 175
    time 119, 120, 121, 122, 125,
        186
levy 116
ligaments 22, 26, 27, 28, 29, 63,
    99, 100, 103, 169, 170, 179
    cruciate 29
Lilleshall 108, 113
limited channel capacity 76, 78
liver 20, 43, 44
local authority 113, 114, 116, 118,
    124, 143, 187

loyalty 140, 141, 188
lung 20, 21, 22, 34, 41, 42, 44, 45,
    48, 49, 50, 51, 52, 53, 85, 98,
    167, 168, 169, 181
    (total) capacity 51, 52, 53
lymphocytes 45, 46

maximum heart rate 67
measurement 86-95
media 131, 137, 138, 166, 178
membership fees 129, 131, 137,
    187
memory 76
    aids 16
meniscal tears 100
menstrual cycle 82, 83
mesomorph 81, 82, 85, 184
metacarpals 22, 23, 26
metaphysis 24
metatarsals 22, 23
minerals 56, 59, 79, 102, 181
mobility 62
motherhood 144
motivation 77, 78, 79
    extrinsic 77, 78, 183
    instrinsic 77
motor racing 135
motor unit 39, 40, 180
mouth 21, 48, 49, 54, 55
    to mouth ventilation 98
muscle 20, 22, 29, 31, 32, 34, 35,
    36, 39, 40, 41, 45, 47, 51, 55,
    57, 61, 62, 63, 66, 69, 72, 73,
    82, 85, 100, 103, 161
    cardiac 31, 35, 168
    cells 33
    fibres 31, 32, 35, 39, 40, 65, 69,
        73, 180
        fast twitch 32, 35
        slow twitch 32, 35
    intercostal 169
    skeletal
        (voluntary/striped/striated) 31,
        32, 35, 36, 102, 168, 180
    smooth (involuntary) 31, 35, 36,
        168, 180
muscular system 19, 31
myofibril 31, 32
myosin 31, 32

nasal
    cavity 21, 49
    passages 21, 48, 49, 53, 181
National Census 121
National Coaching Foundation
    109, 110, 111, 164, 174, 185
National Governing Bodies
    of Sport 106, 107, 108, 109,
        111, 112, 126, 164, 175, 185
National Lottery 109, 117, 118,
    124, 130, 131, 185

National Parks 110, 111, 112, 175
National Playing Fields
    Association (NPFA) 113, 118,
    185
National Sports Centres 108, 111
nerves 19, 31, 37, 38, 39, 40, 100
    connector 38
        effector (efferent/motor) 38, 39,
        40
        sensory (afferent) 38, 39
nervous system 19, 37, 38, 39, 40,
    101, 162
netball 164, 166, 175
neurones (nerves) 37, 39
newspapers 134, 135
nicotine 85
normal state 61
nose 21, 38, 49
nucleus 31, 45
nutrients 44, 45, 46, 55, 161

oesophagus (gullet) 21, 59, 54, 55,
    181
Olympics 60, 79, 84, 127, 128,
    132, 133, 135, 136, 137, 139,
    144, 145, 146, 161, 164, 186,
    187
Opening Doors 124
orbit 23
origin, point of 33, 35
osteoblasts 25, 179
outdoor pursuits 166, 185
output 75, 76, 77, 78, 173, 183
overload 65, 66, 68, 69, 73, 163,
    171, 172
oxygen 20, 34, 35, 36, 43, 44, 45,
    50, 52, 60, 66, 84, 85, 168,
    170
    debt 35, 36, 52, 60, 62, 68
    uptake 50, 53, 181

pacing (control) 74
patella 19, 22, 23, 27, 29, 161, 163,
    167
patronage 132
pectorals 19, 31
pelvic girdle (hip girdle) 22, 23,
pelvis 26, 82
perception 76
performance processing 77
perimysium 31, 33
periosteum 24, 32
peristalsis 55, 56, 59
Persil Funfit 124
phagocytes 45, 46
phalanges 22, 23
pharynx (throat) 21, 48
Physically Handicapped and
    Able Bodied (PHAB) 148
physiology 64
Plas y Brenin 113

Index

politics 136, 137
polypeptide hormones 85
power 63, 64, 72, 172
Premier League 131, 135
press-ups 91
prime mover 33
private sector 117, 118, 176
prize monies 131, 132, 135, 145
professional 126, 127, 129, 131, 132, 133, 137, 138, 141, 142, 187
progression 65, 66, 73, 86, 172, 182
promotional campaigns 124, 125, 164, 165, 175, 178, 186
proprioceptor 38, 75
protective equipment 80, 96, 104
protein 32, 56, 59, 79, 181
providers of sport
    commercial 112, 118
    local 112, 113, 118
    national 112, 113, 118
    voluntary 112, 116, 118
provision of sport 112-118, 121, 165
psychology 57, 63, 64
pull-ups 91, 172
pulmonary circulation 41, 170
pulse rate 42, 43, 44, 47, 60, 64, 67, 93, 98, 168, 171, 182
pyruvic acid 34, 35, 180

quadriceps 19, 29, 31, 170
quango 108, 110

race (nationality) 142, 148
radio 134, 135, 164
radius 22, 23, 26, 33
Rand, Mary 145
reaction time 39, 40, 63, 64, 85, 180
receptor 39, 77
reciprocal innovation 33, 180
recovery position 99
recreation 116, 119, 120, 125
reflex
    action 39
    arc 39, 40
Registrar General 121
relaxation 31, 33, 35, 36, 46, 51, 102
religion 142, 143, 148, 174
repetitions 69, 172
residual volume (RV) 52, 53
resistance 61, 72
respiratory
    system 21, 48, 49, 52, 53, 61, 161, 169
    tract 49, 53
response, nervous 39, 40

rest 67, 68, 73, 79, 85
reversibility 65, 66, 73, 172
revision 16, 17
ribs 18, 21, 22, 48, 50, 51, 103, 167
RICE formula 97, 98, 100, 104, 184
rotation 27, 28
rowing 62, 63, 143
rugby 62, 81, 99, 102, 116, 121, 123, 127, 136, 137, 166, 183
    league 131, 134, 135, 143
    scrum 62
    union 131, 133, 143, 176
rules 80, 96, 104, 120, 126, 128, 129, 137, 138, 141, 175, 187
running 62, 67, 94, 101

sacrum 22, 23, 25, 169
sailing 143
scapula (shoulder blade) 18, 23, 24, 33
scholarship 132
school 124, 125
    public 126, 127, 128, 187
sex (see also gender) 82, 172
Sheldon, William 81
shin splints 101, 103
shock 42, 101, 161
shooting 85, 128
shot put 32, 62
shoulder girdle 22
shoulder lift 86, 87, 88, 95
shuttle run 68, 177, 183
side to side bend 69, 71
sit and reach 87, 88, 95, 171, 184
sit-ups 67, 68, 90, 91, 95, 172
skating 63
    rinks 116, 185
skeletal system 18, 22
skeleton 22, 23, 25, 29, 161
    axial 22, 23, 29
    appendicular 22, 23, 29
    thoracic 22
skiing 143
skill 74, 75, 79, 86, 95, 164, 173, 183
    closed 75, 79, 183
    open 74, 79, 183
    pendulum 75
skin 38, 46, 56
skipping 68
skull 18, 22, 24, 25, 28
smoking 85, 169, 172, 177, 183
soccer 35, 63, 64, 76, 80, 81, 84, 86, 102, 103, 108, 116, 120, 121, 131, 122, 123, 132, 134, 135, 138, 139, 140, 142, 176
soft tissue injuries 99
somatotypes (see also body type) 81, 82

soleus 31
solvents 84
specificity 65, 66, 73, 172
spectators/spectatorism 105, 126, 127, 129, 131, 135, 139, 141, 164, 175
speed 32, 35, 39, 61, 62, 63, 64, 66, 68, 72, 74, 95, 181
spinal cord 19, 37, 38, 40
sprains 81, 100, 103
sprint 32, 34, 62, 68, 177, 183
spirometer 51, 52
sponsorship 117, 130, 131, 132, 133, 134, 137, 138, 145, 164, 166, 185, 187
sport, definition of 120
Sport For All - Disabled People 124, 146, 147, 168, 175, 176
Sportify the Over 45s! 168
Sports Aid Foundation 109, 110, 111, 185
sports centre 113, 123
Sports Council 107, 109, 111, 113, 117, 118, 124, 125, 130, 131, 146, 147, 148, 161, 165, 178, 185
Sportsmark Scheme 125
sportswear 123, 186
squash 108, 115, 116, 118, 121
stamina (see also endurance) 32, 57, 61, 62, 63, 64, 68, 72, 95, 163, 169, 172, 181
standing high jump 89, 90, 91, 95
standing long jump 89, 91, 95
step test 93, 94, 95, 171
    Harvard 163, 171
step-ups 68
sternum (breast bone) 18, 22, 23, 30, 167
stimulants 84
stimulus 35, 39, 63, 75, 76, 169
stitch 101
Stoke Mandeville Games 147
strains 66, 99, 100, 103
strength 61, 62, 63, 64, 65, 66, 67, 68, 72, 73, 85, 86, 95, 163, 171, 172, 181, 182
    explosive 61, 62, 64, 89, 182
    dynamic 61, 62
    static 61, 62
    tests of 89-93
stress 66, 67, 68, 77, 82, 83, 96, 120, 170, 171
stomach 21, 44, 45, 47, 54, 55, 56, 69
stroke volume 47, 60, 64, 182
subsidy 124
sumo-wrestling 81
suppleness (see also flexibility) 61, 62, 63, 64, 72, 73, 95, 181, 182, 184

Index

tests of 86-88
swimming 62, 63, 64, 67, 68, 108, 113, 118, 128, 131, 132, 145, 147, 163, 166
   synchronised 175
synapse 38
synaptic cleft 38
synovial
   fluid 27, 30, 169, 170
   membrane 27, 169, 170
systemic circulation 41, 170
systolic pressure 46

table tennis 108, 167
tarsals 22, 23
taxation 117, 118
television 134, 135, 137, 139, 141, 164, 187, 188
tendon 27, 29, 32, 33, 35, 42, 63, 99, 103, 170
   Achilles 19
tendonitis 100
tennis 74, 116, 134, 143, 145, 167
ten pin bowling alley 116, 185
tensiometer 93
thombin 46
thoracic cavity 48
tibia 22, 23, 27, 29, 103, 179
tidal volume (TV) 51, 52, 181
Tour de France 139
toxins 46
trachea (windpipe) 21, 48, 49, 53, 169, 181
tradition 140, 141, 142, 143, 148, 174, 186, 188
training 79, 83, 86, 96, 104, 163, 165, 177, 184
   activity 72
   circuit 67, 72, 73, 177, 182

fixed load 68
individual load 68
continuous 67, 68, 72, 73, 177, 182
duration 65, 69, 172
fartlek 67, 68, 72, 73, 177, 182
frequency 65, 69, 171, 172
intensity 65, 69, 171, 172
interval 67, 72, 73, 177, 182
programme 65, 66, 80, 83, 84, 86, 95, 164, 172, 173
threshold 67, 73
weight 69, 72, 73, 163, 172, 182
   isometric 69, 73
   isotonic 69, 73
trapezius 19, 31, 36, 169
triceps 19, 31, 33, 169
trunk extension 88, 95
tug of war 62
12 min run test 94, 95, 184
two hands curl 69, 70

ulna 22, 23, 26, 33
unemployed/unemployment 120, 125, 147
United Kingdom Sports Council 107
user groups 121, 122, 125, 186

validity 86
valve
   mitral 42
   semi-lunar 42
   tri-cuspid 42
   watch-pocket 44, 45
vein 42, 43, 44, 47, 169, 181
   inferior vena cava 42, 43
   pulmonary 42, 43, 44, 49

superior vena cava 42, 43
ventricle 42, 60, 170, 181
vertebral column (spinal column) 18, 22, 24, 162, 179
vertebrae (spine) 30, 40, 62
   atlas 26
   axis 26
   cervical (neck) 23, 169
   lumbar 23, 169
   spinal 18, 25, 169
   thoracic 22, 23
vital capacity (VC) 52, 53, 181
vitamins 56, 59, 79, 85, 181
volleyball 81, 121

warm up 72, 80, 88, 96, 100, 104, 182, 183
water-sports 108, 122
weight-lifting 28, 60, 63, 66, 82, 128, 184
weight loss 57, 84, 85, 165, 176
Wenlock Games 127, 128
What's Your Sport? 124, 168, 175, 176
winding 101, 104
women (see also gender and sex) 82, 123, 128, 143, 144-146, 148, 164, 175, 188
   men's attitude to 144, 146, 148, 187
working
   life 120
   week 120
wounds
   closed 99, 100, 104
   open 99, 104, 181
wrestling 128, 134
wrist 24, 25, 26